Praise for *Religion of Love*

This succinct, meticulously researched, and well-written study offers a fresh glimpse into the life and thought of ʿAṭṭār of Nishabur, one of the most influential Sufi authors of all time. Treating ʿAṭṭār's writings as 'a treasure-hunt for the Real that is full of revealed clues and natural signposts,' and utilizing his own knowledge of philosophy and theology, Zargar opens new vistas to rethink concepts such as 'religion,' 'infidelity, 'union,' and more."

— Fatemeh Keshavarz, author of *Lyrics of Life: Saʿdi on Love, Cosmopolitanism and Care of the Self*

"Farīd al-Dīn ʿAṭṭār occupies a crucial place in the history of Sufism. Cyrus Zargar's *Religion of Love* helps us see the full contribution of ʿAṭṭār as the essential 'merging of the two oceans' through whom the worlds of poetry and Sufism mingled in the ripe and lifegiving form that would continue through the centuries through Rumi and others. Zargar makes a unique contribution by centering the religion of love (*Madhhab-i ʿishq*) not as a path of sentimentality but a divine journey of transformation. In Zargar, ʿAṭṭār has found a profoundly creative, thoughtful, and sensitive contemporary interlocuter. Most enthusiastically recommended for all!"

— Omid Safi, Professor of Islamic Studies, Duke University; Director, Illuminated Courses and Tours

"*Religion of Love* will be around as an unmatched work for a long time to come. With great lucidity and insight, Cyrus Zargar explains the relevance of the difficult and nuanced teachings and ideas of ʿAṭṭār, deftly relating them to our fundamental lived experience as human beings and probing wider questions pertaining to the meaning of religion in the modern world."

— Mohammed Rustom, author of *Inrushes of the Heart: The Sufi Philosophy of ʿAyn al-Quḍāt*

Religion of Love

SUNY series in Islam

Seyyed Hossein Nasr, editor

Religion of Love

Sufism and Self-Transformation in the Poetic Imagination of ʿAṭṭār

Cyrus Ali Zargar

SUNY
PRESS

Cover Credit: Original artwork by Moselle Singh, supported by the Persian Heritage Foundation

Published by State University of New York Press, Albany

Printed in the United States of America

For information, contact State University of New York Press, Albany, NY
www.sunypress.edu

Library of Congress Cataloging-in-Publication Data

Name: Zargar, Cyrus Ali, author.
Title: Religion of love : Sufism and self-transformation in the poetic imagination of ʿAṭṭār / Cyrus Ali Zargar.
Description: Albany : State University of New York Press, [2024] | Series: SUNY series in Islam | Includes bibliographical references and index.
Identifiers: ISBN 9781438498676 (hardcover : alk. paper) | ISBN 9781438498683 (ebook) | ISBN 9781438498669 (pbk. : alk. paper)
Further information is available at the Library of Congress.

Contents

List of Abbreviations vii

Acknowledgments ix

Introduction: The Religion of Love 1

Chapter 1. Who Was ʿAṭṭār? 7

Chapter 2. ʿAṭṭār's Writings 13

Chapter 3. The City and the Saint 21

Part I: Religion

Chapter 4. Religion, Then and Now 39

Chapter 5. *Dīn, Dunyā,* and the Pious Life 45

Chapter 6. Sciences of Empty Reasoning 53

Chapter 7. Beyond the Limits of Intelligence 59

Chapter 8. The Religion of Old Women 67

Part II: Love and Infidelity

Chapter 9. Love Beneath the Cloak of Infidelity 79

Chapter 10. The School of Love in History 85

Chapter 11. Metaphorical Spaces of Love and Infidelity 91
Chapter 12. Finding the Real in Byzantium 105

Part III: Union

Chapter 13. ʿAṭṭār and Mystical Experience 119
Chapter 14. Ascents to the Real 125
Chapter 15. Celestial Journey Literature 129
Chapter 16. Union in *The Book of Affliction* 137
Chapter 17. The Source of Affliction 157
Conclusion 163
Notes 169
Bibliography 203
Index 215

Abbreviations

AN: *Asrār-nāma* (ed. Muḥammad-Riḍā Shafīʿī-Kadkanī)

DW: *Dīwān-i ʿAṭṭār-i Nīshābūrī* (eds. Mahdī Madāyinī and Mihrān Afshārī)

EIr: *Encyclopædia Iranica*

Iḥyāʾ: Abū Ḥāmid al-Ghazālī, *Iḥyāʾ ʿulūm al-dīn*

IN: *Ilāhī-nāma* (ed. Muḥammad-Riḍā Shafīʿī-Kadkanī)

MKH: *Mukhtār-nāma* (ed. Muḥammad-Riḍā Shafīʿī-Kadkanī)

MN: *Muṣībat-nāma* (ed. Muḥammad-Riḍā Shafīʿī-Kadkanī)

MT: *Manṭiq al-ṭayr* (ed. Muḥammad-Riḍā Shafīʿī-Kadkanī)

Q: *al-Qurʾān al-karīm* (the Qurʾān)

TA: *Tadhkirat al-awliyāʾ* (ed. Muḥammad-Riḍā Shafīʿī-Kadkanī)

ZP: Shafīʿī-Kadkanī, *Zabūr-i Parsī*

Acknowledgments

I thank the Gerda Henkel Foundation for a generous research grant, one that allowed me the time and resources needed to bring this book to completion. Similar recognition goes to the Persian Heritage Foundation for a grant in support of this book's cover art. Furthermore, I must acknowledge the Al-Ghazali Islamic Studies program at the University of Central Florida, for its institutional support throughout the writing process.

A number of friends offered feedback, either on drafts or on presentations related to the book, and to them I am grateful: Hamid Algar, Susan Bachelder, Nicholas Boylston, William Chittick, Fatemeh Keshavarz, Christian Lange, Gregory Lipton, Ali Altaf Mian, Mehrnaz Monzavi, Shankar Nair, Mohammed Rustom, Omid Safi, Saʿdiyya Shaikh, and Abdulkader Tayob. My wife Shirin offered her unending support, leaving me as indebted as always. This book simply would not appear in its present form without the tireless efforts of Moselle Singh, who was much more than an editor. I thank her for never allowing me to settle for phrasings or structures that were mediocre or ambiguous, though what remains mediocre or ambiguous in this book is entirely my own doing. I also thank her for creating the book's marvelous original cover art. Finally, I must recognize all the saintly folk of Nishapur and the Khorasan region, from before the time of ʿAṭṭār until today. The nobility displayed in their lives, sayings, and writings made ʿAṭṭār's books possible and inspired me to write this one. This is most true for the saint now revered as the "Shāh of Khorasan," ʿAlī b. Mūsā al-Riḍā (d. 203/818), to whom this book is dedicated.

Introduction

The Religion of Love

This is a book about one of the world's great literary voices, one whose name might not be immediately familiar to an English-speaking audience. Those who do know of him often acknowledge him as one of seven or so of the most important poets in Persian literature.[1] If one limits that list of Persian poets to classical Sufi poetry, then he is arguably one of two, along with Rūmī. In terms of the sheer magnitude of what he left behind, this poet's confirmed verse compositions add up to nearly 34,600 double lines, something close to seventy thousand units of verse.[2] As a point of comparison, Homer's *Odyssey* and *Iliad* combine to a little less than twenty-eight thousand lines. For thematic depth, our poet would rival any premodern or even modern writer in ethical and one might say moral-psychological complexity. Finally, in terms of cultural influence, our poet's legacy spans western, central, and southern Asia, as well as Europe. His impact is especially pronounced in Persian, Turkish, and Urdu literature, where his imagery, stories, and style inspired generations of artists, even to this day. Yet what makes our poet perhaps most extraordinary is the insight he offers in terms of Islam as it has been understood theologically, ritually, and ethically. ʿAṭṭār's (d. 618/1221) works of poetry and his book in prose, as I will describe them, outline an ethical journey of love that he saw as an interpretation of Islam. This pathway to reality might sometimes seem strange when compared to the "Islam" many of us recognize, the "Islam" that emphasizes sobriety and self-restraint. Nevertheless, as we will see, its foundations lie in teachings communicated through Islam's revealed sources, the Qur'ān and Ḥadīth, as well as the lives and teachings of its saints. For this reason, our poet's "religion of love" is the topic of this book.

The three coming chapters will introduce you to the poet, the little we know about his life, the content of his poetry and prose, and the historical circumstances in which he wrote. After these introductory chapters, the book is divided into three sections focusing on three themes that prevail in ʿAṭṭār's writings, namely, religion, love, and union. These sections unite several chapters that study ʿAṭṭār as not just a poet but also a thinker, a person with deeply held views on what I have labeled "The Religion of Love."

The Religion of Love

This book is not a biography. Most of the salient available information on ʿAṭṭār's life is offered in chapter 1. It is also not an English-language introduction to his works. For the most part, that can be found in Hellmut Ritter's *The Ocean of the Soul*. Rather, this book introduces ʿAṭṭār as a contributor to Islamic thought, one whose viewpoint, questions, and formulae for a reflective and pious life still have something to offer the contemporary reader. One might say that I will try to imagine ʿAṭṭār as a "philosopher of religion," in the mold of other poets and artists whose work captures and transforms the ideas of their age.

This phrase, "philosopher of religion," comes with the caveat that ʿAṭṭār had a pronounced intellectual aversion to the philosophical approaches of his age. He would have balked at being called a "philosopher" (*faylasūf*), or, even worse, a "Sophist" or *sūfisṭānī*, a designation ʿAṭṭār used to identify the most egregious case of rationalism and skepticism. Yet he would have probably embraced being called a "thinker" (*mutafakkir*). As a thinker and as one who often developed the ideas of others in poetry, ʿAṭṭār offers his readers insights into the God-human relationship, scripture, divine law, cosmology, ethics, epistemology, the nature of love, and human suffering.

One might, and in fact should, wonder what it means when someone describes an artist as a thinker or a philosopher, since the aims of poetry often differ quite observably from those of intellectual, prosaic treatises. First of all, the two were not so disparate in ʿAṭṭār's cultural milieu. Didactic poetry and homiletic poetry—poetry that teaches and poetry that preaches—were quite common at the time, and much of our poet's work falls under those categories. In fact, Austin O'Malley has explored the homiletic dimensions of ʿAṭṭār's writings in an excellent new book, and, as he points out, many classical Persian poets bore the honorary title "sage" (*ḥakīm*), synonymous with "philosopher."[3] This was because of an interdependent relationship between eloquent speech and wisdom in the Persianate literary tradition. Secondly, many Sufi treatises cannot be placed nicely in the category of "scholarly prose" because of the literary and even metaphorical nature of those Sufi prosaic treatises.[4]

It does, in fact, matter that ʿAṭṭār was an artist and not a philosopher, theologian, or legal specialist. As an artist, the imaginative worlds that ʿAṭṭār created relied on his engagement with emerging trends in Persian poetry: the trope of the antiheroic lover, the erotic-spiritual *ghazal* lyric, the frame-tale narrative, and the allegorical journey of the soul. Moreover, the "religion of love" described in this book would not be possible without contradictions, emotive language, personal stories, metaphors, allusions, intertextuality, and personification, among other literary devices. As a poet and hagiographer, ʿAṭṭār employed the intellectual and saintly contributions of his age just as a poet makes use of these devices. His biographer, Dawlatshāh, describes his efforts as a "compiling" of Sufi writings on more than one occasion, and the poet does not seem to have been driven by a desire to be original in any learned sense. Nor does ʿAṭṭār express the need to argue or provide much evidence, since his role is to provoke and inspire the sentiments and imaginations of his readers, not to convince them.

In this regard, ʿAṭṭār might be thought of as a philosophical artist similar to others who have been recognized as such and studied for their contributions to intellectual history. As an example, Benjamin Boysen's *The Ethics of Love: An Essay on James Joyce* unravels the theme of humanist love in the face of the erasure of metaphysical meaning within James Joyce's (d. 1941) fiction.[5] Joyce's representations of life in early twentieth-century Dublin embrace our temporality as individuals and highlight our dependence on the world we encounter for our ego identities. We have the opportunity to go beyond our sense of selfhood by loving entities other than ourselves—loving other human beings. This message and this philosophy rely on the novel and the short story. It needs fiction to exist. Through Joyce's stream-of-consciousness style, something comes to life that would not otherwise have life: the profusion of actions and reactions within human thought. Through narratives, those thoughts surround and describe the phenomenon of human-to-human love as a tapestry of images and ideas.

So, too, do ʿAṭṭār's reflections on love rely on the sort of cognitive superabundance that poetry can create. There is a sense that the reader can join the poet in the pits of Hell or soar to the majestic Mount Qāf in the course of one narrative. And, in all this, the poet helps the reader interpret the meanings of such multiplicity. The ultimate meaning is quite the opposite of what Boysen sees in Joyce, even though it is also a philosophy of love. We embrace the eternal within ourselves by transcending the temporal, including the temporal self. Yet, again, love liberates. Love cures us from selfishness. Love speaks to us from beyond everything we see, hear, and know. Amazingly, Joyce and ʿAṭṭār, separated by so much more than just time, share such themes. This coincidence might tell us something about the venture of great literature. Perhaps their mutual concern with liberation from egocentricity is no accident and might help us have a sense of how literature elevates us from certain norms.

There is another caveat to the phrase "philosopher of religion," as well. Because the world has changed so much since ʿAṭṭār's time, one cannot simply reach into ʿAṭṭār's writings and extract translatable ideas. The word "religion" reflects that problem more vividly than most other terms. "Religion," as I will discuss, carries baggage in modern English that the word *dīn* did not in ʿAṭṭār's Persian. That baggage includes the modern state and its concomitants, namely, nationalism, popular culture, and codified laws. "Religion" also carries something that we collectively imagine: a secular domain in which myth and magic have no place. This too would have been strange to our poet. Much of what we designate as "secular" had, in the time of ʿAṭṭār, been intertwined with what we designate as "religious," that is, notions of God, scripture, and pious authority, whether one called oneself Muslim, Christian, or Jewish.

Neither "religion" nor ʿAṭṭār can ever appear to us fully unveiled by modern prejudices. Yet, with some amount of work, a reader can perhaps begin to lift the veil. Historians lift that veil by trying to uncover the context of a poet's writings. The coming pages will offer some of that context. We can also, however, read ʿAṭṭār and explore "religion" in an imaginative way that teaches us something about our own veils of prejudice, thereby shifting our perspective about the world around us. This is the central goal of this book. Reading and analyzing ʿAṭṭār may expand (1) the way we locate devotion in public life, especially when faced with expressions of rationalism that create doubt; (2) the way we draw the borders between belief and disbelief, especially in the complications and perplexities that come with loving God; and (3) the meaning of religious experience, especially in the context of the limitations of human knowledge.

With these matters in mind, three major themes in ʿAṭṭār's thought will provide structure to the coming parts and our exploration of ʿAṭṭār's worldview: (1) religion, (2) love and infidelity (which are, from a certain perspective, two sides of the same coin), and (3) union. Part 1, on religion, will consider the ways in which ʿAṭṭār defines ideal modes of life and piety. In reacting to the rationalisms of his time, he offers those of us who live in the predominance of scientific standards of truth much to consider. Part 2, on love and infidelity, delves into that which has made Persian Sufi poetry so appealing. I explore here the ecstasy of finding God in the world around us, as well as the symbols of that ecstasy. Part 3, on union, ponders what it means to become "one" with the divine. Union resolves human suffering and caps the universal quest to become whole. In the chapters of each of these three parts, I will touch on the views of contemporary theorists of religion, philosophers, and historians. This is not done to make matters more complicated or as mere comparative dressing. Rather, it is done in the spirit of bringing to light the social and intellectual realities in which we read ʿAṭṭār. In this way, perhaps ongoing conversations—at our universities, among our intellectuals, and in our social communities—can include ʿAṭṭār's contributions. Such comparisons can breathe new life into the ways we think, or, at least, expand our views to include what had been untranslated and uninterpreted. But first let us discover the life, circumstances, and saintly legacy of ʿAṭṭār.

1

Who Was ʿAṭṭār?

The most well-known name of the poet in question is ʿAṭṭār, which simply means "the Druggist" or "the Apothecary," that is, a person who specialized in and sold concoctions, herbal remedies, and fragrances. One of the few things we know about his life is that he was the son of an apothecary, probably an apothecary himself, and thus a member of the shopkeeper class.[1] He might have been born in the year 1158, in a village near eastern Iran's major metropolis at the time, Nishapur, a city whose inhabitants were slaughtered during the Mongol invasions. That city never again returned to its former size or prominence. ʿAṭṭār was one of those killed during the invasions, which places his death at the year 1221, though some have raised the (unlikely) possibility that he was killed in a later Mongol excursion in 1230. I will discuss these possibilities, but what we know of ʿAṭṭār tends to circle around these key aspects of his life: his occupation, the city in which he lived, the time of his life and death, and, of course, his works. The fact that we know so little about one of Persian literature's greatest poets is certainly frustrating, but I will do my best to bring forth a vivid picture of his time, place, and legend.

ʿAṭṭār's name was Muḥammad, though sometime in his life he acquired the epithet Farīd al-Dīn, "Peerless in Devotion." He was born to a very pious father, Shaykh Ibrāhīm, also an apothecary, who himself was the son of a man named Isḥāq.[2] (The word "shaykh" in front of ʿAṭṭār's father's name can refer to a master or spiritual trainer, or simply be added to one's name to indicate honor, learning, or leadership.) ʿAṭṭār's father was affiliated with and perhaps a disciple of Quṭb al-Dīn Ḥaydar (d. ca. 618/1221).[3] Ḥaydar had a leading role in an expression of Islamic piety that was rising during ʿAṭṭār's lifetime, a sort of untamed piety that ʿAṭṭār embraced metaphorically in his poetry though perhaps did not put to action in real life. Dervishes traveled in poverty, begged, and engaged in socially unaccepted behavior, such as body piercings, public nudity, and the use of psychedelics. Ḥaydar, the son of a Turkic sultan, is said to have abandoned the opulence into which he was born in order to live as a dervish.[4]

Other than his own father, ʿAṭṭār's earliest spiritual influences are largely speculative. One of ʿAṭṭār's two main premodern biographers reports that a young ʿAṭṭār had written a long poem dedicated to his father's guide, Ḥaydar, called *The Book of Ḥaydar* (*Ḥaydar-nāma*).[5] Generally, scholars of Persian literary history have considered this farfetched and lacking evidence.[6] Nevertheless, conjectures regarding the circumstances of ʿAṭṭār's spiritual upbringing remain valuable, considering the dearth of information on his life. We do know that ʿAṭṭār's father had an influence on his spiritual life, important enough for the poet to include a very rare autobiographical account mentioning him in one of his poems. At his father's deathbed, ʿAṭṭār beseeches him for one last word of advice. His father replies with a profound reflection about the futility of human speech: "I wasted a whole life in heedlessness, so what can I say? I spent my whole life in useless prattle."[7] He remains silent, ending his last moments by praying for blessings to descend upon the Prophet Muhammad, to which ʿAṭṭār's mother responds, "Amen." ʿAṭṭār makes much of his father's final prayer, ending his poem with its mention and calling it a "talisman of the way" to God. In part, this is because ʿAṭṭār sees any prayer spoken by a "frail and elderly couple" as replete with sincerity, but also because of the poet's real concern for God to "erase the sins" of a father who was so incredibly "goodhearted."[8]

Moving on from his childhood, we do not have a clear picture of ʿAṭṭār's spiritual formation and allegiances as an adult. Such confusion led the famous German scholar of Persian literature, Hellmut Ritter, to assert that ʿAṭṭār was not a committed Sufi. [9] Yet evidence points quite to the contrary. Ritter misinterprets an autobiographical statement in ʿAṭṭār's collected biographies of Sufi saints wherein he declares, "I am not one of *them*, but I strive to be similar to them."[10] Here, "them" refers not to the Sufis, not to all those committed to the path, but to the great saints (*awliyāʾ*) of Islam reviewed in ʿAṭṭār's book. ʿAṭṭār's only claim to sainthood or to such levels of ethical greatness is entirely aspirational. Indeed, his penchant for self-deprecation forces him to declare a few pages later, "I am nobody," and that any value that he might have comes from his being among "the King's [God's] nobodies."[11] Such language should not be taken literally, as it is part of his own spiritual practice of degrading the ego. Even once we establish his ties to the Sufis of Nishapur, trying to pin down ʿAṭṭār's precise lineage presents difficulties, as the sources do not reveal much. Some evidence suggests ʿAṭṭār was a spiritual disciple of Shaykh Jamāl al-Dīn Muḥammad ibn Muḥammad Nughundarī Ṭūsī, called "Imām al-Rabbānī."[12] Little is known about this shaykh. From Imām al-Rabbānī, the chain of ʿAṭṭār's spiritual teachers would go back to the famous Sufi saint Abū Saʿīd ibn Abī al-Khayr (d. 440/1049).

Offering perhaps some clues, ʿAṭṭār sometimes seems to imply affiliation to others, or, at the very least, special reverence. For example, he wishes God's satisfaction upon Abū ʿAlī al-Faḍl ibn Muḥammad Fārmadī (or Fārmadhī, d. 477/1084) of the village of Fārmad near Ṭūs. Fārmadī is also the only source he cites in his entry on the female saint Rābiʿa.[13] Fārmadī was purported sometimes to be a master to Abū Ḥāmid al-Ghazālī (d. 505/1111), and sometimes to be an associate of his brother Aḥmad al-Ghazālī (d. 520/1126).[14] Fārmadī himself was a student of a major spiritual trainer or "shaykh" named Abū al-Qāsim Kurrakānī (d. 469/1076–1077), to whom many well-known Sufi figures traced their disciplinary lineage. Fārmadī seems to be a spiritual forebear to ʿAṭṭār, if only at least in a citational sense, that is, as a source for his writings.[15]

Indeed, in terms of influence, there might be a subtle indication that ʿAṭṭār's primary mode of interchange with the Sufi tradition was a literary one—through books. He says himself, "For no particular reason at all, from the time I was a child, love for this [Sufi] band (*ṭāʾifa*) swelled in my being, and, at all times, the only thing that brought relief to my heart were their words."[16] He points here not to one particular master, nor to a particular source, but rather to the plurality of the "words" of the entire "band," that is, it would seem, to a transmitted tradition. Elsewhere he tells his audience that those who seek the "words" of these saints should look in the "books of both bygone and recent writers of this band."[17] One biographer describes the "four hundred volumes of Sufi texts" that ʿAṭṭār studied and summarized.[18] This interest in books, compounded with the many instances when he borrows from the writings of others, suggests that he was an avid reader of the tradition, with books serving as perhaps his main lifeline of engagement.

Of course, ʿAṭṭār was much more than merely a writer. He doubtless had a circle of followers, whom he identifies twice as those who encouraged him to compose *The Memorial of God's Friends*.[19] They were a select group of "confidential friends" (*aṣdiqāʾ-i maḥram*), whom he calls elsewhere his "beloved companions, prescient affiliates, and agreeable intimates," and who seem to have appreciated his poetry, reading his long poems in their entirety and showing concern for their preservation.[20]

ʿAṭṭār's circle of followers would have been drawn to his eloquence but also to the depth and breadth of his learning. He lived, after all, in one of Islam's centers of learning and spiritual development, indeed the hub of such learning in the East, distinguished by its many schools, Sufi lodges, and eminent scholars. Using what we know of instruction in Nishapur, it is likely that he began teaching classes in his fifties or sixties, though he was perhaps older when a young and soon-to-be famous philosopher came to visit.[21] That philosopher, Naṣīr al-Dīn Ṭūsī (d. 672/1274), reported that he became quite enamored by ʿAṭṭār's words while sitting in on his lectures concerning the spiritual way.[22]

Ṭūsī's interest in the Sufi sciences must have drawn him to the poet, for he certainly could not have sought ʿAṭṭār to quench his thirst for philosophy. ʿAṭṭār was, after all, quite outspoken about his antipathy toward philosophy (*falsafa*), including his distaste for the words of a famous philosopher from his own home city of Nishapur, ʿUmar al-Khayyām (d. 526/1131). ʿAṭṭār went so far as to say that, in knowing God, "the 'D' of Disbelief does better than the 'P' of Philosophy."[23] His assessment of the limits of philosophy, so often repeated in his works, shows some influence of another figure celebrated by Sufis, a scholar of eastern Persian origins—Abū Ḥāmid al-Ghazālī.

ʿAṭṭār's admiration for Abū Ḥāmid al-Ghazālī and the way in which he expressed that admiration indicates much about the intellectual climate in Nishapur as experienced by ʿAṭṭār. References in ʿAṭṭār's body of work to al-Ghazālī's writings, or to those attributed to him, further support the sense that ʿAṭṭār aligned himself with a certain intellectual wave in Nishapur. Along with other Sufi-leaning scholars, ʿAṭṭār seems to have embraced al-Ghazālī's interest in tempering the rational sciences, such as philosophy and theology, by emphasizing the ways pious practice outdoes the rational sciences. In fact, ʿAṭṭār recounts two different accounts about al-Ghazālī—and one about his brother, Aḥmad—in *The Book of the Divine*.[24] In one of those accounts, al-Ghazālī hides at home because of a warning that he will be assassinated by a "heretic" (*mulḥid*). Desperate, he seeks help from a certain "mentor" (*ustād*) of his from a place called Kūshahd. The mentor advises him wisely to leave matters of death to God, who gave him life, therein freeing him from his deep anxiety. That mentor might have been another major Ashʿarī-Shāfiʿī figure, namely, Abū Maʿālī al-Juwaynī (d. 478/1085), known as the Imam al-Ḥaramayn or "Imam of the Two Sanctuaries (in Mecca and Medina)."[25]

From this story, we might extract two things about our poet, substantiated by other pieces of evidence from his writings. First, ʿAṭṭār had sympathies for al-Ghazālī. Second, the denominational factionalism in Nishapur troubled him. The Ismāʿīlī assassin seems to symbolize all the dangers that ʿAṭṭār and the other inhabitants of his home city had retained in their cultural memory. The story might have some basis in history or at least lore, but ʿAṭṭār also seems to be doing here what storytellers often do. He takes an overwhelming and tangled social issue and captures it in a simpler tale, where friend encounters foe. He attributes the threat of violence to a religious group that he and his audience see as radical and heretical, the Shiʿi Ismāʿīlīs, who, in fact, were also often advocates of philosophy.

Yet the historical reality for the scholarly and the pious in Nishapur was that threats often came from those deemed brothers in Islam, as we will discuss. Scholars akin to al-Ghazālī faced persecution, arrest, or even death, at the hands of those belonging to a not-so-distant school of thought. ʿAṭṭār's concern with the hazards faced by al-Ghazālī (the most prominent teacher and writer of the

Ashʿarī theological school and the Shāfiʿī legal school) might reflect his concern for the hazards others who belonged to that school had faced. This included al-Juwaynī, who fled the city in the face of arrest, along with three prominent Ashʿarī-Shāfiʿī scholars who were arrested.[26] ʿAṭṭār's sympathies to these Ashʿarī-Shāfiʿī figures might suggest that he adhered to the Ashʿarī-Shāfiʿī school himself. If so, he seems to have been quite careful not to show his hand.[27] Perhaps it was the city's history of sectarianism that kept ʿAṭṭār from delving into such matters.

Yet the real window into ʿAṭṭār's world lies in his writings. During his long life in Nishapur and the surrounding areas, ʿAṭṭār wrote four long narrative poems, two collections of short poems, and one book in prose recounting the lives of Sufism's great saints. Those will be reviewed in the next chapter.

2

ʿAṭṭār's Writings

There are many texts falsely attributed to ʿAṭṭār. The acclaim that ʿAṭṭār garnered for himself led to borrowings of his name, as well as false ascriptions—a common feature of medieval authorship. Moreover, the popularity of his poetry among Sufi practitioners meant that his poetry was read and shared frequently. This resulted in lines being added to his poems, which contemporary editors have had to identify and remove from critical editions. By his own account, in an introduction to *The Choice Book of Quatrains* (*Mukhtār-nāma*), ʿAṭṭār lists the following existing compositions as his, dividing them into two categories. The first category comprises (1) *The Book of the Divine* (*Ilāhī-nāma*), also known as the *Khusraw-nāma*; (2) *The Book of Secrets* (*Asrār-nāma*); and (3) *The Speech of the Birds* (*Manṭiq al-ṭayr*). The second category comprises (4) *The Book of Affliction* (*Muṣībat-nāma*); (5) *The Collected Poems* (*Dīwān*), a collection of shorter poems in a certain style, called *ghazal*s, as well as longer poems, called *qaṣīda*s; and (6) *The Choice Book of Quatrains* (*Mukhtār-nāma*), a collection of quatrain poems or *rubāʿīyāt*.[1] It seems possible that he considers the first three as master works and the latter three as secondary, though why he divided them as such is not entirely clear. While not listed by the poet, there is also his prose composition, (7) *The Memorial of God's Friends* (*Tadhkirat al-awliyāʾ*), a recounting of the lives and marvels of Sufism's great saints.

Thus, while legend has it that ʿAṭṭār composed 114 works, his confirmed works are seven. He confesses to having destroyed two of his own compositions, *The Book of Gems* (*Jawāhir-nāma*) and

An Exposition on the Heart (*Sharḥ-i qalb*).[2] Using medical terms to describe his purge of these works, he says that these two long poems "suffered from their very beginning from excessive black bile, so that they were treated by water and fire."[3] This statement implies a careful composition process to ʿAṭṭār's poems, and ʿAṭṭār even describes himself as an exacting editor of his own poetry. He describes the process of selecting quatrains for *The Choice Book of Quatrains* as starting with six thousand double lines (*bayt*s) of poetry, leaving "one thousand *bayt*s to be washed away, for they were unworthy of this world."[4] Then, from the five thousand remaining, the poet undertook an even more rigorous process of selection, choosing the best quatrains for his book, and leaving the rest for his *dīwān*, or general collection of poems. Judging from the current edition, he seems to have kept only around half of those five thousand double lines. Unlike Rūmī's *ghazal*s, which were sometimes recited—at least in part—extemporaneously, or some of the writings of Najm al-Dīn Kubrā (d. 618/1221), which seem to have been lecture notes, ʿAṭṭār's authorship of poems seems meticulous and carefully planned.

The contents of ʿAṭṭār's seven books are as follows:

1. *The Book of the Divine* (*Ilāhī-nāma*) was originally titled *The Book of Khusraw* (*Khusraw-nāma*), and it is the latter title that appears in the poet's own list. *Khusraw* refers to a "ruler," and in this case a kingly caliph is the narrative's main protagonist.[5] Editors later settled on *The Book of the Divine* as a title, perhaps as a clarification that its themes are more world-renouncing and divinely focused than they are courtly or kingly. It is one of three of ʿAṭṭār's "frame tale" poems, long poems that include multiple narratives within one overarching narrative. This one describes a caliph with six sons, each of whom expresses their utmost desire. Their requests lead to a discourse between each of them and their father about the futility of what they pursue. Therefore, ʿAṭṭār's book—again, a collection of poetic narratives—considers the proper end of human pursuits, or, put differently, the meaning of life. One son seeks the daughter of the fairy king (*shāh-i parīyān*), a woman of peerless beauty, representing natural desire as its own end. Another seeks magic, representing knowledge through which one acquires earthly power. A third seeks the Cup of Jamshīd (*jām-i jamshīd*, or *jām-i jam*), a legendary goblet in which one can see the entire universe.

This represents the desire for knowledge that lies beyond human capability, which ends in thwarted pride. The fourth son seeks the Water of Eternal Life (*āb-i ḥayāt*), a "Fountain of Youth" that, like the Cup of Jamshīd, comes from Near Eastern and Mediterranean legends. This represents the desire never to die, or, rather, endless desire and greed that becomes its own form of suffering. The fifth son seeks the ring of Solomon, from which the Biblical king derived his ability to control the jinn (protean, sentient, nonhuman beings mentioned in the Qurʾān) and rule over the world. Here the object is absolute earthly dominion, which—his father warns him—is ephemeral and subject to the grand reversal after death and upon resurrection. The sixth and last son wishes to learn alchemy, which signifies knowledge that brings wealth and fame. He plans to use alchemy for that purpose—to bring wealth to many and have his name spread far and wide. This occasions a reflection on the way desires must be made singular. As revealed in the Qurʾān, a lover cannot be committed to two things at once—the worldly and God—and so must choose.[6] This poem is 6,685 double lines long.[7]

2. *The Book of Secrets* (*Asrār-nāma*) differs from *The Book of the Divine* in that it has no framing narrative. Rather, it comprises eighteen poetic essays in the same *mathnawī* style of rhyming couplets as his framed narrative poems. Beginning with a profound exposition of *tawḥīd*, that is, a recognition of God's oneness, ʿAṭṭār lays out an elaboration of theology informed by Sufi cosmology (study of the universe), psychology (study of the soul, as well as its faculties and its modes of being), and theories of love. One might call it a primer on theoretical Sufism with two major exceptions. First, there is much practical advice in the work, drawing from the lives and legends of saints and others, even animals. Indeed, most theoretical observations are illustrated by a corresponding micronarrative that illustrates the point within the context of lived experience. Second, ʿAṭṭār delves so deeply at times into the nature of reality, making controversial statements about the cosmological nature of love, that the topic at hand can quickly shift from introductory material to metaphysical complexities. Love, in this poem, is a cosmological force that outstrips the intellect. The human reality is to break through normal means of perception—especially the focus on external "form"—to perceive supersensory "meaning," or spirit. It is 3,307 double lines in length.

3. *The Speech of the Birds* (*Manṭiq al-ṭayr*) is ʿAṭṭār's most famous composition and the one most often translated into European languages, including numerous English translations.[8] The author refers to this text both as *The Book of Birds* (*Ṭuyūr-nāma*) and *The Stations of the Birds* (*Maqāmāt-i ṭuyūr*), using the phrase *The Language of the Birds* (*Zabān-i murghān*) as well, though not as a title.[9] This frame tale tells the story of a flock of birds, varying in species, who elect to set out to meet the mysterious and awe-inspiring Sīmurgh, a creature with resemblances to the phoenix and the griffin. Each bird embodies a certain ethical or spiritual shortcoming, one congruent with their depiction in folk wisdom. The journey involves valleys that represent the major stages of the spiritual path. The hoopoe, guide to the birds, addresses various spiritual challenges through storytelling. Most do not survive the trip, but those thirty who do then realize that the Sīmurgh reflects the essence within themselves. That is, the Sīmurgh is in fact *sī-murgh,* that is, *sī* (thirty) *murgh* (birds). The poem runs 4,724 double lines in length.

4. *Dīwān* is a collection of ʿAṭṭār's *ghazal*s and *qaṣīda*s. A *dīwān* in Persian and Arabic literature refers to a poet's collected works, usually excluding longer poems in rhymed couplets, especially longer narrative ones. Most poets did not compile their own poems into a *dīwān,* an action usually undertaken after the poet's demise. ʿAṭṭār, however, arranged his own *dīwān,* as he tells us himself.[10] This collection of ʿAṭṭār's shorter, non-narrative poems—especially amorous poems—left a noticeable mark on the Persian art of poetry, itself highly influenced by themes in the poetry of Majdūd ibn Ādam Ghaznawī "Sanāʾī" (d. ca. 525/1131) and the flowing, lucid style of Awḥad al-Dīn Muḥammad Anwarī (d. ca. 582/1186).[11] Drawing from his poetic predecessors, ʿAṭṭār furthered a language of love and an embrace of nonconformity through symbols of infidelity. This was all part of a poetic style that would later become synonymous with classical Persian love poetry. In ʿAṭṭār's *Dīwān,* certain places and objects become pronounced that would also become hallmarks of a classical Persian poetics of love. Those hallmarks included non-Muslim worship sites, clothing, priests, and even idols, as well as the tavern with its wine, wine servers, and drunkards. This language is more than mere metaphor aimed at curbing pietism and hypocrisy. As we will see, it is a complex ethical and psychological commentary

on the pitfalls of asceticism and the wisdom of God's allowance for disbelief. These were not new symbols by any means. Wine imagery, like erotic expressions of human beauty, were a common feature of Persian love poetry well before ʿAṭṭār, and some bore the marks of Arabic poetic influence.[12]

Through the collected poems of his *Dīwān*, ʿAṭṭār explored the evocative and powerful blending of two poetic traditions he had inherited. The first was the aforementioned courtly tradition of wine and love poetry. The second was a (mostly Sufi) tradition of contemplating the difficult path to God. The mixture of the two was not new.[13] Rather, the depth of ʿAṭṭār's knowledge of Sufi terms, ethics, and theology—a theology of divine love—makes his commitment to this emerging poetic style truly pioneering. Erotic poems aside, many poems in his *Dīwān* are elaborations on states and stations of the path. States (*aḥwāl*) describe fluctuations of the heart, and stations (*maqāmāt*) describe the more lasting formations and stages of God-oriented character. States often show the effects of the lover's sense of distance or proximity to the beloved. Stations mark the lover's lifelong progression to union with the beloved. In ʿAṭṭār's *Dīwān*, the movements between states and stations appear as the difficulties of being enamored with a transcendent deity. This collection of poems, in one edition, totals 10,346 double lines.[14]

5. The third and final frame tale poem is *The Book of Affliction* (*Muṣībat-nāma*), a poem that borrows from Islam's rich tradition of heavenly ascent narratives, most prominently, of course, the night journey and ascent or *miʿrāj* of the Prophet Muhammad himself. The poet tells us of the journey of a suffering protagonist, the "wayfarer of contemplation" (*sālik-i fikrat*). The wayfarer, guided by his unnamed master, visits forty entities, from the angels, to the heavens, to the elements, geographical features, plants, animals, jinn, humans, prophets, and finally the psychological faculties. Each of these entities engages in a dialogue with the wayfarer, declines his request to end his existential suffering, and becomes the subject of learning when the wayfarer consults his master. The Prophet's intercession leads to the wayfarer's redirection into the soul and to his final five dialogues with the psychological faculties. The wayfarer goes from sense (*ḥiss*), to imagination (*khayāl*), to intellect (*ʿaql*), to heart (*dil*), and finally to spirit (*rūḥ*). There, within spirit, the wayfarer undergoes union. It is 7,425 double lines long.

6. *The Choice Book of Quatrains* (*Mukhtār-nāma*) is a collection of ʿAṭṭār's quatrain poems or *rubāʿīyāt*. The Persian quatrain form, in a manner similar to Latin epigrams, emphasized a poet's wit. The form has become most famous in Edward Fitzgerald's poetic translations of quatrains attributed to the scientist and philosopher ʿUmar al-Khayyām. So widespread were ʿAṭṭār's quatrains that they made their way into the collections of others. Some quatrains mistakenly attributed to al-Khayyām were indeed ʿAṭṭār's. Here, in fifty chapters, ʿAṭṭār preaches on and explicates some of the finer points of Sufi thought, many of which are also addressed in *The Book of Secrets*. These include *tawḥīd*; annihilation of selfhood (*fanāʾ*); union with the divine; bewilderment; the spirit; complaints against the lower self; ethical points to consider on the path toward God; the intricacies of the lover-beloved relationship; meditations on the beauty of the beloved, anthropomorphic descriptions of divine beauty, and the states inspired by that beauty; celebrations of metaphorical infidelity; wine poetry; and extended reflections on the candle and its metaphorically rich relationship with the moth. ʿAṭṭār's sincere sense of spiritual struggle comes out clearer in his quatrains, because of their brevity, than in his other writings, which are already quite earnest.

> Having not exchanged my being, what's left for me to do?
> Because I have no place in all this, what's left for me
> to do?
> They tell me, Come! Come see the fire of God's presence
> that Moses saw!
> But with this Pharaoh sitting beside me, what's left for
> me to do?[15]

Here, as in many other quatrains, the poetic persona wrestles with his propensity to wickedness. The collection is 2,280 double lines long.

7. *The Memorial of God's Friends* (*Tadhkirat al-awliyāʾ*) is a major prose work, an oddity in ʿAṭṭār's corpus both for being prosaic and for being completely devoted to the lives of saints. Before ʿAṭṭār, there were other such compendiums of Sufi saints' lives and deeds. As Paul Losensky explains in an introduction to his English translation of much of this work, ʿAṭṭār's project was largely one of "rewriting" previous collections of the lives of Sufi

saints, a genre that flourished in his hometown.[16] For ʿAṭṭār, this process meant collecting accounts from previous such works and creating a myriad of biographies in Persian. He made it accessible to a wide audience by adding expository comments for technical language and by excluding chains of transmission. This tells us that ʿAṭṭār's audience was invested in Sufism as an expression of Islamic piety, but they were not necessarily committed scholars of the Islamic sciences. Moreover, ʿAṭṭār found ways to shape the narratives to emphasize themes in his interpretation of Islamic spirituality. For instance, placing the Prophet's eminent great-grandson Jaʿfar al-Ṣādiq (d. 145/765) first, despite a break in chronology, allows him to highlight the primacy of the Prophet's family. Having an extended, sympathetic, and even moving account of the martyr Ḥusayn b. Manṣūr al-Ḥallāj (d. 309/922) allows ʿAṭṭār to highlight his loyalties to a love-centered interpretation of Sufism that favored metaphors of heresy and infidelity to represent the sincere lover. Most manuscripts of *The Memorial* would end with this very account of al-Ḥallāj.[17] In part, this created a sense of a very powerful ending, because no other chapter rivals the al-Ḥallāj chapter's emotional depth. ʿAṭṭār borrowed material from *The Ranks of Sufis* (*Ṭabaqāt al-ṣūfīya*) by Abū ʿAbd al-Raḥmān Muḥammad ibn al-Ḥusayn al-Sulamī (d. 412/1021), as well as a Persian translation of al-Qushayrī's *Epistle on Sufism* (*al-Risāla al-qushayrīya fī ʿilm al-taṣawwuf*). He borrowed heavily from *The Unveiling of What Is Veiled* (*Kashf al-maḥjūb*) of ʿAlī ibn ʿUthmān Hujwīrī (d. ca. 463/1071). The first two of these three were from ʿAṭṭār's own city of Nishapur, while Hujwīrī hailed from farther east, namely, the city of Ghazni (Ghazna). The charm of ʿAṭṭār's version lies in his storytelling abilities, as well as his clear and often poignant writing style, which give each account a literary quality not found in the sources from which he borrows. This prose composition includes the author's introduction and ninety-seven biographical entries.

In the coming chapters on ʿAṭṭār, I will offer original translations, drawing from each of these sources, as well as from those of other Persian and Arabic authors, often with ties to the Sufi tradition.[18] I have focused on some texts more than others, for this book is not an introduction to all of ʿAṭṭār's themes and thoughts. Rather, each of the various topics at hand within the larger framework of ʿAṭṭār's "religion of love" has guided me in choosing which passage or text to highlight.

3

The City and the Saint

ʿAṭṭār's writings are in many ways the product of his place and time, even as he aimed to transcend both. From a historical perspective, his residence in a place of intellectual vibrance—premodern Nishapur—helped create the richness of characters and places in his poems and book of prose. Nishapur's climate also contributed to his breadth of knowledge on theology, ethics, and saints' lives. For that reason, in this chapter I will attempt to recreate two facets of ʿAṭṭār's background: the historical, insofar as it offers a glimpse of medieval Nishapur, and the hagiographical, insofar as it presents the life and legend of ʿAṭṭār as captured in premodern biographies.

ʿAṭṭār was born in Kadkan, which was a satellite village to the metropolis of Nishapur (Nayshābūr or Nīshābūr). His village sat in a quarter of larger Nishapur called Shāmāt, in the area of Rukh.[1] He seems to have lived, worked, and died in Nishapur, more specifically, in a section of Nishapur called Shādyākh. There is some confusion about the location of his tomb relative to the original city of Nishapur. According to his biography by Amīr Dawlatshāh (d. 900/1494 or 913/1507), ʿAṭṭar's shrine was originally erected outside of Shādyākh, that is, outside of Nishapur, at a place called Shahr-i Bāzargān.[2] Later, in 891/1486, the Turkic poet, litterateur, and architect Amīr ʿAlī-shīr Nawāʾī (d. 906/1501) built a replacement shrine for ʿAṭṭar at the same location. Nevertheless, the original perimeters of Shādyākh remain murky, so it is quite possible that his shrine's location falls within the area of Shādyākh.[3]

Most people in ʿAṭṭār's time lived in villages and rural areas, not cities. So, to understand Nishapur's true size and significance, one must also consider its many villages and neighborhoods, such as Kadkan. The roughly 1,700 villages surrounding Nishapur had an average population of about three hundred people per village, which adds up to around five hundred thousand people. ʿAṭṭār's native village, Kadkan, was home to around two or three hundred families. Nishapur itself, situated on a stretch of land that measured around 6.5 square miles, had a population that was two hundred thousand at its highest, around a century before our poet was born, and which hovered around one hundred thousand, a number quite high for a medieval city.[4] It was composed of sixty smaller neighborhoods.[5] It was not only the largest but also the most scholarly active city of what we might call "the Persianate world," or the area that was then called *diyār al-ʿajam* (Land of the Non-Arabs) or *Īrān-shahr* (Iran).[6]

Eastern Iran: ʿAṭṭār's Home, Sufism's University

Nishapur was known for its legacy of Sunni scholarship, its sheer cotton fabrics and silks, its ceramics and turquoise, its famous and even edible clay, but also for its many earthquakes.[7] In fact, those earthquakes come up repeatedly in its history and seem to have been a major challenge for its inhabitants. It was a center of activity, both cultural and economic. One thousand camels would make their way into the city daily, carrying, among other necessities, the fruits of the farms around the city.[8] Those farms, like the city itself, were watered by one of ancient Iran's most impressive technological feats: the qanat watering system, which transferred water from aquifers through underground, interconnected passageways, using the force of gravity. There was a sense, in that time, that cities served a purpose beyond economics. Merchants and aristocrats, through their donations and vows, supported religio-scholarly institutions. This meant that their activities in the market and in the public domain aimed at something higher than life within the city.

In ʿAṭṭār's day, however, Nishapur had lost much of its glory due to attacks on the city from the outside, as well as violent rivalries within the city. During his parents' lifetimes, and perhaps during his early childhood, a group of nomadic raiders attacked

Nishapur, leaving much of it in ruins. These were the Oghuz (Oğuz, or Ghuzz) Turkmen. Hostilities had begun earlier with a dispute and confrontation between the Oghuz chieftains and Aḥmad b. Malikshāh Sanjar, the Seljuk ruler of the Khorasan region from 1097 to 1118.[9] Having already conquered the capital of Khorasan, Marv (or Merv), as well as the city of Ṭūs, the Oghuz raided Nishapur during the year 548/1153. Records of the occupation describe pillage, rape, and torture, as well as a famine that followed the carnage. Residents witnessed a pile of the corpses of 15,000 men that accounted for only two quarters of the city. They also recounted the razing of institutions and buildings, including twelve libraries, twenty-five seminaries, and countless private residences.

Matters did not improve once the Oghuz attacks were over. Local gangs took advantage of the mayhem and wrought their own destruction on the city. Fighting between the city's Shāfiʿī and Ḥanafī factions, two schools of legal interpretation within Islam, led to even more disorder and ruin. At one point in these interdenominational rivalries, the district housing the apothecaries' shops burned down, with it, in all likelihood, that of ʿAṭṭār's own father. This was in the year 553/1158.[10]

From this situation, Shādyākh, once a western suburb of Nishapur, rose to become a replacement for the city's previous center. It was a location attached to the outer gate of the city, that is, adjacent to Nishapur but still outside it.[11] Within, one would have found mostly gardens and a retreat for some of the city's elites. After the events that followed the Oghuz raids, Shādyākh's walls were rebuilt, and the city's remaining population relocated here. This new Nishapur was a much more modest and smaller Nishapur than what had been.[12] It was leveled, after ʿAṭṭār's lifetime, by an earthquake in 669/1270, after which point it had to be built again.[13]

For Nishapur's residents, despite the carnage their parents and their grandparents had described when remembering the Oghuz, nothing compared to the Mongol invasions. It took the invaders only three days to overwhelm the city, which happened on 10 April 1221 (15 Ṣafar 618). That was a Saturday. The massacring of residents continued for four more days, until the morning of Wednesday, when only four hundred craftsmen were allowed to live. Those killed in Nishapur and its surrounding areas, including

ʿAṭṭār, supposedly numbered an almost unbelievable 1,747,000 people.[14] Even today, with our massively sized cities, that is a staggering number. Yet, at the time, it must have seemed apocalyptic. Location after location westward from Nishapur fell to the Mongol victors after that. Around thirty years following the fall of Nishapur, the Mongols arrived at and began the siege of Islam's number one city, Baghdad, on 29 January 1258 (22 Muḥarram 656). In this way, ʿAṭṭār's death marks the beginning of a new era in the political and social history of Islam.

Despite their contentions, the Ḥanafī and Shāfiʿī schools had contributed greatly to the flourishing intellectual climate of Nishapur. At one point, these two branches of Sunni jurisprudence laid claim to so many institutions that the turmoil of the aforementioned Oghuz Turkmen raids wreaked destruction on no less than eight Ḥanafī seminaries and seventeen Shāfiʿī seminaries.[15] What Nishapur left to the world, beyond its institutions, were the scholars shaped by them. One could, indeed, create a long list of scholars, saints, poets, and politicians who shifted the trajectories of Islamic thought and came either from this city or one of its satellite villages. That list would include the famous author of *Ṣaḥīḥ Muslim*, Muslim b. al-Ḥajjāj (d. 261/875), the great Shāfiʿī legal scholar Imām al-Ḥaramayn al-Juwaynī, and many others, especially—as we will see—contributors to the legacy of Sufism.

Nishapur matters to us both as ʿAṭṭār's place of origin and as a location for lasting cultural, scholarly, and literary changes within Islam itself. Thus, the aforementioned phrase "Sufism's university" alludes to the Khorasan region, that is, eastern Iran, as a site of development in Islam's intellectual history, a region that included important cities such as Nishapur, Marv, Ṭūs, Balkh, and Herat. Among these cities, Nishapur was quite prominent, and the religious, cultural, and intellectual changes in that city (as in Khorasan more broadly) allowed for the development of Sufism, the branch of knowledge most pivotal to ʿAṭṭār's writings.

What we call "Sufism," or *taṣawwuf*, is intertwined with early Islamic movements to worship God and even know Him in a special sort of way, that is, in a way above and beyond the modes of practice, meditation, and contemplation required by Islamic law. Each school of law present in Nishapur had teachings regarding what advanced devotion might entail. There were, though, three movements that most left their mark on Sufism in Nishapur.

Three Devotional Movements in Nishapur

One major movement in Nishapur was the Karrāmiyya. This group of pious men and women had their own distinctive legal school and theological creed, and were considered, in many ways, revolutionary. This was, in part, because the Karrāmiyya encouraged public displays of piety. They were easily identified by their white cone-shaped hats, sheepskin clothes, and public acts of asceticism, especially public preaching.[16] Moreover, they promoted a life withdrawn from earning a living. The Karrāmiyya's message seems to have appealed to the city's poor, which meant their presence was focused in Nishapur's more impoverished northwest quarter—a district that was undesirable because it lacked water canals, so water had to be carried to one's home.[17] Their views on avoiding work and rousing the underprivileged created great opposition in a city with a powerful merchant class that served as a locus of trade between China and western Asia.

The Karrāmiyya movement was founded by Abu ʿAbdallāh Muḥammad b. Karrām from the Sistān or Sijistān region. He was a man of the people. He had no interest in keeping his own wealth, which he sold, devoting his time to preaching. It was in Nishapur—the home of Ibn Karrām's teacher, the world-renouncing Aḥmad b. Ḥarb (d. 234/848–849)—that the Karrāmiyya movement grew into a real sociocultural force.[18] In 488/1095, however, that came to an end, when the Karrāmiyya were expelled from the town, as their theology and way of life were seen as a threat to others in Nishapur. Hostility against the Karrāmiyya almost definitely stemmed from their opposition to aristocratic and mercantile values of Islam upheld in Nishapur, the very same mercantile values that would give our Sufi poet the penname "The Apothecary," wherein one's profession indicates one's identity. The Karrāmiyya's strengths also made them threatening. They were organized and outspoken, being the first to build *khānaqāhs*, which were places of worship and group management—a practice that would later be taken up by the city's

Sufis. The *khānaqāh* is just one of their legacies in Sufism and in Nishapur, and it is a common symbol in ʿAṭṭār's poetry: a place of austere worship for the committed ascetic. Their most lasting legacy may have been the ongoing debate among Sufis about the value of avoiding work for the sake of trust in God, a topic found in the sayings of countless early Sufis and in the writings of ʿAṭṭār and Jalāl al-Dīn Rūmī (d. 672/1273), among others.

A second movement that shaped Nishapur and our poet was the Malāmatiyya, which refers not to an individual's name, as was the case with the Karrāmiyya, but rather to their manner of observing piety. Malāmatiyya means "People of Blame," the word "blame" here signifying "avoiding esteem," referencing this group's deep suspicion of acclaim. In the premodern city, social recognition for one's piety could turn one into a medieval rock star, such as was the case with Aḥmad b. Ḥanbal (d. 241/855), Abū Saʿīd b. Abī al-Khayr, and countless others. Even if not to that degree, public piety could make a person famous in one's neighborhood or extended family. This created a crisis of intention: trying to reach the highest echelons of the God-human relationship meant risking one's sincerity. One could, even unwittingly, begin to play the piety game for the sake of recognition. As a protective measure, the Malāmatiyya advocated a complete veiling of devotional activity and achievements. They sought sincerity of intention (*ikhlāṣ*), which for them was in opposition to pietistic ostentation (*riyāʾ*). Public *dhikr*, that is, public evocation of God's names, was avoided, as were the other sorts of observable actions that groups like the Karrāmiyya undertook, such as distinctive dress, preaching, visible poverty, or the composition of treatises. Earning was not discouraged but, to the contrary, an inalienable part of the Malāmatiyya piety, where a person might be a weaver by day but secretly—in the seclusion of a prayer niche—a weeping saint by night.

This sort of "Malāmatiyya" piety pervades ʿAṭṭār's poetry and also serves as the basis for his veneration of the martyred saint al-Ḥallāj, who eschewed the praise of others to such a degree that he associated himself with the damned. Moreover, Malāmatiyya-style piety corresponded perfectly to the deeply ingrained spiritual component in eastern Iranian trade and artisanry, which usually involved a code of virtuous conduct specific to each profession through which one sought God's approval.[19]

The Malāmatiyya was a movement native to Nishapur that unfortunately has not left us much in writing, probably because of its emphasis on confidentiality, but also because Sufis eventually claimed it as their own after they became the dominant school of piety in Nishapur. The Malāmatiyya instead relied on charismatic teachers, Abū Ḥafṣ al-Ḥaddād (d. ca. 270/879), Ḥamdūn al-Qaṣṣār (d. 271/884), and Abū ʿUthmān al-Ḥīrī (d. 298/910), whose instruction benefited a network of righteous craftsmen and merchants.[20] What these teachers lacked in terms of learning and the mastery of Arabic vis-à-vis their Sufi counterparts in Baghdad they made up for in their commitment to an earnest relationship with God bereft of display. Their approach was preserved in a treatise by Abū ʿAbd al-Raḥmān al-Sulamī (d. 412/1021), a Sufi with familial ties to the Malāmatiyya, but their approach also emerges in ʿAṭṭār's poetry as a preoccupation with unwavering sincerity.

Eventually, however, one expression of piety came to the fore in Nishapur, absorbing some of those that existed before it. It was taught and practiced by those adhering to the Shāfiʿī legal school. This group was the Ṣūfiyya, which we can call "Sufism" proper, a movement that began in ninth-century Baghdad but borrowed much from Basra and even from Nishapur. They were more public than the Malāmatiyya but also more reserved and respectful of the mercantile status quo than the Karrāmiyya. Their connections to the highly organized and erudite Shāfiʿī-Ashʿarī scholars, along with their reputation for a long tradition of pious saints, helped the Ṣūfiyya gain traction in Nishapur. While early Sufism (or *taṣawwuf*, the act of practicing Sufism) was associated with Baghdad and the famous al-Junayd (d. 298/910), Nishapur became its cultural hub once Shiʿi Buyids began to rule Baghdad, drying up patronage for Sunni learning. Many Sunni scholars and renunciants sought such patronage in Nishapur, the capital of eastern Iran or "Khurāsān."[21] As it developed, two of the most important figures in the consolidation of Sufism were from Nishapur. The first was al-Sulamī, whose writings helped solidify a sense that Sufism had historical continuity and deserved its place at the table of Sunni normativity. The second, his student Abū al-Qāsim ʿAbd al-Karīm ibn Hawāzin al-Qushayrī (d. 465/1072), furthered the process of consolidation in his writings, including Sufi readings of the Qurʾān. Nearby, in Ṭūs, were such figures as

Abū Naṣr al-Sarrāj (d. 378/988), Abū Ḥāmid al-Ghazālī, and his brother Aḥmad al-Ghazālī. These writers contributed to a process of institutionalization centered in eastern Iran by which Sufism became what we know it to be today.

Indeed, three centuries after al-Junayd and the early Sufi masters, Sufism's true period of consolidation was happening around the time of ʿAṭṭār and the century following, with Nishapur as an epicenter of such activity. Loose relationships of mentorship became solidified as chains of authority linking a mere pupil to the Prophet himself through a wise master. Sufis went from having little discernible organization, with the spiritual life mostly revolving around key saintly figures, to existing in orders, with various established forms of succession and with shaykhs serving as teachers to a much larger number of students.[22] Especially in Nishapur, the role of such teachers began to change from a once hands-off approach to very particular and exacting styles of spiritual training.[23] This made writings on moral psychology and the stages of the soul, such as ʿAṭṭār's, incredibly valuable. Politically, because of the respect that many Muslims had for pious Sufis and their methods, the Sufis went from being suspect and, because of such suspicion, secretive, to becoming moral advisors to kings and viziers.[24] Genres of writing blossomed or were adapted to convey what were once oral teachings: Qurʾānic commentaries, epistles, handbooks, hagiographies, and poems. Persian began to appear as a language suited for books and manuals on the teachings of the Sufi path, while such writing was once exclusively undertaken in Arabic. ʿAṭṭār embraced this, especially in terms of poetry. He not only innovated Persian literary Sufism, he advanced it.

In many ways, ʿAṭṭār's writings aim to transcend Nishapur and even Sufism. This book, in fact, will focus on the transcendent vision for human development that ʿAṭṭār puts forward in his poetry and book of prose. In his thought, Sufism is a means to the completion of human potential. This is why, at times, ʿAṭṭār mentions Sufism in idealistic terms, as the best approach available for training the soul. In this spirit, he quotes Ibn ʿAṭāʾ Aḥmad Ādamī (d. 309/922), a Baghdadi saint who defended ʿAṭṭār's hero al-Ḥallāj and was condemned to the same fate of execution: "Sufism (*taṣawwuf*) means being hitched to the Real (*ḥaqq*) in companionship."[25] (Sufis and others who claimed to have a special relationship with

God or intimate knowledge of God used the name "the Real" to refer to "God as Reality" as opposed to "God in creation.") On the other hand, ʿAṭṭār frequently alludes to the "Sufi" as a person on the path, but with flaws both ethical and intellectual. In one story, a Sufi beats a dog with his cane for rendering his clothes impure.[26] He is chastised by the great Abū Saʿīd b. Abī al-Khayr, as well as by the dog herself, who proclaims the man unworthy of Sufi attire that should indicate care and kindness. Here Abū Saʿīd, ʿAṭṭār's own spiritual forebear, is something more than a mere Sufi: he is a wise judge who stands between two of God's creatures, the Sufi and the dog. Moreover, because the saint intercedes on the Sufi's behalf, Abū Saʿīd is also an intermediary between God and humans. In this way, ʿAṭṭār never idealizes the Sufi as a Sufi. The poet implies, in this, that reality and the institutions aimed at uncovering reality will never coincide perfectly. Rather, human traditions such as Sufism aim to create knowers of God who might resemble saints like Abū Saʿīd.

Historical Legends about the Druggist of Secrets

ʿAṭṭār did more than relate the exemplary lives of the saints of Sufism's past. He was himself remembered as a saint, consistently referred to as "Shaykh" or "master" in the medieval biographical literature. One of his biographers was the later Sufi poet, Nūr al-Dīn ʿAbd al-Raḥmān Jāmī (d. 898/1492). Like ʿAṭṭār before him, and al-Sulamī before ʿAṭṭār, Jāmī contributed to his vision of the Sufi tradition by compiling a book of saints' lives. That book, *Wafts of Intimacy from the Realms of Purest Sanctity* (*Nafaḥāt al-uns min ḥaḍarāt al-quds*), became an abiding version of Sufi history, and one of two well-known, if historically flawed, versions of the life of ʿAṭṭār.[27]

Jāmī hints at ʿAṭṭār's role in the history of Sufism by where he places the poet. First, Jāmī situates ʿAṭṭār's biography between that of Sanāʾī and that of Musharrif al-Din Muṣliḥ Saʿdī (d. ca. 690/1291). Neither of those two is a renowned Sufi master with a long line of spiritual descendants. Both, however, are major contributors to Persian Sufi poetics. The difference with ʿAṭṭār, however, is that his poetry cannot be likened to that of other such poets, even that of literary giants. ʿAṭṭār's lines have, after all, a sense of spiritual insight that distinguishes ʿAṭṭār from others that Jāmī knows. In Jāmī's words, "The sheer number of secrets regarding God's absolute oneness, or realities of experience and of ecstasy, that one finds in his rhymed-couplet poems, or his shorter lyrical *ghazals*, cannot be matched by the written legacy of anyone else in this Sufi faction."[28] Considering the prominence of ʿAṭṭār within Persian Sufism, the lack of visible connections between ʿAṭṭār to familiar Sufi masters is a problem that Jāmī attempts to solve.

In order to bring to light ʿAṭṭār's ties to the Sufi tradition, Jāmī includes two possibilities for ʿAṭṭār's line of saintly transmission back to the Prophet Muhammad—what is called a "chain," or *silsila*, by which some holy personage would bridge ʿAṭṭār to the institutionalized Sufism known by Jāmī. The first possibility Jāmī offers is that ʿAṭṭār might have been a disciple of the famous Kubrawī master known as Majd al-Dīn Baghdādī (d. 616/1219). Jāmī bases this possibility on a mention in the poet's introduction to *The Memorial of God's Friends*, in which ʿAṭṭār describes having visited the master and having had a conversation with him. The encounter, a rare autobiographical moment in the author's preface to his masterpiece on saintly lives, does certainly seem significant.[29] Yet the figure that Jāmī identifies as the famous Majd al-Dīn Baghdādī, whose full name was Abū Saʿīd Sharaf b. al-Muʾayyad b. Abī l-Fatḥ al-Baghdādī, was probably in reality a saint more local to ʿAṭṭār's Nishapur. ʿAṭṭār identifies him only as "Majd al-Dīn Khwārazmī." The confusion, it seems, stems originally from a possibility raised by a certain Shaykh Ādharī-Ṭūsī (d. 866/1461–1462), author of *Gems of What Has Remained* (*Jawāhir al-āthār*). The author of this book argues that ʿAṭṭār refers to the renowned Sufi teacher Majd al-Dīn Baghdādī, despite the naming discrepancy, because Majd al-Dīn Baghdādī did indeed hail from "little Baghdad," a neighborhood of Khwarazm, which would explain ʿAṭṭār's reference to him as "Khwārazmī" instead of "Baghdādī."[30] This somewhat farfetched theory has been rejected by contemporary scholars of Persian literature, who have identified this "Majd al-Dīn Khwārazmī" as other alternatives, such as an Arabic grammarian who lived in Nishapur, or a virtually unknown student of Majd al-Dīn Baghdādī named Aḥmad Khwārī.[31]

Of course, even Jāmī seems to realize that this encounter is not weighty evidence of an affiliation, and so Jāmī offers another alternative, one reflective of ʿAṭṭār's particular approach to human-divine relationships as evidenced in his poetry. Jāmī tells us that "some have said that ʿAṭṭār was initiated by an Uwaysī connection."[32] By this, Jāmī references the Prophet Muhammad's companion from Yemen, Uways al-Qaranī (d. 37/657), who never met the Prophet in person. Within Sufi practices of initiation, it is possible to have a master-disciple relationship with a person who has passed, even if they have died long ago, much as Uways in Yemen learned from the Prophet in Medina through a link that transcended physical presence. "One finds in the lectures of Mawlānā Jalāl al-Dīn Rūmī, God bless his saintly heart," Jāmī reports, "that the light of Manṣūr al-Ḥallāj, even 150 years after his execution, disclosed itself to Farīd al-Dīn ʿAṭṭār's spirit and trained him on the path."[33] For obvious reasons, a historical analysis of this claim is impossible. Judging from ʿAṭṭār's devotion to al-Ḥallāj and many poetic celebrations of condemned lovers of God, Jāmī's claim certainly makes sense.

Another famous account of ʿAṭṭār's life appears in a collection called *The Memorial of Poets* (*Tadhkirat al-shuʿarāʾ*) by Amīr Dawlatshāh b. Amīr ʿAlāʾ al-Dawla Bukhtīsha al-Ghāzī al-Samarqandī. Dawlatshāh was a Timurid courtier born to a prominent and politically connected family, who seems to have had trouble finding financial support for his poetry. Perhaps as an alternative, he produced a compendium of lives of Arabic and Persian poets, with samples of their work.[34] Generally, scholars of Persian literature have seen Dawlatshāh's account of ʿAṭṭār's life as fanciful. Dawlatshāh has, for example, a brief consideration of ʿAṭṭār's possible links to Sufi masters. Like Jāmī, he mentions Majd al-Dīn Baghdādī but connects him to ʿAṭṭār only insofar as Baghdādī (a major Kubrawī master) gave ʿAṭṭār a "cloak of blessings," which is not the same as a direct affiliation.[35] ʿAṭṭār's first trainer on the path was a certain Shaykh Rukn al-Dīn Akkāf, to whose Sufi monastery he fled after his repentance and his initial embrace of the spiritual way.[36] After spending several years with Akkāf, he undertook the Hajj pilgrimage, returned home to Nishapur or thereabouts, and became engaged in his work of collecting and conveying the lives and wisdom of Sufi saints.[37] Toward the end of his life, he abandoned the writing of poetry.[38]

A Sufi saint needs a conversion story. More than merely a literary trope, conversion stories are a reflection of Sufi ethical theory. Some repentance or awakening marks the beginning of the path and the abandonment of heedlessness. To say that a person has no conversion story, no repentance, is to imply that they are either unaware of their imperfections or somehow born perfect, and neither applies to the saint. ʿAṭṭār himself will always include each saint's conversion story, if available, in *The Memorial of God's Friends*. Dawlatshāh and Jāmī have very similar conversion stories for ʿAṭṭār. Jāmī's is quite short:

> They say that the cause of his turn toward the way of spiritual refinement was as follows. One day he was busy in his apothecary, madly absorbed in trade and profit. A dervish came to his shop, seeking charity, saying a few times,
>
> "Anything for God?"
>
> ʿAṭṭār gave him nothing.
>
> "Sir! How will you die?" the dervish asked.
>
> "Just like you will," ʿAṭṭār replied.
>
> "Can you die in the same way that I will?" the dervish said.
>
> The dervish had a beggar's wooden bowl, which he thereupon placed beneath his head. He cried, "Allah!" and surrendered his spirit to death.
>
> ʿAṭṭār took on a changed state, closed his shop, and started out upon this path.[39]

The contrast is vivid. While ʿAṭṭār is not willing to part with even a small amount of wealth "for God," the dervish yields his life to complete his return. The dervish's visit was, in fact, one in which the poor man sought not to take something from ʿAṭṭār but rather to give something to ʿAṭṭār, to give to ʿAṭṭār an awakening under the guise of taking his charity. Dawlatshāh's account includes more detail but has the same major themes:

> The reason for the shaykh's repentance was that his father had a large, successful, and busy apothecary. After his father's passing, ʿAṭṭār followed in his father's footsteps, and his own apothecary was quite beautiful. People came from all over to enjoy its sights and fragrances.

> One day the shaykh was sitting very regally at the front of his shop, when some rascally young men with belts [of the antinomian lovers of God] approached, in front of whom suddenly appeared a madman of the Farzāna Order. This man arrived at the door of ʿAṭṭār's shop. The man was looking closely inside his shop. His eyes filled with tears, and he let out a sigh. The shaykh [ʿAṭṭār] said to that dervish:
>
> "Why are you staring? It would be better for you to pass by here quickly."
>
> The madman said:
>
> "Dear sir! I travel lightly. I have nothing but this cloak on my back.
>
> O sir whose sack is filled with aromatic drugs
> What's the plan when it's time to depart?
>
> I can leave this bazaar in a flash. But you need to think about managing your stockpiles and burdens. Use insight to ponder your own spiritual state!"
>
> ʿAṭṭār asked:
>
> "How can you leave as suddenly as you say?"
>
> He replied:
>
> "Like so."
>
> Then he removed his cloak, put it beneath his head, and gave up his ghost to the Real. The shaykh ached in wonder at the words of this mad lover of God. His heart burned up and acquired the scent of the potpourri incense (*muthallath*) he sold for healing. The worldly became for him as cold as the camphor he sold for purifying the dead. He forsook the shop and was fed up with the bazaar of worldly affairs.[40]

The nature of his conversion, and even some of its details, might be based in historical reality. Nevertheless, we do know from ʿAṭṭār's writings that he did not flee from his shop. Rather, he maintained his apothecary as he wrote poetry.[41] Indeed, by ʿAṭṭār's own description, the wealth made from his business, and probably also from a small farm that he mentions, freed him to write poetry without the need of a patron.[42] This was a fortuitous state of affairs for Persian poetry, both because in general Sufi poetry on love, saints, and metaphysics did not pay, and also because Nishapur during ʿAṭṭār's lifetime saw numerous upheavals in power—not the sort of climate conducive to courtly literature.

Dawlatshāh also provides a moving account of ʿAṭṭār's death. It is an event commemorated in a verse engraving at the mausoleum in Nishapur built by Nawāʾī.[43] Dawlatshāh's account tells of the poet and Sufi master's well-known beheading at the hands of invading Mongol soldiers:

> During the invasion of Genghis Khan, the shaykh was taken captive by the Mongols. He was martyred in the widescale slaughter of the city's inhabitants. He was martyred because the parrot of his blessed spirit had grown weary of being jailed in the cage of his body. It longed to be in the sugarcane field of union [with God], so ʿAṭṭār sought to hasten his death. It is said that a Mongol wanted to kill him, but another Mongol said,
>
> "Do not kill that old man—I will give you one thousand dirhams for him."
>
> The Mongol was about to sell him and thus leave off killing him when ʿAṭṭār said,
>
> "Don't sell! They'll pay a better price for me elsewhere."
>
> Someone else said, "Do not kill that old man—I will give you a sack of chaff for him."
>
> The shaykh then said, "Sell me! For I am worth no better than this."
>
> The shaykh then drank the elixir of martyrdom, reaching thereby the rank of the felicitous.[44]

Dawlatshāh tells us that the poet's martyrdom took place on 10 Jamādī al-Thānī 627 (or 3 May 1230). All historical accounts, however, report that this raid occurred in 618/1221. It seems unlikely that the Mongols would sack Nishapur once again when they already came through the city in 618/1221, which makes Dawlatshāh's idea that ʿAṭṭār was killed during a later raid, and hence at a later date, rather dubious.[45]

Today, historians do not give much substance to these two traditional accounts of ʿAṭṭār's life. Both Jāmī and Dawlatshāh lived centuries after ʿAṭṭār, and neither tell us very much about their sources. Considering, however, the lack of other useful accounts of ʿAṭṭār's life, as well as the way in which these depictions have shaped the remembrance of ʿAṭṭār and the legend of ʿAṭṭār, they merit mention. They also merit mention because elements of these traditional narratives seem to arise from sources available exclusively to these premodern biographers that are no longer available today. According to Muḥammad-Riḍā Shafīʿī-Kadkanī, Dawlatshāh is especially useful when it comes to ʿAṭṭār's years of birth and death (while the editor of Dawlatshāh's text—Edward Brown—dismisses Dawlatshāh as "not a very accurate writer").[46] This is because Dawlatshāh only specifies the day, month, and year of birth and death for three poets in his *Memorial of Poets*: three out of around 140 names mentioned. Those three are Kamāl Ismāʿīl Iṣfahānī, Amīr Ḥusaynī Harawī, and our very own ʿAṭṭār. Iṣfahānī (d. 635/1237) was a poet and panegyrist, and Harawī (d. 719/1319) was a poet most famous for posing the seventeen questions that led to Maḥmūd Shabistarī's (d. ca. 720/1320) well-known versified reflection on Sufi metaphysics, *The Garden of Secrets* (*Gulshan-i rāz*). Shafīʿī-Kadkanī asks a legitimate question: Why would Dawlatshāh forge dates for these three poets—two of whom are rather minor poets—and not create such dates for the likes of Sanāʾī, Rūmī, or Ḥafiẓ? Rather, it is quite possible that Dawlatshāh had access to a text currently unavailable to us today, especially since he disagrees—seemingly intentionally—with the year of death chiseled on ʿAṭṭār's tombstone, 586/1190.[47] As mentioned, Dawlatshāh's proposed year, 627/1230, only works if one imagines that there was some later Mongol onslaught on Nishapur, for which there is no evidence. Concerning the poet's birth year, while Dawlatshāh's text has 513/1119, a textual misreading makes it quite easy to mistake 553 for 513, giving us as a date of birth of 6 Shaʿbān 553 (9 September 1158), and a much more realistic lifespan of sixty-three solar years for ʿAṭṭār—as opposed to the now famous 114 years of life, equaling the number of chapters in the Qurʾān.

Even if their accounts lack historical accuracy, Jāmī and Dawlatshāh lived in circumstances, times, and places that resembled ʿAṭṭār's—in ways that our modern situations do not. Hence their biographies of ʿAṭṭār can offer us a sense of the significance of his life and death for the generations who followed him. Take for example the death of ʿAṭṭār at the hands of Mongol soldiers. Certainly, as historians, we can dismiss certain folkloric elements of the story, especially the shaykh's self-deprecating maneuver of trying to convince the Mongol soldier to sell him for less. The report is too poetically perfect and too difficult to report to be believable. What does seem to be the case, however, is that ʿAṭṭār was indeed killed during the Mongol invasions or soon thereafter—a set of invasions that meant the death of nearly every resident of that city, if the reports are to be believed. The city, Nishapur, would have to be rebuilt and would never again achieve its former glory.[48] Thus, the larger message of this narrative—its very meaning and its reason for existence—is that ʿAṭṭār's death marks the simultaneous end of one of Islamic civilization's major cities and also the end of one of Sufism's two birthplaces. Dawlatshāh's account so ably conveys this message that one wonders how much it matters whether the story is historically true.

Part I

Religion

4

Religion, Then and Now

Writing about a "religion of love" in ʿAṭṭār's works creates a dilemma. The word "religion" has acquired certain modern connotations through the course of history. This has brought some historians to declare that careful scholars should almost never use the word "religion" as a translation for any premodern word. Assumptions about "religion," they say, usually privilege a Protestant Christian point of view, and Protestant Christianity is a relatively recent and European phenomenon in comparison to global intellectual movements of one thousand years ago or more. "Religion," according to a Protestant point of view, is interior and often private, with beliefs mattering more than practices.[1] Premodern philosophies and modes of worship, however, were often public and part of many facets of everyday life. Despite this difference between past and present, as historian Brent Nongbri argues, "religion" has become a universal term to describe dissimilar phenomena, even when the word "religion," as a translation for other historically indigenous terms, does not fit. Latin's *religio*, Greek's *thrēskeia*, and Arabic's *dīn* comprise his central examples. The last of those three, *dīn*, is an important part of ʿAṭṭār's poetic vocabulary, even if its signification had changed somewhat for ʿAṭṭār and his audience in the six centuries since the age of the Qurʾān.

The "modern" and the "Protestant," I contend, should have no monopoly over "religion" as a word or concept. ʿAṭṭār's way of love describes a psychological, ethical, and practical reality for which we might have no better word than "religion." His overarching theory of love and union is a "moral universal," in that it presents a way of living and being that includes all people and all potential acts. That is, in a way that many Muslims and Christians imagine their respective religions, ʿAṭṭār offers a "religion" wherein love of God and for God is the reality behind the message of all the prophets, the end of all good actions, and thus a way of life. Also, while I will offer some discussion of the word *dīn* (closest to "religion") in his thought, one should not suppose that this is just a matter of translating one specific term in ʿAṭṭār's vocabulary. The word "religion" best describes the overall message that ʿAṭṭār has for his audience. Love goes beyond the word *dīn* for ʿAṭṭār. This is because love—as discussed in this book's second part—shifts paradigms, transforming and awakening a person to realities beyond everyday human experiences:

> Today I'm the one who's enamored, perplexed—
> without *dīn*, without heart, without disbelief or belief,
> entirely lost, needy, and agitated,
> unable to do anything, absolutely confused.[2]

As we will see, *dīn* gives order to those seeking God, whereas love disrupts that order. Both are essential components of ʿAṭṭār's conception of the path to God that I will call "religion."

"Religion" can be used when conveying ʿAṭṭār's views on the way to God, as long as the reader becomes aware of its ambiguities and imperfections. Translating between languages, times, and cultures will always present us with such compromises. For example, the word I translate as "love," the Persian (and Arabic) *ʿishq*, has a difficult history in Islamic theology.[3] Words for love abound in Persian and Arabic. Among them, *ʿishq* signifies a passionate, torturous, desirous, and even dangerous type of love. But I translate it as "love," just as I translate many other terms as ably as I can. If important enough, the term might receive a note or in-text explanation, as *ʿishq* enjoys here. Otherwise, I might simply highlight the original word using parentheses. This notifies specialists of the word's origin, while allowing general audiences to circumnavigate confusion, so that they can learn other things until they take interest in such details. In this case, the word "religion" allows me to describe a related set of the poet's commitments most analogous to the concept of religion, despite the challenges that such a term presents.

This is because, historically speaking, discovering our connections to the past can often be as useful as emphasizing the differences between past and present. Many of the boundaries we have drawn between present and past, West and East, our world and ʿAṭṭār's, are imagined. Pious practice, social boundaries, ritual, and many of the other elements that we now see as comprising "religion" have morphed but did exist in the time of our poet. Historians Carlin Barton and Daniel Boyarin make this argument in their study of ancient life and the place of "religion." They remind us that the word "religion" evolved over time, as did our word "superstition." Religion (*religio*) came to mean solemn observation of duty, while superstition (*superstitio*) came to mean excessive *religio*, that is, excessive cultic zeal.[4] All elements of religion existed back then—myth, ritual, architecture, social contracts, and norms—even if people did not distinguish them from other life practices as "religion." Yet it would be mistaken to claim that religion did *not* exist before modernity. The concept of heresy existed, for example, in order to demarcate Christianity in a way that would exclude Jews who might revere Jesus. Even today such demarcations inform our categories of "religion," "Christianity," and "Judaism." This renders us unable to say that religion somehow suddenly came to exist at a certain point in time.[5]

In a sense, religion both does and does not exist in the past. Religion does not exist in the past because ancients (and premodern Persians such as ʿAṭṭār) partitioned their lives differently than we do. In their lives, temporal power, magic, rituals, laws, and institutions blended worldly and otherworldly concerns more closely. When one goes back many centuries, science cannot be neatly separated from religion; history cannot be neatly separated from myth; and law cannot be neatly separated from God's will. Yet religion does exist in the past insofar as we can locate its constituent elements there. We might envision ancient "religion" as a series of buds from which grew the conceptions that inform "religion" today. In imagining religion this way, we realize how our own present reality occurs within a historical trajectory of concepts and practices and is a blend of old and new. Some of those older "religious" concepts from ʿAṭṭār's eastern Iranian Islamic milieu will appear in the next chapter's discussion of *dīn*.

In fact, there is no clean break between the premodern and the modern. History schoolbooks taught us that one thing led to another in a chain to create the supposedly scientific, ordered, rational, and free lifestyle that is "modern."[6] Yet, in reality, just as the traits of our biological ancestors appear in new genetic configurations, concepts of the past usually inform modernity. What changes is the grand narrative, or what philosopher Jason Josephson-Storm has called the "master paradigm." For example, superstition (*superstitio*) was once the counterpart to true Christianity. It was unorthodox, extreme, and demonic. It included magical practices and mythical tales.[7] Today, superstition is the counterpart to "science," which has often come to mean empirical forms of investigation. Since the scientific excludes the religious, religion—once the counterpart to superstition—can now be equated with superstition.

Again, what has changed is the overarching narrative by which we see the world. Modernity, then, is how we choose to label and see things, religion among them. It is not so much that we *are* modern, but that we *do* modern; modernity is something that we impose on the world around us through our perceptions, as opposed to something that asks to be seen.[8] Modernity might be imagined as a curtain that alters the sunlight we strive to see, with religion as one of many patterns on that curtain.

When I think about history as a continuum—when I consider the lack of any concrete division between the premodern and the modern—my reading of ʿAṭṭār changes. In this newer context, his observations on *dīn*, on love, and on embracing the limits of human understanding have relevance for my modern reality, which often seems dominated by a drive to be scientific, factual, objective, and hence free from religious delusions. In contrast, this first part of the book, on religion, will introduce ʿAṭṭār's view that learned intellectuals often delude themselves, while simple-minded lovers of God enjoy inner enlightenment. That easily might be as true today as it was in the thirteenth century.

Finally, to clarify something important, ʿAṭṭār's religion of transcendent and universal love is Islam. Yet it has surprises for those expecting the normative Islam described by theologians and legal scholars. His *dīn* certainly includes normative Islam but aims beyond it at something less easily understood than normative Islamic beliefs and practices. In fact, because this Islam-as-religion-of-love escapes all understanding, ʿAṭṭār sees love as being hindered by intellectualism. Theories and practices of love only flourish when one throws off the shackles of trying to understand.

5

Dīn, *Dunyā*, and the Pious Life

A number of terms inform ʿAṭṭār's views on the pious life, even if the closest actual word to "religion" in ʿAṭṭār's poetry is *dīn*. ʿAṭṭār places *dīn* within a constellation of related terms, especially *ʿaql* (intellect), *khirad* (intelligence), and *ʿishq* (love).[1] There is also the *madhhab* (way) one chooses to interpret life and the world, something akin to a religious school of thought or a denomination within Islam. There are words such as *millat* (nation), *kīsh* (confession), and, rarely, *ā'īn* (custom), usually used interchangeably with *dīn*. In ʿAṭṭār's language, *dīn* itself signifies one's commitments to God as communicated by prophets. As the heart tries to find its way to reality, *dīn* is a revealed roadmap, a program on how to please God. Thus, *dīn* directs the heart to what lasts and is meaningful. *Dīn* contrasts with *dunyā*, which signifies the parts of living in this world that pass when we die. The *dunyā* encompasses passing pleasures that enthrall us temporarily. If *dīn* is a roadmap to salvation and even reality, *dunyā* resembles the appealing, distracting, and potentially fatal sites along the way to our otherworldly destination with God. Hence, I translate *dunyā* as the "worldly."

Most of all, *dīn* represents the most fundamental choice a believer makes every day to live for something beyond life's pleasures. That is, *dīn* requires a commitment to God, divine law, and self-restraint when faced with the allures of the fleeting material world, namely, again, the *dunyā*. This *dīn-dunyā* binary has a long history of usage in medieval Persian and Arabic literature, including the Ḥadīth.[2] Usage shifts, though, from that found originally in the Qurʾān. In the Qurʾānic sense, *al-dunyā* or *dunyā* does not stand in contrast to *al-dīn* or *dīn*. Rather, *al-dunyā* stands in contrast to *al-ākhira* (the hereafter). The Qurʾān warns against *dunyā* as a bad investment: people who willingly commit acts of evil and ignore the warning of the prophets for restraint have "bought this worldly (*al-dunyā*) life using the hereafter (*al-ākhira*)."[3] They have chosen the immediate gratification of sin over the delayed satisfaction of eternal grace. They have exchanged their felicity for mere distraction.

ʿAṭṭār's vision of *dīn*, however, shifts emphasis away from the afterlife. He urges practitioners to focus less on rewards or punishments in the afterlife, less on *ākhira,* hence his understatement of the hereafter. Yet he still extends the Qurʾānic theme of *dunyā* as poor choice-making, drawing *dīn* into his rebuke of *dunyā*-loving dupes. He personifies both *dīn* and *dunyā* in *The Book of Secrets*:

> O treacherous *dunyā*, how you flaunt yourself before *dīn*!
> But you wouldn't be a vulture, had *dīn* not become a corpse.[4]

For ʿAṭṭār, *dīn* and *dunyā* counteract one another—strengthening one weakens the other. One might be tempted to think of the modern dichotomy between the "religious" and the "secular," but that does not hold here.[5]

To presume that *dīn* is *religion* and that *dunyā* is something like the *secular* would be a misreading of ʿAṭṭār's message. The "religious" and the "secular" oppose each other in a different way than *dīn* and *dunyā*. When a friend tells you that she and her family "are not very religious," a counterbalance to "religious" often comes to mind—the "secular." Your friend might have difficulty describing "secular," except that it is different and separate from "religion," and that it is a pervasive part of a contemporary way of life.[6] Yet when ʿAṭṭār pits *dīn* against *dunyā*, he does not mean that "religion" can help a believer curtail her "secular" impulses. He means that God tries to speak to humans through *dīn*. They, in turn, tend to ignore that call because the glitter of *dunyā* distracts them. The "secular" means "devoid of religion." The *dunyā*, however, can include many elements we would consider parts of religion. Among the most dangerous snares of the *dunyā*, for example, can be religiosity, when that religiosity becomes self-ignorant pietism or corrupt asceticism. As an example of this, ʿAṭṭār gives us Iblīs (Satan), who prostrates out of habit, for such was his wont before the fall:

> The accursed Iblīs (Satan) was prostrating on the earth.
> Jesus asked him, "What's this that you're up to?"
> Iblīs said, "From a time before anyone else existed, a long life ago,
> I have made a regular habit of prostration;
> It's become a habit. That's what keeps me prostrating.
> Yet even if each is a real prostration, I still have to pay the price of damnation."
> Jesus, the son of Mary, said to him: "What blunder!
> You know nothing, so you've made the Way into one of error.
> Be certain that in the path to Him,
> all habit is unworthy of His courtly threshold.
> Those things that happen as habits over time
> have no relationship at all with Reality."
> Iblīs will leave you no bequest whatsoever but *dunyā.*
> You keep stealing from him, here and there,
> but a person who steals property from Satan
> will know the next day plights that no one else can!
> Were Iblīs to disappear from the bazaars,
> when would trade flow through the marketplace?
> Because the *dunyā* is his market, through and through;
> most buying and selling is his handiwork.
> He and only he is the boss of each and every market.
> No affairs of the *dunyā* happen without him, not for a heartbeat.[7]

Even acts of worship, when done only habitually, can constitute the *dunyā.* Prostrations can be as worldly as the marketplace. It is difficult, at first, to discern the connection between the mindless, almost ritualistic prostrations of Satan and his lordship over the marketplace. The two are, however, connected in that the market is a place of habits, a place where people act without much awareness of intention. No unmindful deeds, whether rituals or transactions, will earn a person eternal happiness. According to a saying that ʿAṭṭār attributes to the early saint al-Ḥasan al-Baṣrī (d. 110/728), "Endless and eternal Paradise lies not with these meager daily deeds. Rather, it lies with good intentions."[8] Both the prostrations of habit and the trade of the market aim at rewards without higher awareness, such that both can be *dunyā*-oriented acts. Iblīs is mildly disappointed that his prostrations cannot save him from damnation, because he sees worship as transactional, as many worshipers do. In the bazaar, there is also a thoughtless, almost ritualistic attempt to gain wealth and even happiness in people's quotidian comings and goings. The promises of wealth and happiness can bring one to transgress upon the rights of others, or, at the very least, become heedless of God's remembrance. As such, the bazaar becomes part of the "bad deal" of exchanging nearness with God for the sake of immediate gain, much like the bad deal that Satan made when choosing his pride over eternal felicity.

These facets of the *dunyā* would have been familiar to ʿAṭṭār. On one hand, he lived in the pious setting of Nishapur, surrounded by men and women of learning and praxis. He would have also known some false claimants to piety, who directed their worship not toward the Eternal but toward reputation or mere habit, that is, ephemeral matters. Such performative worship failed to take aim at anything transcendent. On the other hand, he almost definitely faced the moral challenges of the marketplace, having owned and managed his own apothecary among the shops. There, he would have noticed the way buying and selling could entrance a person, which perhaps contributed to his conclusion that worldly striving often means rubbing elbows with Satan. The bewitching attraction of commerce sometimes brings ʿAṭṭār to depreciate the goal of economic success: "For those great ones whose goal was *dīn* / the losses of their *dunyā*-related efforts were profit."[9]

The markets aside, the *dunyā* extends to all distractions from ultimate reality, which is the Real, or God. Even becoming "busy with oneself" counts among its trappings.[10] Some acquiesce and give themselves to the love of *dunyā*. Others who do not, however, still often find themselves drawn by the *dunyā*. They become torn by the gravitational pull of two powerful inclinations, seeking God versus seeking temporal pleasures. Reality lies in the natural propensity to know and love God through *dīn*, but that propensity becomes sullied by an unsound appetite for the lure of the worldly:

> O you who have placed your head on the pillow of
> forgetfulness,
> leaving *dīn* to the wind, for the sake of *dunyā*!
> Does *dīn* suit you, you—with all your possessions of
> *dunyā*?!
> Do you genuinely need *that*, as much as you need *this*?
> You are [by nature] a seeker of *dīn*, even if your heart's
> drunk on *dunyā*.
> Don't you know that that collection of opposites would
> never hold its hand out to help?[11]
> Your heart became preoccupied by two-facedness,
> leaving you beneath a mountain of self-regard and
> conceit:
> You've oriented one of your faces toward *dunyā*,
> the other you've oriented toward *dīn*.
> In the end you will say—after forcefully abandoning
> such two-facedness:
> "One had been enough. One, in the end."
> Disgrace has befallen your heart because of your
> two-facedness;
> For [it has been said in a ḥadīth], "The worst of humanity
> are those with two faces."[12]

The soul becomes split between fidelity and temptation. This renders the person a hypocrite of sorts, having to play two roles in life, failing to do justice to the only role that matters, namely, being aware of God. The heart's struggle between *dīn* and *dunyā*, as described by ʿAṭṭār, occurs within all spheres of life, even if today we attempt to divide those spheres neatly into the religious and the secular. In fact, one wonders if the religious-secular binary has created a newer and more potent expression of "two-facedness."

For ʿAṭṭār, the word *dunyā* represents that which is sensory, material, impermanent, and meaningless. Because the human senses delight in variety and outer beauty, the *dunyā* can become addictive. A person addicted to *dunyā* gradually begins to lose sight of the inner meanings of things. Their senses and outlook become externalized, unable to see beyond surface beauty. In declaring this, ʿAṭṭār expands on a message conveyed by the Qurʾān itself, namely, that the gold and silver that bedazzles our senses has no real value:[13]

> Another said, "I'm a gold-lover—
> the love of gold has become like the kernel within the
> shell of my being.
> Me without gold is like the rose without its yellow
> filament;
> When gold's not in my hands, then, I can't be as gratified
> as the laughing rose.
> The love of the worldly (*dunyā*), the gold of the worldly,
> has changed me,
> filled me with false claims and emptied me of meaning."
> The wise one replied, "Oh besotted by form!
> Hidden from your heart is the dawn of [divine] attributes.
> Whether day or night, you can't overcome your
> day-blindness,
> clinging to form like an ant to its grain.
> Be a man of meaning! And don't entangle yourself in
> forms.
> What is meaning? The root. What is form? Nothing.
> A stone materialized to take on the color gold—
> like a child, you're fixated on mere color."[14]

The phrase "emptied me of meaning" matters in the preceding poem. In ʿAṭṭār's conception, there is a reality that might also be called "spirit" or "meaning." (Meaning, in ʿAṭṭār's world, comes to light; it is not made, it lies with God and is discovered.) "Meaning" is interchangeable with the word "attribute," because all things derive their meanings from the attributes of God. Fixation on the outer forms of things—their colors, shapes, and other deteriorating properties—is a form of blindness. Specifically, it is a blindness to daylight, or hemeralopia, the daylight here representing God's manifest presence. Attachment to outer forms, which is the very essence of a worldly or *dunyā*-oriented mentality, can consume a person from the inside out. The gold lover here confesses that these desires have overcome the very core of his being and have begun to define him. They have emptied him of meaning, because the meaninglessness of the *dunyā* has a compulsive quality to it: it promises more, so one seeks more; one remains unfulfilled, increasing one's need for that which the *dunyā* promises. That which rescues a person and recalibrates them, redirecting them toward the true meaning in all things, is the pursuit of God, His remembrance, as well as the program laid out by Sufi masters, and, even more basically, the program laid out in the *dīn* of Islam.

Finally, because of all the pitfalls, tempters, and false beliefs in human communities, a person must be protective of their *dīn*. ʿAṭṭār wrote during a time of the Crusades, a time of Christian hostility that affected his writings, as we will see in this book's next part. Above that, though, ʿAṭṭār wants to exhort his audience to be—as the Qurʾān says—uncompromising toward those who wish to enshroud God's *dīn* in denials, lies, or false beliefs.[15] In *The Book of Secrets,* for example, ʿAṭṭār tells us of a story narrated by a certain man "of saintly miracles."[16] In that story, a Jewish man went to the "ruins" (*kharābāt*), a place of ill repute in which one might find gambling, alcohol, and other vices. There he gambled away everything, including his home, a garden, and one of his eyes. Yet, when those present told him to "become Muslim and bet away your *dīn,*" he grew angry and "punched the Muslim in the eye," warning him, "Do whatsoever you like / but do not speak to me about my *dīn.*"[17] ʿAṭṭār uses this as an opportunity to urge his audience to have a protective attitude toward their own *dīn*:

> That Jewish man in his Jewishness acted like so,
> I do not know what I should expect from a person of *dīn*.
> All that he had he lost, including an eye.
> But he'd never peel his heart away from his *dīn*.[18]

The way ʿAṭṭār describes it, there are two *dīn*s in these lines about the Jewish man. The first is the universal *dīn* of truth, which is Islam and which ʿAṭṭār attributes to himself and his readers. The second is a localized *dīn* that every devotional tradition claims. This protective attitude that ʿAṭṭār expects his readers to have toward this universal *dīn* can often assume a homiletic tone. When it comes to *dīn,* ʿAṭṭār has no qualms about preaching to and even shaming others.[19]

6

Sciences of Empty Reasoning

ʿAṭṭār's writings encourage us to find our way back to God through a revealed path. In a word, that revealed path is *dīn*. Because *dīn* has been elaborated in the Qurʾān, Ḥadīth, Islamic sciences, and teachings of Sufi saints, ʿAṭṭār wants his audience to appreciate such wisdom and to avoid the tendency to construct one's own reality using philosophical reasoning, that is, a reasoning process untethered from and unguided by revelation. Revelation for ʿAṭṭār would be the Qurʾān and the Prophet Muhammad's way, or *sunna,* as captured in the Ḥadīth, since the Prophet embodied the Qurʾān in his lived example.

ʿAṭṭār expresses the superiority of revealed learning to the rational sciences quite clearly in *The Book of Affliction*:

> Be a man of *dīn*! On intimate terms with the secrets,
> and estranged from the imaginings of the philosopher.
> No human being remains further than the philosopher
> from the revealed law (*sharʿ*) of the Hāshimī prophet.[1]
> Revealed law means obedience to the message bearer,
> while the philosopher's lot will be to rub the dirt of
>   regret on his head.
> Think of the philosopher as following the manner of
>   Zoroastrians,[2]
> turning his back toward the revealed law.
> For the philosophical one, the Universal Intellect is
>   enough;

for our intellect, the command "Say" is enough.
In reality, the hundred worlds of the Universal Intellect
become lost in awe of the one command to "Say!"
If the divine command never brings the intellect to life,
then when will the intellect ever practice servitude?[3]

ʿAṭṭār takes aim at advocates of the rational sciences, especially Islam's most renowned philosopher Abū ʿAlī Ḥusayn ibn Sīnā (d. 428/1037), known in English as Avicenna. During ʿAṭṭār's time, these rational sciences would comprise philosophy and those speculative interpretations of Islamic theology that—in his opinion—read the scriptures allegorically in order to give preference to logical arguments.

Intellect, for Ibn Sīnā and the philosophers, is the faculty that comprehends universals. It is superhuman. There exists in the universe a perfect or "first" intellect that the human soul can try to approach. That first intellect is the Universal Intellect.[4] The human soul approaches that most sublime intellect by mirroring the intellect closest to human capabilities, called the Active Intellect. The Active Intellect might be thought of as the human-facing side of that perfect first intellect that is so sublime that only God lies beyond it. Mirroring occurs as the process of making logical deductions and inductions sharpens the rational part of the soul—in this process, the human soul begins to acquire universals. This aids it along the mirroring process, as it gradually resembles the Active Intellect. When mirroring has become complete and total, the human soul, called the rational soul (*al-nafs al-nāṭiqa*), itself becomes an intellect. This is the highest achievement in Ibn Sīnā's philosophy.

It is not clear the degree to which ʿAṭṭār has studied the concept of "intellect" in Ibn Sīnā's writings, or those of other philosophers. Poets under the influence of Sufism, such as Sanāʾī, ʿAṭṭār, and Rūmī, tended to prioritize the all-consuming power of love over the abilities of the intellect as described by the philosophers, especially Ibn Sīnā.[5] Yet often these poetic criticisms fail to communicate that, for Ibn Sīnā and others who agreed with him, "intellect" was not simply a mechanical, discursive faculty, but rather a supersensory reality with similarities to the Neoplatonic nous.

Nevertheless, ʿAṭṭār, in the preceding lines, means that God's words as spoken to the Prophet Muhammad communicate what no human soul can comprehend, however awakened by and similar to the Active Intellect a philosopher might think that soul has become. In fact, he does not accept Ibn Sīnā's structure of the universe as being surrounded by ascending intellects and seems to use the phrase "Universal Intellect" ironically, only to dismiss it. ʿAṭṭār wants to deny that the universe is a descent of high intellects to lower ones, a descent from intellected universals to particulars. Rather, descent applies to God's pure words sent down to those ready to receive them.[6] The command "Say" (*qul*), which appears frequently in the Qurʾān, conveys God's direct command to the Prophet Muhammad to share God's words with the Qurʾān audience. For example, God commands the Prophet to describe Him: "Say: 'He is God, the uniquely one.'"[7] The Prophet becomes a conduit for God's voice through this command to "say" or "tell them." One must breathe in such divine words, ʿAṭṭār says, study them, and let them guide all ideas and actions. This is why ʿAṭṭār proclaims that "for our intellect, the command 'Say' is enough."

God's revealed words appear as matters of obedience in Islamic law. They appear directly in the text of the Qurʾān. They appear as matters of character in the life of the Prophet and the saints who imitated him, thus in Sufism. With this tradition in mind, ʿAṭṭār highlights three sciences as sciences of *dīn*, namely, *fiqh*, *tafsīr*, and *ḥadīth*, or, the study of Islamic law, the exegesis of the Qurʾān, and the study of Ḥadīth. "Reasoning," by which I mean a logical, proof-based often syllogistic method of drawing conclusions (sometimes called *istidlāl*), has its place but cannot serve as some alternative or preferred route to ultimate realities about God and the soul.[8] There is no alternative to the Qurʾān, Ḥadīth, and their lived realization in the ways of the Sufi saints, which is why ʿAṭṭār seeks to elevate the revealed sciences above the rational sciences. ʿAṭṭār's view of reasoning processes devoid of revealed guidance shapes the sciences he accepts:

> Do not reckon knowledge as part of anything other than
> the Real's being alive.
> Do not think your *Salvation* will come from reading *The Healing*!
> Knowledge of the *dīn* is the study of Islamic law, the
> exegesis of the Qurʾān, and the study of Ḥadīth!
> Anyone who studies other than these becomes sullied.

The man of *dīn* is a Sufi, an expert in Qurʾān recitation, and a legal scholar (*faqīh*);
If you don't study these, I'll keep calling you a fool.
These three pure sciences lay claim to the kernel of salvation,
the excellence of virtuous character traits, and the exchange of attributes.[9]
These three sciences are the root—these three are the water-spring source!
Anything beyond these belongs to the category of "no benefit."[10]

Here *Salvation* (*Najāt*) and *The Healing* (*Shifā*) are titles of Ibn Sīnā's two most famous books on his philosophy. They offer nothing to the person of *dīn*, who devotes time instead investigating those sciences that would illuminate God's revealed words.

For ʿAṭṭār, legitimate knowledge must make its way through *dīn*, whether one studies the sciences of *dīn* or uses *dīn* to verify one's intuitions and spiritual insights. ʿAṭṭār himself might have been no expert in the branches of learning that he lauds, *fiqh*, *tafsīr*, and *ḥadīth*, for he describes himself as only being familiar with them: "I have whiffed a scent from each of these sciences."[11] The orientation *toward* these sciences and *away* from the rational ones (philosophy and speculative theology) mattered more to him than actually learning them. The goal was to orient oneself to receiving God's guidance. That could be done by studying the sciences of *dīn*, by learning from those who have studied these sciences, or by one other means. That other means was direct unveiling (*kashf*). Direct unveiling occurs for those who have purified their hearts, often through *dhikr* (the remembrance of God), *khalwa* (meditative retreat), contemplation, good acts, and the experience of love. God pushes aside the curtains surrounding the heart and knowledge springs up from within:

The one to whom certainty appears through the eye of unveiling
has knowledge of *dīn*, upon the straight path.
Even if there are a thousand paths, like a head of hair,
From all that hair, see one cord as the right one![12]

That is, even the person of unveiling or spiritual insight should appreciate the absoluteness of *dīn*. The hidden truth behind *dīn* transcends the religion followed by the masses, but that should not confuse the unveiled heart into supposing there are multiple realities, one reality for the enlightened and one for the unenlightened. God is one and so is His message. A person should seek out and follow God's revealed pathway. From there, one can dive beyond the external forms of that pathway to delve into its inner meanings.

7

Beyond the Limits of Intelligence

Like many other classical Sufi thinkers, ʿAṭṭār sees a limited role for Islam's rational sciences: ultimate success rests with the simple God-conscious person, who ponders the mysteriousness of life within a framework of humility and who puts love of God into practice. As a pathway to truth, the *dīn* of this simple practitioner will always outrival insatiable intellectualism. By "simple," I do not mean lacking in depth, wisdom, or the knowledge that comes from an intimate relationship with God. Rather, I mean unpretentious and unfazed by attempts to argue about what lies beyond human understanding.

In opposition to the simple practitioner of *dīn*, for ʿAṭṭār, was the insatiable and misguided philosopher or intellectual. Most of us can recall thinkers who could be contained by no religious or spiritual tradition because their scope of inquiry was just too wide. From a perspective similar to ʿAṭṭār's, one might say that their skepticism constantly undid the solid ground upon which they could build the skills and traits needed to become adept at an inherited tradition. Sometimes we even see these figures lament their inability to accept any answer. Here I speak not of the self-assured atheist, but rather the philosopher so absorbed by questions and sometimes doubts that she or he acknowledges the pains of ceaseless rationality. As an example, David Hume (d. 1776) ruminates on a mood that at times overcomes him:

> Where am I, or what? From what causes do I derive my existence, and to what condition shall I return? Whose

> favour shall I court, and whose anger must I dread? What beings surround me? and on whom have I any influence, or who have any influence on me? I am confounded with all these questions, and begin to fancy myself in the most deplorable condition imaginable, inviron'd with the deepest darkness, and utterly depriv'd of the use of every member and faculty. Most fortunately it happens, that since reason is incapable of dispelling these clouds, nature herself suffices to that purpose, and cures me of this philosophical melancholy and delirium. . . . I dine, I play a game of back-gammon, I converse, and am merry with my friends; and when after three or four hour's amusement, I wou'd return to these speculations, they appear so cold and strain'd, and ridiculous, that I cannot find in my heart to enter into them any farther.[1]

Engrossing doubts bring no sense of inner harmony, though a philosopher might respond that they do impel a person toward something arguably more valuable, a sense of reality. Yet Hume at least finds solace from the doubts of unremitting philosophical inquiry in the human capability to be distracted by pleasure. The restlessness of such philosophizing types would, for ʿAṭṭār, point to the futility of their questions. Neither philosophy nor the distractions of the *dunyā*'s pleasures can substitute for *dīn*.

Ibn Sīnā became, during ʿAṭṭār's time, the epitome of the sort of complete confidence in reasoning that ʿAṭṭār disparaged. The philosopher seems to have had an insatiable and exceptionally brilliant mind, having (according to his own account) mastered in a year and a half all the philosophical sciences "as much as is humanly possible."[2] Ibn Sīnā was perhaps too self-assured to suffer from excessive doubts. He believed in the power of intelligence and clearly expressed the absolute necessity of intelligence for an awareness of reality. For example, the way in which God knows things in a universal way, and yet also knows even the most minute of particular things, could only be comprehended by "the subtlety of an inborn, acute intelligence (*luṭf qarīḥa*)."[3] "The best among people," Ibn Sīnā says, "is the one whose soul is perfected by becoming an intellect."[4] Such perfection, however, is an opportunity not suited for everyone. Rather, it is for "those naturally disposed toward theoretical reflection," that is, those innately drawn to abstract matters and innately able to draw logical conclusions, namely, the intelligent.[5] There seemed to be little room for simple practitioners in his thought when it came to the human calling to realize transcendent truths.

Even before Ibn Sīnā, the philosopher al-Fārābī (d. 339/950) believed religion (*dīn*) existed for the masses and spoke to human imagination, imagination being incompletely suited for grasping reality.[6] Imagination is for al-Fārābī a faculty situated between sense and the rational faculty; it converts sensory data into forms and impressions but cannot comprehend universals, that is, universal truths. Imagination aids intellectual contemplation in making connections to what humans know in the sensory world, but higher-level thought needs engagement with the intellect. Abū Naṣr Muḥammad al-Fārābī saw prophethood (*nubuwwa*) as the height of imagination's powers, or, in his own words, "the most complete level at which terminates the imaginative faculty and the most complete level which a human can reach through the imaginative faculty."[7] Prophets had more than simply intellectual strengths, they had powerful imaginations. Because of their imaginative strengths, prophets could communicate philosophical truths to those less suited to grasp them—through allegories and symbols (which engage the imagination). Religion was, as such, a simplified and allegorical version of philosophy, since philosophy spoke to the intellect itself and to those intelligent enough to benefit fully from it. Religion was, in other words, philosophy for the less intelligent.

This should not lead us to suppose that reasoning and revelation were at odds in the Islam of ʿAṭṭār's day. Every branch of Islamic learning used reasoning in different ways and some even engaged in it to make substantial arguments about God, divine justice, and human will. Theologians, for example, embraced reasoning, but they also embraced the doctrinal boundaries of their schools, what we might call "dogma." Yet Ibn Sīnā's philosophy seemed to threaten the dogma of Islam's theological schools.[8] ʿAṭṭār's literary response to such intellectual confusion was a rejection of the philosopher's unending need to question everything. Freedom from doubt and skepticism provides a person with the freedom to move vertically and to advance the completion of the soul and the pure connection of the spirit. That is, in stark contrast to al-Fārābī,

Ibn Sīnā, and their ilk, ʿAṭṭār exalted *dīn* above the variety of learning espoused by the philosophers. He preferred the insights that revelation gave to everyone—including the simpleminded—to the specialized claims of philosophers and those theologians who resembled the philosophers in their emphasis on reasoning.

ʿAṭṭār was not alone in this. He was part of a larger intellectual climate in eastern Iran, where prominent theologians and thinkers expressed concerns about the overreach of reasoning. One such figure was Abū Maʿālī al-Juwaynī, who proclaimed at the end of his life that he regretted pursuing theology instead of attaining the "simple faith" of the old women of Nishapur, a theme in ʿAṭṭār's writings as well.[9] The "religion of old women" forms the backdrop of ʿAṭṭār's conception of a proper *dīn*. Even if it is identified by specialists in Ḥadīth as spurious, it comes from a saying of the Prophet: "Adhere to the religion of old women" (*ʿalaykum bi-dīn al-ʿajāʾiz*).[10] This has been traditionally interpreted as a reference to the piety and simple theological beliefs associated with elderly women, often unschooled and sometimes unlettered but earnest. These "old women" as imagined by those who circulated this ḥadīth—or by al-Juwaynī here, as well as by ʿAṭṭār, who provides a commentary on it—lack the hubris of men, whether that hubris comes from their learning, or their social power, or both. Their relationship with God is thus a direct one, unmediated by either self-conceit or rationalized conceptions. In fact, al-Juwaynī lauds the religion of simple old women as superior to the pursuit of truth as expounded in fifty thousand books of intellectual speculation.[11] Like al-Juwaynī, his student Abū Ḥāmid al-Ghazālī had serious questions about the limits of reasoning as a pathway to knowing reality.[12]

Al-Ghazālī famously championed inspiration (*ilhām*) over the rational sciences. In his *Incoherence of the Philosophers* (*Tahāfut al-Falāsifa*), among other places, al-Ghazālī complains about philosophers' tendency to explain matters they do not truly understand, including revelation and divine law. As he explains, this takes them into uncharted waters, where they use guesswork to dismiss what the experts in God's law (*ahl al-sharʿ*) have proclaimed about revelation and the unseen.[13] In fact, al-Ghazālī went through a process of engaging with philosophy—studying and even embracing some aspects—though later in life, he favored knowledge acquired through God's direct unveiling of realities for those who were pious and mindful.[14] This is not quite the "religion of old women" proclaimed by his teacher al-Juwaynī and later by his admirer ʿAṭṭār, but one can see parallels in ʿAṭṭār's advocacy of truths accessed by the purehearted who know little or nothing of the rational sciences. In fact, as we will explore in this book's last part, ʿAṭṭār extols the intellect but places the heart and the spirit well beyond its reach.

Sounding like al-Ghazālī, ʿAṭṭār responds negatively to attempts to understand the universe, its origins, or its purpose using human reasoning. He tells the story of an "unripe soul," that is, a naïve young man with philosophical questions. This unnamed youngster poses his questions to the great Sufi saint Bāyazīd Basṭāmī (d. 234/848 or 261/875), asking him, "Why is the world like this, in that there is one sky and one earth?"[15] The young man continues to inquire about the nature of the universe, until the saint replies boldly: "For the reasons you see—nothing else!"[16] This leads ʿAṭṭār to a discussion of the limits of understanding causality, and—when it comes to *dīn*—the limits of reasoning. He calls reasoning the "philosophical intellect" (*ʿaql-i falsafī*), which suggests that ʿAṭṭār wants to distinguish this intellect (*ʿaql*) from the spiritually perceptive faculty of intellect mentioned in some of the sayings of Sufi saints that he and others, such as al-Ghazālī, value.[17] ʿAṭṭār is clear on the pitfalls of excessive reasoning. Speculation on the underlying purpose of creation is not only a distraction, it is an obstacle:

> Once the philosophical intellect fell into Cause,
> it became deprived of the *dīn* of Muṣṭafā [the Prophet].[18]
> The problem was neither in *dīn* nor in Cause,
> but rather that this *dīn* and this devotional collective (*millat*) are nothing but surrender (*taslīm*).
> Beyond the intellect, there's a castle for us,
> but philosophy gives you only one eye to see the way to it.
> Whenever someone says, "Why?" they err—
> Instead say: "Why should I ask why?"
> "Why" and "because" are plants that grow from the earth of estimation (*wahm*)—
> Only a person with pure discernment will grasp this.[19]

ʿAṭṭār is not promoting ignorance. Rather, he is teaching his audience the limits of an outlook. Philosophers and others entranced by the power of intelligence overestimate rational knowledge, characterized by cause and effect, while underestimating revelation. Revelation is the highest form of inspired knowledge. Only those who surrender (perform *taslīm*) to revelation, from an openhearted and even simplistic position, benefit from it.

ʿAṭṭār does indeed value reasoning, even if he declares that what the seemingly simpleminded "know" can outshine what the rationalists (those who put more value in reasoning than revelation) think they know. Their "reasoning" is more like guesswork, because unseen realities remain beyond the reach of reasoning. In fact, "estimation" (*wahm*) refers in these lines to the ability to know things in a vague way, one conducive to error.[20] Positive use of reasoning is to contemplate God's creation, while acknowledging the limits of human reasoning. A person should apply their senses to perceiving the world as a showcase for God's signs, by looking at the world with a receptive heart, humbly and thoughtfully.

In this disparaging view of philosophical arguments as rational sleight of hand, ʿAṭṭār's perspective follows closely the case made by Abū Ḥāmid al-Ghazālī against the philosophers in many places—such as in *The Deliverer from Error* (*al-Munqidh min al-ḍalāl*). Like al-Ghazālī, ʿAṭṭār wants his audience to seek a reality within oneself to which reasoning has no access, one that only blossoms through righteous and God-conscious practices and perception. One should beware of those who make persuasive arguments for their own understanding of the nature of reality. ʿAṭṭār labels these smooth talkers "Sophists" (*sūfisṭānīyān*), by which he means the philosophers:

> Peer upon the Real's fabrications, until you discern
>   secrets,
> and you will see anew the reality of things.
> If things were, in reality, as they appear
> how would Muṣṭafā's [the Prophet Muhammad's] request
>   ever be valid?
> No! For that most exalted one of *dīn* said, "Dear God,
> show me things as they really are!"[21]
> If you dissect the heart one hundred times,

you still won't be able to see what the heart really is.
This very eye, this very hand, this very ear,
this very soul, this very intellect, this very acuity (*hūsh*):
If, from all these, you have not found a way to awareness,
still, do not pave your path to the Sophists!
God knows the nature of things as they are,
for things become, by necessity, inverted in your eye.[22]

For ʿAṭṭār, *dīn*—and nothing else—can open one's eyes to realities that evade reasoning, because those realities are only made visible to the heart. To make his point, ʿAṭṭār uses his knowledge of human physiology, in the way the eye's curves create an image on the retina he describes as "inverted." This is strongly reminiscent of Abū Ḥāmid al-Ghazālī's argument that humans cannot rely on sensory data because the most powerful sense, that of sight, mistakes shadows as still and stars as tiny.[23] In like manner, even sleep can beguile reasoning such that the sleeper cannot discern dreams from reality.[24] Conversely, when one reads the world through one's heart and through the *dīn*'s proclamations, mysteries will come to light, so that "if the eye of your heart opens itself to *dīn*," as ʿAṭṭār says, "it will extract from a tiny little atom one hundred secrets."[25]

8

The Religion of Old Women

To capture *dīn*'s liberation from the boundaries of human reason, ʿAṭṭār offers his audience the trope of the unlettered "old lady." The phrase "old lady" renders the Arabic word *ʿajūz*, which derives from a root signifying weakness and inability. The word conveys the bodily frailty and social marginalization of elderly women. ʿAṭṭār's admiration for elderly women's simple mode of worship comments not only on reasoning in matters of *dīn* but on Islam's spiritual elites. When some specialize in "knowing God," they run the risk of veering from a straightforward sincerity that ʿAṭṭār saw as natural to Islam. Others have expressed this sentiment for similar reasons. For example, Taqī al-Dīn Aḥmad ibn Taymiyya (d. 728/1328), according to his student Shams al-Dīn ibn Qayyim al-Jawziyya (d. 751/1350), once commented that "the common people worship God," while so-called Sufi masters "worship themselves."[1] Such self-proclaimed elites (elite in their experiential knowledge of God) worship themselves by exaggerating their achievements and spiritual status, while depreciating the piety of commonfolk.

ʿAṭṭār's response to the bravado of philosophers, self-styled Sufi masters, and pietistic worshipers is to remind his audience of a simpler relationship with God. The Prophet himself endorsed that simpler relationship in the aforementioned saying: "Adhere to the religion (*dīn*) of old women." Old women were thought to have no aspirations for empty reasoning or for social power. That was the source of their sincerity and wisdom, a special kind of knowledge of *dīn*. After all, *dīn* stands outside of what the intellect comprehends. To make this point, ʿAṭṭār compares *dīn*'s secrets to the belt or girdle, called the *zunnār*, that Christians wore to designate their non-Muslim status. Children lack the sophistication to appreciate the *zunnār*'s symbolism as a mark of Christian commitments. They would see nothing more than a belt. So, too, the secrets that lie within *dīn* are beyond the intellect:

> To try to impose the form of these secrets on the Intellect
> would be like binding the *zunnār* girdle around Christian children.
> Beyond the Intellect, there are many more modes of being,
> in bottomlessness much deeper than the faculty of Estimation (*wahm*).[2]

ʿAṭṭār responds to the classical Islamo-Arabic philosophical model of the intellect as a site upon which are impressed forms, which constitute knowledge. The secrets embedded within *dīn*, even if they could be forcibly placed as forms onto the intellect, would be indecipherable to the intellect. The intellect's comprehension is only as wide and deep as its faculties, which include the faculty of estimation, the faculty that discerns intentions and meanings. Estimation can no better measure the secrets of reality than a cup could measure the ocean. Acknowledging the intellect's limitations leads ʿAṭṭār to the *dīn* of old women:

> Allow me to divulge my beliefs to you,
> but, really, when will this change happen for you?
> The very school (*madhhab*) that a group of old women follow
> is my school of thought, and this is a statement true!
> Know it well. And become, like me, an unable one (*ʿājiz*).
> In reality, this is the *dīn* of "unable old women."
> All of those old women have confessed to
> what you, on the path [to Him], piece by piece, deny,
> because you're stuck in seeking the causes of how and why.
> Yet if you cannot arrive without causes, then you cannot arrive.[3]

ʿAṭṭār plays on the word used to signify frail old women, so that *ʿajūz* (old woman) becomes *ʿājiz* (an unable person)—a person unable to understand the intricacies of reality, aware of the impotence of such pursuits and yet willing to move along the path of *dīn* regardless. Thus, the inspirations and insight that come to those who practice the "*dīn* of old women" stem from their recognition of their own intellectual limits, which results in sincerity and a lack of affectation.

ʿAṭṭār expounds upon the ascendancy of the simple old woman in detail in his famous chapter on the female saint Rābiʿa al-ʿAdawiyya (d. ca. 185/801) in *The Memorial of God's Friends* (*Tadhkirat al-awliyāʾ*). As the only entry in this collection on a female, the chapter on Rābiʿa presents her as a paradigm for other women, which is further underscored by ʿAṭṭār's comparisons to Mary, the mother of Jesus, and ʿĀʾisha, the wife of Muhammad. She, like them, is a female ethical exemplar in a literary world otherwise focused on the achievements of men. ʿAṭṭār proclaims this rather explicitly:

> If someone were to ask, "Why have you mentioned her in the ranks of men?" I would reply, "The liege of the prophets himself, blessings and peace be upon him, has said, 'God does not look upon your forms.'"[4] That is, it is intention that matters to Him, not external form. Likewise, he [the Prophet] has said, blessings and peace be upon him, "People will be gathered according to their intentions." If it is acceptable to acquire two-thirds of the religion (*dīn*) from ʿĀʾisha the Ever-Truthful [two-thirds in terms of her narrations of Ḥadīth], may God be pleased with her, then it is perfectly acceptable to find religious (*dīnī*) benefit in a serving girl from among the servants of ʿĀʾisha.[5] When a woman is a man on the path to God, one cannot even call her a woman. In this manner, ʿAbbāsa Ṭūsī[6] has said, "When tomorrow on the bare plains of the Resurrection, a voice cries, 'O men!' the [only] person who will step foot at the rank of men will be Mary."[7]

Rkia Elaroui Cornell argues that Rābiʿa's status as serving girl to ʿĀʾisha tells us something important about ʿAṭṭār's account, one that becomes the standard and the basis for almost all accounts of Rābiʿa that follow.[8] According to Cornell, ʿAṭṭar conflates this Rābiʿa with the earlier Muʿādha bint ʿAbdallāh al-ʿAdawiyya (d. 83/702 or 101/719), who was indeed a student to the Prophet's wife, a relater of Ḥadīth that ʿĀʾisha narrated, and a pioneer in the world-renouncing women's movement of Basra, which Rābiʿa eventually would come to represent.[9] This explains how Rābiʿa appears much older than al-Ḥasan al-Baṣrī in ʿAṭṭār's version of her life, even though—historically speaking—she would have been a young girl at the time of his death in 110/728.[10] Another possibility is that ʿAṭṭār seeks to fit Rābiʿa within the mold of the pious elderly woman and does so by presenting her as older than al-Ḥasan and other early Muslim world-renouncers.

Her simplicity and humble status are woven into every element of his account. According to ʿAṭṭār, Rābiʿa was born into a very poor family, where she ended up being sold into slavery. Devoting herself to God, she became renowned for her poverty, frank observations, and friendship with God. ʿAṭṭār describes her as constantly enamored by God and willingly entrenched in the barest sort of life, avoiding meat, marriage, and wealth. Unimpressed by her own saintly miracles, she even helps the great al-Ḥasan al-Baṣrī become unimpressed by his. According to ʿAṭṭār, when al-Baṣrī wants to upstage her by throwing his prayer rug on the water to pray, she ends up upstaging him. She throws her prayer rug to levitate in the air, where she climbs upon it and challenges him to join her. He lacks the spiritual ability to do so, so he remains silent. She reminds him that God's favors are best saved for the afterlife and best kept private. Yet she also consoles him by telling the saint, "O Ḥasan, you did what fish do. And I did what flies do. True exertion is completely beyond either of these two things. One must busy oneself with exertion!"[11] The spirit of the *dīn* of old women lies entirely in such self-effacing focus on service and simplicity.

Earlier accounts of her life confirm ʿAṭṭār's depiction of her as an earnest lover of God. Al-Sulamī, for example, begins with Rābiʿa in his *Dhikr al-niswa al-mutaʿabbidāt al-ṣūfīyāt* (*Accounts of Devoted Sufi Women*) and reports many sayings from her, including one when questioned about why she was swaying back and forth one morning: "Last night I became drunk on the love of my

Lord, and I woke up still intoxicated by Him."[12] Others revered her as well, including the litterateur Abū ʿUthmān ʿAmr ibn Baḥr al-Jāḥiẓ (d. 255/868), the moralist Ibn Abī al-Dunyā (d. 281/894), the Ḥanbalī scholar Abū al-Faraj ʿAbd al-Raḥmān ibn al-Jawzī (d. 597/1200), and the Sufi author al-Qushayrī, among many other scattered references in Sufi writings.[13]

Contemporary English-language scholars of Sufism and Islamic studies have taken great interest in her, as well. The historian Margaret Smith (d. 1970) saw Rābiʿa as emblematic of the spiritual life's possibility to exist outside the confines of traditional gender roles.[14] Michael Sells, in his essay introducing ʿAṭṭār's passage, as translated by Paul Losensky, sees ʿAṭṭār as subverting stereotypes about women, albeit within a medieval framework.[15] (In fact, an English version of ʿAṭṭār's account of Rābiʿa's life can be found in both Sells's anthology and Losensky's translation.)[16] Claudia Yaghoobi compares the life of Rābiʿa and that of the English mystic Margery Kempe (d. 1438), focusing on the manner in which both challenged patriarchal authority and broke through gender boundaries.[17] Tamara Albertini discusses the historical Rābiʿa's contributions to Sufism's language of love.[18]

Finally, very worthy of mention is the comprehensive book on Rābiʿa and the study of Rābiʿa by Rkia Cornell, which includes lengthy treatment of ʿAṭṭār's account, namely, *Rabiʿa from Narrative to Myth*. Interest in Rābiʿa comes from much more than her status as one of the few female saints given extended consideration in early texts. It is, rather, her ability to challenge and even at times subvert expectations that makes her a fascinating historical and literary figure. For ʿAṭṭār, that power of subversion comes from the freedom that being a "weak woman" (*ḍaʿīfa*) gives her, since she is outside of and in many ways exempt from male-dominated circles of authority. Yet Cornell also shows us the ways in which Sufi accounts single out great women in a spirit of exceptionalism, leaving male excellence as a standard of virtue.[19] Zahra Ayubi provides an extended consideration of the workings through which Islam's most celebrated medieval ethical treatises sustain men and their male traits as norms.[20] ʿAṭṭār's depiction of Rābiʿa leaves no doubt about his and his audience's expectations of male normativity, as seen in the aforementioned question he asks about Rābiʿa: "Why have you mentioned her in the ranks of men?"[21]

As a hagiographer, ʿAṭṭār elevates Rābiʿa's humble devotion, describing her as "hidden behind the veil of sincerity (*ikhlāṣ*)" and "incinerated in passionate love and longing for God."[22] In order to show his audience how earnest simplicity surpasses self-involved pietism, ʿAṭṭār will often have Rābiʿa—described often with the Persian equivalent of *ʿajūz*, namely, *ḍaʿīfa* (weak old woman)—outdo self-assured, pious men. She will correct and even chastise them, including saints respected enough to be among Sufism's major founding figures. ʿAṭṭār does so in part to make the case for a simple yet profoundly personal interpretation of *dīn*, one focused on love, direct discourse with God, and, usually, obedience. This is not unusual. Even the much earlier Sufi writer al-Sulamī saw in Rābiʿa an embodiment of *taʿabbud* (selfless servitude), a virtue that al-Sulamī associates with ideal women.[23] As ʿAṭṭār illustrates, Rābiʿa excels in the domain of service to God, because she does not allow herself to be drawn into ambiguities:

> It has been reported that Rābiʿa's serving girl was making barley-and-onion porridge after days of Rābiʿa's not having any food.[24] They needed onions.
>
> The serving girl said, "Let me ask the neighbors."
>
> Rābiʿa replied, "Forty years ago I promised the Real, exalted be He, never to ask anything of anyone but Him. Forget the onions."
>
> At that very moment, a bird flying overhead dropped a peeled onion into the pot.
>
> Rābiʿa said, "I'm not invulnerable to tests."[25]
>
> She ordered her to give up the porridge completely, and she ate plain bread.[26]

Rābiʿa prefers the rigors of obedience even to a clear sign of God's favor, shown by food falling from the sky—one of a few occasions wherein ʿAṭṭār makes subtle comparisons to her and Moses.[27] She makes promises directly to God and keeps those promises without any sense of hubris. While her food is simple, there is no sense of self-admiration in that simplicity. In fact, she guards herself vigorously against the conceit that may result from accepting divine gifts, such as onions from the sky.

Rābiʿa's religiosity has no need for the rational sciences, nor even the traditional sciences, such as law or Ḥadīth. In accounts other than ʿAṭṭār's, she chastises prominent pious men for engaging in the worldly activity of collecting and evaluating ḥadīth reports.[28] Such superfluous learning has no appeal to one who speaks to God directly. Rābiʿa's relationship with Him is unmitigated by such filters. Moreover, Rābiʿa flips the power dynamic involved in her status as female and elderly, as well as the simple view she has of God. She makes use of such vulnerability to highlight her sense of neediness toward God. In this way, she weaponizes that dependence, emphasizing the contrast between her weakness and His power, thus arousing His mercy:

> After she had died, someone saw her in a dream and asked her, "How did you find deliverance from Munkir and Nakīr [the two angels who interrogate people in their graves]?"
>
> She replied, "When those two fine young men came and asked, 'Who is your Lord?' I said, 'You go back and tell God, "My God, you never forgot a weak old woman, among a million of your creatures. In this whole wide world, I have no one but you, so how could I forget you for you to send someone to ask, 'Who is your Lord?' "' "[29]

The questioning of the grave is supposed to be a terrifying stage of the afterlife. For Rābiʿa, however, it is like a lover's quarrel. Her position with God is such that she can reprimand Him for even daring to ask how she might forget Him, so profound is her need for Him and so earnest her love. This guileless declaration of need, more than the arguments of theologians or philosophers, can rescue a person after death, for it arouses divine mercy, a theme found in other Islamic and Sufi texts as well.[30]

Through Rābiʿa, ʿAṭṭār advocates knowing God by means of a disposition, a highly attuned outlook. That outlook—grateful, receptive, intellectually simple, reliant on God and in constant conversation with Him—is the "religion of old women" that she embodies. She teaches it to others, often through edifying admonitions:

> When she saw a man with a compress wrapped around his head, she said:
>
> "Why are you wearing this compress?"
>
> He replied, "I have a headache."
>
> Rābiʿa said, "How old are you?"
>
> He said, "Thirty."
>
> She said, "For thirty years, you have been healthy, and yet you never once wrapped the compress of gratitude around your head. Now He gives you a headache for one night, and you put on the compress of complaint?"[31]

In medieval Persianate medicine, a physician or healer might treat a headache with a cold or warm compress on the head, along with a foot massage using essential oils, salt, and chamomile for a number of hours, and by limiting movement in the limbs and submerging them in lukewarm water.[32] Substances were applied directly to the patient's head, held by a wrap, that included (depending on the type of headache) sesame, spearmint, artemisia, camphor, cannabis, henna, tar, bird suet, cow bone marrow, and water-lily oil.[33] As an apothecary, ʿAṭṭār would have known and even sold many of these medicinal substances. Rābiʿa seems simultaneously unappreciative of medical treatments and yet acutely aware of the ethical motivations behind them. That is, she seems both simpleminded and spiritually profound. Her reading of all events as interactions between God and servant renders her oblivious to the mundane workings of cause and effect that have preoccupied those around her.

Finally, there is an important psychological component to ʿAṭṭār's valorization of the *dīn* of old women, and, in its most emblematic form, the practices, words, and life of Rābiʿa. The very objective of the path to God is to become absolved of ego, and, in this, the unassuming elderly female devotee has an advantage of character. ʿAṭṭār shows Rābiʿa's lack of conceit as an especially female quality, one expressed when she responds to the boasting of men:

> It is narrated that a group went to her to assess her and sought to hear some statement from her. They said, "All virtues have been showered upon men. Only men have

> been crowned with prophethood (*nubuwwat*). Only men have been girdled with extraordinary miraculous deeds (*karāmat*). No woman has been appointed to the rank of messengership (*payghāmbarī*)."
>
> Rābiʿa said, "All this is true, but the ego of conceited selfishness found in 'I am your Lord most high' has not emerged from any woman . . ."[34]

Here Rābiʿa reminds her male audience of the abject arrogance of Pharaoh, whom the Qurʾān quotes as making a declaration that he—and not God—is worthy of obedience and worship. If men have been charged with prophecy and miracles, so be it. They have, in being cognizant of such a capacity for greatness, played a high-stakes game that can lead to damning pride. Rābiʿa's wisdom, the very wisdom doubted and yet sought by these male visitors, comes from her humble and honest awareness of her place in the larger scheme of things. She is like Moses in her fearless verbal opposition to the tyranny of men. Rābiʿa thus stands for the subversive power of earnest humility, a power that is one of the many hidden secrets of *dīn*. Those secrets open themselves up to Rābiʿa not in spite of the simplicity of her approach toward God but indeed because of that simplicity.

Beyond his account of Rābiʿa, ʿAṭṭār offers a *dīn* that requires little of a person other than a sincere embrace of their own weaknesses, their utter dependence on God. This *dīn* lacks the elitism of the philosophers, for whom intelligence was mandatory for knowing and encountering the Real. ʿAṭṭār's *dīn* is not quite egalitarian, however, since it certainly still privileges some above others, as making male traits a measuring stick for excellence. Yet, for people seeking to know the Real, ʿAṭṭār's *dīn* negates the need for access to libraries, teachers, and even exceptional intelligence. One can imagine how those of limited means might gravitate toward an interpretation of piety that welcomed them as they were. In fact, in ʿAṭṭār's *dīn*, weakness, shortcomings, and disadvantages become a means to humility and thus a fast track to being loved by God. Perhaps this is one reason among others why ʿAṭṭār's Sufi interpretation of Islam, which resembled that of Abū Ḥāmid al-Ghazālī, rang true for so many: it aimed to be as wide and embracing as the ultimate Truth that it sought.[35]

Part II

Love and Infidelity

9

Love Beneath the Cloak of Infidelity

Proof-based reasoning (*istidlāl*), or what I am simply calling "reasoning," is bounded and has limits. For those not tied down by reason, there is something powerful in an intellectually simple relationship with God. All of this has been established as basic themes in ʿAṭṭār's thoughts about devotion, or, we might say, in ʿAṭṭār's conception of "religion." Now we can devote our full attention to something unbounded in ʿAṭṭār's thought—love.

Love for ʿAṭṭār includes that between humans and humans and that between humans and God. In both cases, love means more than mere attachment, passion, or care. In fact, love's secret, as ʿAṭṭār tells us in *The Book of Secrets*, is that it is wider and truer than the universe itself: "The two worlds are but shadows of the sun of Love; / the two spheres are the eternal presence of Love."[1]

All the things in creation—all that is seen and all that is unseen—are merely shadows when compared to the sun that illuminates them. That sun, that light, that empowering and radiating source, is love. Another cosmological entity that ʿAṭṭār describes in this way is the light of the Prophet Muhammad, whose "light is the basis (*aṣl*) for all existent things."[2] These two, (1) unbounded love and (2) the Prophet's light, might indeed be one thing, one cosmological principle. After all, the Prophet's identity is closely tied to love, as God's named and special beloved (*ḥabīballāh*) and a "mercy to all the worlds."[3]

Love is its own religion, in a sense, for ʿAṭṭār. It has its own practices and even its own scriptures. To begin with, ʿAṭṭār offers a metaphorical equivalent to revelation, the "Psalms of Love," which is legible only for those whose hearts have transformed to receive its message. That is, for love to speak, reasoning must step aside. Love is a language that requires sincerity and a transformation out of one's selfish state of being. These can only happen when one limits one's attempts at reasoning, or, as ʿAṭṭār calls it, "intelligence" (*khirad*):

> Read, like David, the verse of the perplexed!
> Read those Psalms about the love of the distraught.
> Transform words of love into a Litany of Lovers.
> Lose your heart and soul to Lovers' whimsical desire.
> Like incense, become cremated over Love.
> Weep like the candle does: happily.
> Pour the wine of Love into the goblet of Intelligence,
> from that goblet, pour a swig over your very own soul.
> Cut off Intelligence from pure wine, once it's drunk—
> walk it back home to its street, so you don't have to
>   hear it brag much.
> Once Love arrives at the scene, blot out Intelligence's eyes!
> You can arrive at your true self, through Love's red-hot
>   iron poker.[4]
> As forms, Intelligence is water; Love is fire.
> Water and fire are incompatible by necessity.[5]

Love cannot speak until intelligence (or reasoning) becomes intoxicated. Once reasoning loses itself and becomes disengaged, then love can take over the conversation taking place within each of our souls. Once it takes over, love demands pain and confusion, but the outcome justifies the lover's efforts, because love leads to destinations that reasoning cannot begin to fathom. Reasoning is our limited, step-by-step attempt to arrive at conclusions.

Reasoning or intelligence presents two major problems in matters of love. First, even though love's domain lies far beyond reason's reach, reasoning will nevertheless always try to get involved, make sense of things, and manage things. For this reason, ʿAṭṭār suggests blinding it, rendering it unable to interfere. Second, reasoning is all about validating the self. When stuck in the realm of reasoning, we want to understand for ourselves and prove ourselves right in argument. Moreover, we do so with the resources immediately around us, the things we see and hear. The higher truths of love, however, do not work like that. For love, we need to let go. We need to rise above our immediate surroundings. We need to let love come to us, take possession of us, and even incinerate us:

> Intelligence sees nothing but the outer of both worlds,
> whereas Love sees nothing but the Beloved.
> Intelligence is a sparrow trapped in the snare of inability,
> whereas Love is the majestic Sīmurgh of meanings.
> Intelligence is but a preamble to a *dīwān* that describes
> a foothill meadow,
> whereas Love is a brilliant star, lantern to the night sky.
> Intelligence is mere reports about the abode of created
> things,
> whereas Love is the very elixir of life!
> Intelligence puts its renunciation on display in every
> neighborhood,
> whereas Love is a ribald, indifferent to reputation.[6]

This last point—the indifference to reputation—results from love's ability to strip one of selfishness, which is, for ʿAṭṭār, the only means to achieve the clarity of vision needed to reach human perfection. Reasoning serves as an obstacle because it forces the believer to acknowledge multiplicity, differences, limits, and impossibilities. Love serves as a remedy, as the universal force of creation, one that works unquestioningly and only demands earnest devotion. Thus, the aspiring lover needs to focus on the object of their love, unconcerned with risks, outcomes, the future, or their reputation.[7]

True love demands sacrifice. The lover must sacrifice reasoning, selfishness, reputation, and even identity. Love can demand the sacrifice of one's religion or faith (*īmān*), as well:

> If you're told, "Abandon your faith (*īmān*)!"
> or if word reaches you to give up your life,
> Who are you to argue? Relinquish them both.

Abandon faith, and give up your very life.
The imbecilic denier will say that this is evil.
"Love," you should reply, "transcends both infidelity and faith."
What does love have to do with infidelity and faith?
Why would lovers need their lives even for a moment?
The lover sets the whole harvest aflame.
They take a saw to the top of his head—he doesn't say a thing.[8]

This may seem contradictory to the previous chapters of this book where I made the case for why "religion" matters to ʿAṭṭār. Yet ʿAṭṭār and other Sufi writers also saw ways in which religiosity, pietism, sectarianism, and ambition ruined many a soul. Traits of ostentation and egoism prevailed among those most famous for being "religious," those lauded for their piety or religious learning. Such traits contradicted sharply with the traits of the lover, liberated from all concerns of self and reputation. Thus, the rejection of religion, or "infidelity" (*kufr*), became the most powerful image to describe the lover's style of life. ʿAṭṭār and other Sufis who promoted themes of infidelity did so metaphorically, at least usually. They generally did not want to encourage the abandonment of Islamic norms but rather the awakening of a sense of liberation from being tied to those norms. ʿAṭṭār wanted his audience to observe *dīn* while setting one's sights beyond *dīn*, in the direction of the Real, that is, God as God, not God just as an object of human worship.

Moreover, as the preceding lines show, ʿAṭṭār wanted his readers to know that, in love, one discovers a reality beyond the religion that they imagine, but also beyond the infidelity that they imagine. "Anyone whose foot becomes firm on the way of Love," he says, "will leave behind both infidelity and Islam."[9] In place of that imagined "good" Islam and that imagined "evil" infidelity, the lover embraces a state of confusion, bewilderment, or "perplexity" (*ḥayrat*). In that perplexity of falling in love, "infidelity became faith, and faith became infidelity."[10] That is, it becomes a necessity to embrace wholeheartedly what would not make sense to the average believer. The most important barrier in Islam, that between humans and God, between created and Creator, between worshiper and Worshiped, comes crashing down in love:

> Love came and did not spare the words "infidelity" or
> "faith";
> It did not leave hidden any self-conceit that was.
> Since It could view the veil of the unseen with direct sight,
> It left the soul not an atom of imagining an Other.[11]

Humans rely on these veils, these false barriers and separations, to make determinations. Yet love floods the lover with the beloved's direct presence, or with the desire for that direct presence. The veils fall; the barriers disappear; things no longer make sense:

> Oppression, justice, evil, good, infidelity, and religion
> all arise from the World of Intellect, to be sure.
> Once you fold and close the World of Intellect,
> an atom of Love will leave them empty-handed.[12]

ʿAṭṭār uses the term "infidelity" to describe the perplexing realizations that love brings—realizations often contrary to normative beliefs.

The perplexing realizations of love also come and go. Sometimes the heart is a good Muslim, observing the proper human-God relationship. At other times, though, the heart becomes an infidel. The veils fall, and (as we will explore further in part 3) God becomes omnipresent, or present in the beauty of another human being, or even a mirror image of oneself:

> O heart! You'll neither die in infidelity nor in faith.
> Poor helpless you, O heart! That you'll die like so:
> You're neither completely in infidelity, nor in religion;
> sometimes this, sometimes that, you'll die "wavering
> between the two."[13]

Infidelity results from the ecstasy and self-loss of love. Infidelity is love's clearest sign and its major symptom. In the discussion of the coming pages on love, the word "infidelity" might not come up frequently. Yet images of infidelity are everywhere: imbibing alcohol, rejecting norms, embracing other religions, and venturing outside of one's social boundaries. These are all images of infidelity that constitute ʿAṭṭār's language of love.

10

The School of Love in History

One might be tempted to say that the divine essence itself is love, that is, that God is love, as has been implied in other Sufi texts, especially that of Shaykh Aḥmad Ghazālī (d. 520/1126). The famous Shaykh Aḥmad presented perhaps the earliest cosmology of love in his *Inspirations* (*Sawāniḥ*). In this mysterious treatise, God's love for Himself engendered the cosmos.[1] By reflecting upon that love, realizing it, and moving beyond human love for God to God's love for Himself, the aspirant completes the path. Aḥmad's writings are famously terse, even cryptic, leaving their mark not only on the writings of his student ʿAyn al-Quḍāt Hamadānī (d. 525/1131) but also on a Sufi chain of learning and remembrance—the Suhrawardiyya Order—that traces itself to Aḥmad.[2] Despite Aḥmad's influential teachings on love, we cannot identify the divine essence as love in ʿAṭṭār's poetry. In fact, we cannot identify the divine essence with anything at all in ʿAṭṭār's thought. ʿAṭṭār is quite clear that "when it comes to the ultimate truth of His essence, no signifiers exist for anyone / such that whatever you say about it—it's not that."[3] Nothing conclusive can be said about God's essence.

Nevertheless, Shaykh Aḥmad's larger concern—the universal predominance of love—certainly appears in ʿAṭṭār's poetry. This may or may not be due to the historical link between the two. ʿAṭṭār acknowledges Aḥmad, in fact, as a master who taught others about the mysterious subtleties of love.[4] Some have thought that ʿAṭṭār's masterpiece on the theme of union through love, *The Speech of the Birds*, might have been based on Aḥmad's *Treatise of the Birds* (*Risālat al-ṭayr*). Probably, though, ʿAṭṭar's *The Speech of the Birds* adapts a very short *Story of the Birds* (*Dāstān-i murghān*) by Abū al-Rajāʾ Chāchī (d. 516/1122–1123).[5] In gauging intellectual influence, we also should not overestimate the individual thinker. After all, Aḥmad himself drew from a larger love-based intellectual atmosphere in Nishapur and the entire Khurāsān area. Sanāʾī, too, matured intellectually in that atmosphere, picking up on the trend of metaphysical and ethical reflections on love. ʿAṭṭār, in turn, was indebted to Sanāʾī, especially in his symbolic language of love.[6] Hence such theorists of love formed parts of a larger Sufi-influenced, Persian-language network that included ʿAṭṭār. These theorists sometimes referred to their outlook as the *madhhab-i ʿishq*, the "School of Love."

Theirs was not a formal school of thought, with theological doctrines or defined approaches to matters of law, as existed at the time. Most of the aforementioned belonged to real theological and legal schools, or they modified views from within such traditions. Those who promoted this "school" agreed on love's ability to outshine all other ways of knowing and serving God. The doctrine that they shared was belief in the transformative power of love.

In other words, "School of Love" was, as Shahab Ahmed describes it, an "umbrella term" for an "ethos" and an "aesthetic."[7] This ethos and aesthetic resulted from generations of teachings about God's love, flourishing fully in the time of our poet. Leonard Lewisohn has reviewed the major early figures and concepts that contributed to this aesthetic, beginning with two sacred sayings.[8] In the first, from the Qurʾān, God describes His beloveds as taking part in a reciprocal relationship: "He loves them and they love Him . . . and they do not fear the blame of any blamer."[9] In the second, in a ḥadīth, God describes His servant as drawing near to Him with obligatory acts, and then continuing to do so through elective or supererogatory acts, until God loves him. Famously, at that point: "Once I love him, I am his hearing by which he listens, his vision by which he sees, his hand by which he seizes, and his foot by which he walks."[10]

As Lewisohn tells us, a ḥadīth narrated by al-Ḥasan al-Baṣrī raised the stakes, replacing the healthy love (*ḥubb*) described earlier with a desirous and passionate love (*ʿishq*). According to this divine saying, holding the remembrance of God as one's primary concern leads to finding joy in that remembrance. Such remembrance blossoms into a mutual desirous love between servant and Lord, such that "when he desires Me and I desire him, I raise the veils between him and Me, and I become a cluster of knowable things before his eyes."[11] Sufi studies scholar Annabel Keeler has put forward the possibility that—almost a century and a half after al-Baṣrī would have been relating this ḥadīth—Bāyazīd Basṭāmī first began to use *ʿishq* to describe the torrid relationship between God and His human lovers.[12]

Even when using words for "love" other than *ʿishq*, early figures expounded on love as the loftiest station and the most direct way of knowing God, proclamations from which later generations formulated theories of love.[13] Those early figures included Rābiʿa, Jaʿfar al-Ṣādiq, Shaqīq al-Balkhī (d. 194/810), Dhū al-Nūn al-Miṣrī (d. 245/859), and Abū Saʿīd al-Kharrāz (d. 277/890 or 286/899). Of importance in the following later period of formulation were Abū al-Ḥusayn al-Nūrī (d. 295/907) and Abū Bakr al-Shiblī (d. 334/946). But, for ʿAṭṭār in particular and for many others as well, it was the legendary al-Ḥallāj who showed the world through his words and actions what it meant to be God's lover: the sacrifices involved, the pain endured, and, in ʿAṭṭār's version, the condemnations that would lead to his execution. In terms of theory, al-Ḥallāj's love-based framework for the human-God relationship became fodder for the philosophically inclined Abū al-Ḥasan al-Daylamī (fl. 4th/10th century) and the Sufi teacher Abū ʿAbdallāh Muḥammad ibn Khafīf Shīrāzī (d. 371/981).

Of great influence as well for ʿAṭṭār was Abū Saʿīd ibn Abī al-Khayr (d. 440/1048), to whom ʿAṭṭār seems to have traced his spiritual lineage and in whose poetic legacy ʿAṭṭār found a model for teaching the spiritual way through erotic verse. ʿAṭṭār also shows some indebtedness to the psychology of the philosopher Ibn Sīnā, who mused on love and union—especially as it was presented to ʿAṭṭār in the poetry of Sanāʾī.[14] Finally, there are the lingering effects of the teachings of Khwāja ʿAbdallāh Anṣārī of Herat (d. 481/1089) and his student Rashīd al-Dīn Maybudī (d. 520/1126). As Islamic studies scholar William Chittick has discussed at length, Maybudī's forceful proclamations on love resonated long after him. Maybudī often describes love as a revealed way of life, or a sharīʿa, commenting that "bewilderment is a great pillar in the Sharīʿa of Love," and that "throwing away life in the Sharīʿa of Friendship is its religion."[15] The phrases "Sharīʿa of Love" and "School of Love" also appear in the writings of Aḥmad Samʿānī (d. 534/1140).[16] Parallels between Samʿānī and Aḥmad seem not to be a matter of Aḥmad's influence but rather of common origin, as teachings and sayings on the topic of love pervaded the area of eastern Iran where both lived.[17] A fuller account would mention other important figures, but one can find the major themes of this School of Love expressed in the salient figures mentioned: Aḥmad Ghazālī, his student ʿAyn al-Quḍāt Hamadānī, the poet Sanāʾī, and ʿAṭṭār.[18]

The central theme of ʿAṭṭār's entire body of work is "love"—hence the title of this book—and yet he mentions the "School of Love" trope only twice from what I have discerned. In one of the two instances of the phrase "School of Love," ʿAṭṭār speaks mainly to the world-renouncing ascetic who craves reputation, rules, and outward forms of piety:

> Be absolutely certain that here the School of Love
> reigns over the seventy-something others.
> You won't find the ruin-dweller near any bath stove;
> he won't be ripped away from his dear ruins.
> Give me a seat right next to him in the dirt,
> for I'm partial to a sullen drunkenness.
> I must be among the drunken lovers,
> even if the place of ascetics is much closer at hand.[19]

Here the School of Love sounds almost countercultural. Adherents observe drunkenness and shun prestige and even respectability. ʿAṭṭār's use of the word *madhhab* (school) as one of "seventy-something" schools alludes to a saying of the Prophet. Abū ʿIsā Muḥammad ibn ʿĪsā al-Tirmidhī (d. 279/892) reports two versions of this ḥadīth. In the first, the Prophet describes his nation's fate using the word "sect" (*firqa*): "The Jews became divided into seventy-one or seventy-two sects (*firqa*). The Christians did the same. My nation (*ummatī*) will become divided into seventy-three sects."[20]

In another quite similar version of this ḥadīth, the Prophet describes the seventy-three factions using the word *milla*, which we might translate as "denominational community."[21] Because ʿAṭṭār alludes to this narration, we know that he means *firqa* or *milla* by *madhhab*. Thus, we might call ʿAṭṭār's chosen way a "School" or, translated differently, a "Sect," "Denomination," or even "Religion" of Love (*madhhab-i ʿishq*). Any translation of the term should convey a sense of sacrilege, because of the ironic juxtaposition of *madhhab* (which often refers to sober, judicious, and pious scholars debating God's ways and laws) placed next to the word *ʿishq* (which indicates a desirous, all-consuming, and even sometimes libidinous love).

Contributing to that sense of sacrilege, adherents to the School of Love often proclaimed human beauty to convey divine significance. Beauty mattered greatly, since, after all, beauty arouses love. In fact, many of those mentioned earlier, including ʿAṭṭār, praised the devotional contemplation of human beauty. Falling in love with a human being, losing oneself completely to someone else, could be an important rite of initiation in the process of eventually falling in love with God. In this sense, the word *madhhab* made a scandalous substitution, putting the human beloved in God's place as the "highest point of the lover's universe," a tension that Sufi poets utilized.[22] In a poem attributed to ʿAṭṭār, for example, he describes the proper religious "school" as being one devoted entirely to a lock of his beloved's hair.[23]

The School of Love also carried a sense of sacrilege because—rhetorically—it presented itself as an alternative to Islamic norms, that is, to the many established and accepted schools of Islam.[24] The name implied that the followers of the School of Love would face the rejection of those stuck in fixed interpretations of piety wherein rigor mattered more than love. Yet the lovers' devotion to the beloved, their sense of purpose in having fallen in love, prohibited them from fearing reproach. This lack of fear resulted in their freedom. Even if judgmental types closed the door on them, the lovers had only one need—the beloved's face—and hence a multitude of doors, as ʿAṭṭār declares in *The Choice Book of Quatrains*.

> We, the School of Love, have the face of that full moon
> before us—
> we come up short for anything other than that beloved.
> If our door is closed on this journey to love,
> for every step, we have a thousand other doors.[25]

Here we encounter the second mention of the phrase "School of Love" in ʿAṭṭār's poetry—at least as far as I can tell. The word for "door" (*dargah*) in these lines means something like "threshold," usually a portal to a place of courtly or sacred significance. The lovers in this school do not need a place in which to belong or to receive praise. All they need is a place to reflect on the beloved's beauty, which can be anywhere.

The themes of love that appear in ʿAṭṭār's poetry affected many poets and readers for generations to come. One of Aṭṭār's major contributions to Persian poetics was to advance the spiritual dimension of love language. As we will see, ʿAṭṭār accomplished this by accentuating the ironic tension between piety and infidelity in matters of love.

11

Metaphorical Spaces of Love and Infidelity

You may have noticed, in the preceding poems, that ʿAṭṭār describes the School of Love in terms of space or geography. It is *"here,"* ʿAṭṭār proclaims, that "the School of Love reigns." He describes a place where love reigns, where lies dirt, ruins, and wine—a place far different from the mosques and Sufi monasteries in which the "dry ascetic" (*zāhid-i khushk*) worships God.[1] Indeed, ʿAṭṭār often focuses on place in matters related to the School of Love. Places dictate our behavior. We carry ourselves one way in the mosque, another way in the court of a king, and yet another way in the tavern.

The School of Love's spaces of choice are those that require one to take risks with one's livelihood, well-being, and—above all—reputation. In fact, ʿAṭṭār uses another phrase to describe this school in a poem about his drunken visit to the ruins. There the "master of the ruins" (*pīr-i kharābāt*) tells him, "Adopt the School of the Scoundrels of the Ruins (*madhhab-i rindān-i kharābāt*)! / Get up and cast that prayer rug off your shoulder!"[2] The prayer rug (here *muṣallā*) is a portable place of prayer. Casting it over one's shoulder is a way of literally wearing one's religiosity on one's sleeve. The School of Love, however, is associated with the notorious ruins. Another word that appears in this poem, *qalandar*, signifies a wandering group of God's lovers actively engaged in ruining their own reputations. It originally referred to a disreputable section of town. That is, even in the case of the word *qalandar*, identity originally came from place.[3]

ʿAṭṭār refers to ignominious places that existed in the medieval cities he knew, places that were quite real. He draws metaphorical power from these real places, which allows him to communicate the School of Love's unique type of infidelity. Metaphor, in general, hints at something greater than the words that compose it. For example, a mental, image-making process begins when Shakespeare compares his beloved to a summer's day. As Persian studies scholar Fatemeh Keshavarz discusses, this process draws on a long stream of the reader's experiences and cultural associations, as the reader or listener makes sense of tensions in the metaphor, ways in which the metaphor is both true and false; it is true in some associative or emotive way, even if literally false.[4] The beloved is not a summer's day, and yet she somehow is. ʿAṭṭār draws on these powers of association when it comes to the lover by throwing his audience into places where pious men and women do not belong. He takes them into dens of iniquity, taverns, and the houses of idols, because a dangerous, addictive, and yet liberating love is found there.

These metaphorical places are common not just to ʿAṭṭār, but to Sanāʾī and other Persian poets. By considering such metaphorical spaces in ʿAṭṭār's poetry, we can discover the complex and dynamic potential that he and others saw in love.

The Kaaba

ʿAṭṭār might seem, at times, to shun the Kaaba. If that shocks the reader, then the poet has achieved his purpose. He does not mean to disparage Islam's most sacred structure and location. Rather, in ʿAṭṭār's poetry, the Kaaba represents Islam's externalities. He seeks to destabilize symbols of piety, to offer an alternative system of poetic symbols. Famously, for example, ʿAṭṭār has Rābiʿa spurn the Kaaba. When it comes to receive her in person, she declares: "I must come upon the Lord of the House. What do I want with the House?"[5] The House, or the Kaaba, represents a mere building, a mere exterior. Rābiʿa's seeks the ultimate truth behind and beyond such peripheries.

Ritter catalogues cases of lovers of God seeming to give the Kaaba the cold shoulder. One saint tells the Kaaba not to be "haughty," because "if the divine Friend one time says to you: 'My house,' He says seventy times to me: 'My slave.' "[6] Here ʿAṭṭār's saint references the one Qurʾānic mention of the Kaaba as God's "house," versus the countless Qurʾānic mentions of humans as God's beloved slaves.[7] In like manner, ʿAṭṭār tells us that the early Sufi saint Shiblī desired to set the Kaaba on fire to redirect human attention away from a site of worship and back toward the divine. True worship is complete devotion, a theme that ʿAṭṭār sometimes communicates by memorializing Arabic and Persian literature's most famous tragic couple, Majnūn and Laylā. The mad lover Majnūn's devotion to Laylā has consumed him so completely that Majnūn describes the Kaaba as the direction of prayer for the "ignorant," as a mere "stone," while the true lovers' orientation of prayer faces his darling Laylā.[8]

Yet this theme—highlighting the metaphorical nature of the Kaaba as God's house—must be understood within the context of ʿAṭṭār's other symbols, such as the ruins, the tavern, the idol temple, and the church. He is not praising the latter in reality, nor disparaging the Kaaba. Rather, he is preparing his audience for secrets that upend conventional and sometimes insincere understandings of devotion to God. After all, to return to the previous example, Rābiʿa's attitude toward the Kaaba shifts decidedly after God teaches her about spiritual poverty, one's sense of nothingness before God's grandeur. She discovers the distance between her and God, a distance that will not cure her longing for Him, one compared to "a sea of blood, motionless in the sky" and collected from the blood of God's lovers.[9] Thereupon she cries out, "Back in the beginning, I would not accept the House. I wanted You. But at this moment I am unworthy even of Your house."[10]

As a Muslim and—from what his poetry suggests—a pious one, ʿAṭṭār reveres the Kaaba. As a poet, however, the Kaaba as a site of worship presents him with an opportunity: to hint at the bewildering reality encountered by those who fall in love with God. In that reality, God is seen everywhere and, especially in His beauty, appears in beautiful human faces most intensely. If the Kaaba was meant to be God's house, the site of His worship, then for this person who seems to see God, places of beautiful vision become like the Kaaba. God resides there, in His beauty. This allows ʿAṭṭār to use the power of ostensibly heretical language to convey a perplexing and all-encompassing experience. It is an experience that disrupts the everyday ways in which we think of a transcendent God who is very much unlike us. It is the encounter with God as beloved:

> Once I made your face my *qibla*-prayer-direction,
> I took your face as a second Kaaba.
> Once I turned my face toward your Kaaba,
> I performed one hundred varieties of honorable
> prostrations.
> So befuddled I became that, around that Kaaba,
> my circular walks became multiplied each moment.
> One day, not of any volition of my own, I went
> and looked into the book of being-in-love-with-you.
> It seemed as though I'd read for a thousand years
> —until I memorized it all with just one look.
> Once I saw soul and world to be nothing but you,
> I gave up the soul and abandoned the world.
> From the day when I saw soul as a veil covering you,
> I made a hole inside this soul of mine.
> I sat abidingly at the window of myself,
> gearing myself up, all for you.
> Once I saw you as the foundation of all the world,
> I abandoned wrong and right, good and evil.
> That moment when my heart became sunlike,
> as if through a celestial orbit, I traveled within myself.
> They were narrating the story of your dominion:
> I, incinerated, lifted my prostrate head from the soil;
> like the revelers, I made my way to the tavern,
> with the dancers therein, I started moving from my feet
> on up.
> Once I caught a whiff of the wine of love,
> I made myself oblivious to both the worlds.
> Every moment, this broken ʿAṭṭār is being
> restored by me, through love for your face.[11]

The poetic "persona" (a way of referring to ʿAṭṭār as a first-person character in his own poems) has discovered what might be called a new religious world. Before, he would pray toward the Kaaba, and all was well. Yet he discovered a face, a beautiful face, one with which he fell in love. That beautiful face became his new Kaaba. It drew more from him than he had ever given before. His circuits around this Kaaba were like the circuits made by pilgrims in devotion, but superior in intensity, sincerity, and self-loss. Learning, which had been a slow process before, became about sudden realizations, epiphanies inspired by this new and intoxicating love. One of those epiphanies, indeed the greatest of them, was that the only thing separating the persona from his beloved was his own soul. So, he found a way to see through his very soul—an opening, whereby he sits and waits for glimpses of the beloved.

The beloved is more than just one with the persona. Rather, the beloved is the very essence of the entire world, its origin, and reality, or, in ʿAṭṭār's words, the universe's *aṣl* (literally "root," here "foundation"). This realization causes a paradigm shift, in that all that was considered proper, normative, and ritually correct, or—conversely—improper, evil, and blameworthy, ceases to matter. It is only the presence of the beloved that matters. The persona, then, has more in common with dancing drunkards than with pious men of faith. Drunkards, too, revel and lose themselves in a beloved. They, too, care little for formalities. ʿAṭṭār, the pious advocate of renunciation and Islamic devotion, certainly might not condone their behavior. After all, their love is aimed at human beloveds, not the divine beloved; their drunkenness comes from physical wine, not spiritual intoxication; and their dancing is a form of heedlessness, not remembrance. Yet ʿAṭṭār the poetic persona must be honest, in that there is no better way to describe the effects of this love than through the wild freedom with which those drunkards live.

The Tavern and the Ruins

Irony is arguably the most powerful of literary devices, and ʿAṭṭār's poetry presents no exception. With irony, a poet's words veer meaningfully from expectations. ʿAṭṭār relies on our expectations that the mosque is where one finds God; sobriety is how one remains true to Him; and outward forms of worship, such as the ritual prayer, prove one's moral worth. In his poetry, however, the tavern is where one finds God; intoxication is how one intensifies one's love for Him; and the defiance of conventions—dancing, crying of love, or embracing other religions, even idolatry—reveal an utterly sincere moral worth. All this might seem to make light of the Qurʾān's identification of wine, along with gambling (also praised in Persian Sufi love poetry), as "having great wickedness."[12]

From another perspective, however, the sentiment that one finds God among those hated by moral society hearkens to God's own promise in the Qurʾān. To those who abandon their *dīn* (their religious commitments) God has announced that He will bring a group of people "whom He loves, and who love Him."[13] They have a special quality that applies here, in that "they do not fear the blame of any blamer."[14] God's true lovers, in other words, have no concern with what others think about them or say about them. Social norms do not matter to them, especially if others condemn them for their expressions of love for the Beloved. From a historical perspective, some of this sentiment was captured by the Malāmatiyya movement mentioned in this book's third chapter, a spiritual fellowship very active in Nishapur that did their best to hide feats of piety. From within ʿAṭṭār's corpus, the finest example of God's blameworthy lover is al-Ḥallāj. His utterance "I am the Real," which in a way resembles or even exceeds the statement "I am God," is actually an ecstatic expression of love: I am inseparable from the Beloved. For this statement, al-Ḥallāj is condemned not just on the tongues of his contemporaries, according to ʿAṭṭār, but on the gallows. When love is on the line, he makes the ultimate sacrifice in his courageous lack of concern for the hatred of others.

Numerous symbols and places capture this sentiment—the uninhibitedness of the true lover—in ʿAṭṭār's poetry. One of those is the tavern or "wine house" (*maykhāna*). There, one can utterly lose oneself in beauty and ecstasy:

> It's us—we've gathered in the tavern (*maykhāna*) tonight,
> given our ears over to the music (*samāʿ*) of minstrels
> tonight,
> gotten up and left the two worlds, only to sit down
> joyfully
> with the *shāhid*, the wine, and the burning candle
> tonight.[15]

The persona and his friends have abandoned everything for this carousal. ʿAṭṭār lauds such abandonment, the abandonment of all things worldly—an important part of his ethical program. Even otherworldly ambition, all of it is forgotten in the persona's intoxicated infatuation with the *shāhid*. This is freedom. The word *shāhid* is virtually untranslatable: it means "witness," "evidence," or even "testimony." It refers to a person whose beauty testifies to God's presence. In Sufi practice, the face of the *shāhid* might be the site for what is called "witnessing" (*mushāhada*, or *shuhūd*). That is, the *shāhid*'s beauty can allow us to observe in the world around us the secrets that God uncovered within our hearts, secrets unveiled through the practice of remembering Him, a meditative practice called *dhikr*. Yet here such technicalities do not matter much. This quatrain is about jubilation. It communicates the sheer liberation and joy exclusive to those who have flaunted propriety, those who have traded in the admiration of others for something visceral and direct. It is, in other words, an excellent metaphor for encountering God through love and ecstasy. That encounter requires abandoning interest in the esteem of others, letting oneself go and adoring beauty. It also sometimes involves "audition" or *samāʿ*, which is the musical recitation of love poetry, on occasion accompanied by rapturous dance. If the Kaaba is where God's obedient servants gather, the tavern is where His scorned lovers gather.

Other places of iniquity function in similar ways. We can see ʿAṭṭār list them in a description of the fluctuating phases that a seeker of God experiences. These vicissitudes occur in a larger discussion of the long road to perfecting oneself, which leads to unveiling secrets of the physical and spiritual universe, along with a vision of God, for those who have mastered spiritual poverty. Almost like a spiritual diary in brief, ʿAṭṭār's list tells of pains, misunderstandings, and—in this short section—adventures in love:

> Sometimes with the scoundrels, we were in the tavern;
> sometimes we rubbed our faces on the door of the idol temple;
> sometimes we fastened the Christian *zunnār* girdle around our waists;
> sometimes we seated ourselves inside the Christian monastery;

sometimes among hostile disbelievers we were at war;
sometimes along with fire we were lodged in stone;[16]
sometimes we threw our prayer rugs over our shoulders;[17]
sometimes, in the heart's vast ocean, we boiled.[18]

In the idol temple (*butkhāna*) exist beautiful objects of worship. This serves ʿAṭṭār's purpose of describing absolute devotion to sites of God's beauty. Let it be said, though, that at times, even in this very poem, ʿAṭṭār describes the idol as a false object of attention and devotion. He promotes smashing the idol of egoism—the lower self as an overlord—in the manner of Abraham.[19] With the Christian girdle or *zunnār*, ʿAṭṭār proudly wears what should be a mark of shame. The *zunnār* was, at different points of history, enforced as the identifying garb of protected non-Muslims (*ahl al-dhimma*). Such wearing of distinctive clothing often became enforced during times of conflict, such as when hostilities intensified between the Christian Byzantines and the Muslim Abbasids in 191/806.[20] Later again, in 235/850, the presiding caliph ruled that Christians wear a honey-colored hood (*ṭaylasān*) and the distinctive *zunnār*, though Christians were more often associated with the color blue.[21] Sometimes religious minorities wore a patch signifying their religious identity, called a *ghiyār*, the respective color of which denoted their community, yet it was the *zunnār* that captured the creative interest of Persian Sufi poets. Just as the turban became a marker of Muslim group identity, so too did the *zunnār* represent disbelief, non-Muslimness, and disesteem.

In ʿAṭṭār's poetry, as in much Persian Sufi poetry, the disrepute of the *zunnār* is put to good use: the *zunnār* stands for liberation from caring about the opinions of others—an insignia of the true lover. It is worn by those who serve their objects of worship as complete outsiders, even outcasts. Christianity forms an important part of ʿAṭṭār's descriptions of the liberated lover. In the monastery (*dayr*), as ʿAṭṭār often imagines it, one shares ritual wine, served by beautiful Christian boys and girls. Among these Christian monks, worship and wine are intertwined, so that devotion meets inebriation. Translated in Sufi terms, contemplation of the beloved becomes fueled by passion and bewilderment, becoming lost in the signs of God on earth.[22]

Yet there is one symbolic location missing from this list, one that appears quite frequently in ʿAṭṭār's poetry: the ruins, or *kharābāt*. It too is a symbol that ʿAṭṭar has inherited from Persian Sufi writers before him. The ruins harbor the maverick, whose love blurs the line between devotion and infidelity—as told in the writings of Aḥmad Ghazālī, for example, as well as his accomplished pupil ʿAyn al-Quḍāt Hamadānī.[23] Of special influence on ʿAṭṭār in this regard was Sanāʾī. Sanāʾī shows us the meaning of the "ruins" for all lovers in the first few lines of a magnificent poem:

> Since I've taken the tavern as my *qibla*-prayer-direction,
> how can I practice pious self-restraint?
> Love has become my king. So how can I make kingly
> claims?
> My beloved's Kaaba is the ruins; his sanctuaries are sites
> of gambling:
> I've taken that as my religious persuasion, so how can
> I practice pious self-restraint?
> Having been with beautiful-faced Christians in the idol
> temple,
> how can I practice showy asceticism, with sullen-faced
> men of religion?[24]

The ruins are where gamblers, drinkers, and lovers of beauty go. Yet one challenge that scholars of Persian literature have had in describing this term is that the historical *kharābāt* or "ruins" remain elusive. After all, metaphorical spaces derive their rhetorical impact from real spaces. The tavern resonated with ʿAṭṭār's audience because it corresponded to real taverns. Christian houses of worship, in all their mysteriousness and despite fetishizing stories surrounding them, existed in reality. So, too, did the "ruins." Strictly within the context of Persian poetry, the "ruins" can seem vague, often interchangeable with *maykhāna* or "tavern." Or, it can refer broadly to any place of gathering for the disreputable and the morally depraved, especially gamblers. The great editor of ʿAṭṭār's works, Muḥammad-Riḍā Shafīʿī-Kadkanī, echoes some of the ambiguities and confusions I have mentioned about the real-life meaning of *kharābāt*. Ultimately, he defines it in a general sense as any place for the morally depraved.[25]

Kharābāt may originate in a word for literal "ruins" (*kharāba*). In this case, *kharābāt* would denote dilapidated sites, perhaps on the margins of the city, wherein forbidden and blameworthy activities took place.[26] Another possibility is that the word *kharābāt* stems from *khūr-ābād* (sun temple), a place of worship for devotees of the Zoroastrian angelic-superhuman figure Mithra (Mītrā), sometimes called Mehr (Mihr).[27] This is not a farfetched theory, since Persian Sufi poets often associate non-Islamic places of worship with illicit activity—as we have seen with churches and Buddhist temples. If one looks outside of Persian poetry, especially in books of history written near the time of ʿAṭṭār, a somewhat different picture of the distinguishing trait of the "ruins" appears. My own survey of historical sources has uncovered numerous cases in which the *kharābāt* refers to a brothel. Such seems to be the case in a source on Seljuk history, written a little before ʿAṭṭār.[28] The Il-khanid statesman ʿAṭā-Malik Juwaynī (d. 681/1283), writing not long after ʿAṭṭār, uses the word quite clearly in this sense in his history of the Mongols.[29] It is also used as such by the historian Rashīd al-Dīn Faḍlallāh Hamadānī Ṭabīb (d. 718/1318), writing around a century after ʿAṭṭār's passing.[30] Certainly, of course, disreputable places of gathering can offer multiple forms of iniquity. The ruins, like the tavern, probably provided an outlet for numerous such activities, including drinking, music, and gambling, but it is possible that, at least sometimes, its identifying characteristic was as a site of sex trade.

The point here should not be to locate the ruins (*kharābāt*) as an actual place that ʿAṭṭār frequented. It is the associations of this place that matter. As a poet, ʿAṭṭār draws from the infamy of this location to lead the reader to a profound reconsideration of what we might call "religious commitment," as seen in this striking poem from his collection of *ghazal*s:

> Right before dawn, I set out toward the ruins
> to invite its scoundrels to wild words of godly ecstasy,
> cane in hand, prayer rug over my shoulder,
> thinking, "I am a world-renouncer, endowed with saintly
> miracles."
> A ruin-dweller said to me: "O shaykh!
> Tell me what great task brings you here!"
> I replied, "My task is your repentance.
> If you just repent, you'll set right your reputation."
> He said to me: "Get out of here, you dry world-renouncer—

before you're moistened by the dregs of these here ruins.
If I sprinkle just one drop of these wine dregs on you,
you'll abandon the mosque and your intimate, whispered prayers.
Get out! Stop selling austerity and self-display—
because no one's buying your austerity here, nor your obedience.
A person can only ripen into this color,
who, at the Kaaba, would look after the idol."
He said this and gave me just a piece of wine sediment;
my intellect went numb and was liberated from idle fables.
Once I was annihilated of my haggard soul,
a meeting took place between me and the Love of my Life.
Having found deliverance from the Pharaoh of existence,
like Moses, I had a rendezvous at every instant.
Once I located myself above the two worlds,
and once I saw my true self as all those stations of wayfaring,
then a sun rose from my being—
my interior went outside the heavens.
I said to it, "O knower of secrets!
Tell me, when do I arrive at immediacy to that Essence?"
It said to me: "O heedless, self-deceived one!
Does anyone ever arrive? Impossible! Impossible!
You'll see quite a bit of play, moving down and up,
but in the end you'll stay far-flung, until you're finally checkmated."
All the specks of the universe are drunk on love,
left far-flung, between negation and affirmation.
In that momentary position, when the light of the sun shines,
those illuminated specks of dust are neither existent, nor nonexistent.
What, in the end, are you saying ʿAṭṭār!
Who can understand these clues and allusions?[31]

This poem is a clear example of how ʿAṭṭār speaks through symbols. The early stage of his piety, like the piety of so many who have tried to reform themselves, was marked by a certain smug lack of self-awareness. Those who have this trait project their self-esteem outward, judging the world. They are indeed still today known as "religious folk" in many mosques, churches, synagogues, temples, and other places of worship. The "religious" person seems to have a more black-and-white view of life, and they enjoy being on the side of right. Then the persona visits the ruins, a place or state of mind that disrupts norms. There he is pushed beyond black-and-white, and even beyond his intellect. This leads him to transcend his own sense of selfhood, at which point he begins to hope for direct contact with his Beloved. Yet life itself prohibits such direct contact. Like Moses, he is in effect told by the divine voice, "You will not see Me," even if, like Moses, he has conquered the tyrant of selfhood within.[32]

Wine drinking and idol worship would appear—in this poem—to outdo prayer and obedience. This should give us pause, because it is not meant literally. Transgression in ʿAṭṭār's poetry, from a symbolic perspective, can be transformative, as is argued by Claudia Yaghoobi. Drawing from the French philosopher Michel Foucault (d. 1984), among others, Yaghoobi investigates this theme throughout ʿAṭṭār's canon. Love itself, Yaghoobi argues, is transgressive and transformative; it is "a process of becoming oneself."[33] Through transgression—especially sexual transgression—a person discovers the boundaries of selfhood.[34] Importantly, for Foucault, transgression means courting limits, or exposing limits, and not completely undoing them, for to undo limits would be to end any chance to transgress.[35] Here we might think of the relationship between the world-renouncing impulse in ʿAṭṭār's poem and the dangerous liberation offered by the ruin-dweller. These two positions have a symbiotic relationship: medieval Nishapur needs its people of piety, its devout worshipers, but ʿAṭṭār and other poets have found, even if only in poetry, something profound in the subversive. That profundity can only be appreciated by those who have tried to be pious and therein have come to know piety's limitations. Otherwise, subversiveness is not liberatory but rather mere perversity.

Let us, however, go beyond the poetry's social and ethical dimensions and think of it as applying to the God-human relationship. How would those seeking proximity with the Real interpret this ode to the ruins? After all, ʿAṭṭār mentions certain "clues" (*rumūz*) and "allusions" (*ishārāt*) at this poem's conclusion, using terms frequently found in Sufi manuals meant for the initiated. Moreover, he closes the poem by drawing attention to the all-pervasiveness of love for God throughout the cosmos. He touches on the way all things are both *real*, when illuminated by God's glow, and *unreal*, when left in the darkness of themselves. The key to interpreting all this seems to lie in the entity that ʿAṭṭār addresses at the end of the poem. He calls this entity a sort of "sunlight" (*āftābī*) and "interior" (*darūn*), yet it corresponds to what he calls "spirit" (*rūḥ*) in other writings—the infinite reality deep within the human that reflects the Real.

In those rare glimpses of one's spirit, one realizes that human love for God is but an attenuated reflection of God's love for the cosmos and, ultimately, for Himself. That love cuts through and undoes everything, that is, it has a transgressive power, because it is the actual end objective of existence. The spirit, borrowed from God but within the human, is endless and pure, but covered up by layer upon layer of selfhood, ego, and self-regard. That which brings a person to shed those layers is an unveiling or revealing of the spirit. The spirit is revealed but only shines through when the shadowy presence of egoism retreats. This is why the hated, the mocked, the lowly, the drunkards, the gamblers, and the fornicators hold such high esteem in ʿAṭṭār's poetry. Their way opposes egoism. Their way is one that has no desire for acclaim. It is all risk, and that which is risked is reputation, wealth, and well-being, namely, all the main elements of self-regard. All is risked, moreover, for love. This is made nowhere clearer than in ʿAṭṭār's famous case of the Shaykh of Ṣanʿān, whose story and example is the focus of the next chapter.

12

Finding the Real in Byzantium

The three major poetic forms in which ʿAṭṭār wrote provided him with a toolbox of symbols. The erotic *ghazal*, the pithy *rubāʿī*, and the protracted *mathnawī* narrative poem each came with expectations for the poet.[1] In each form, in ways appropriate to that form, ʿAṭṭār drew heavily from a language of infidelity that often made use of Christians and their sacred spaces. In fact, ʿAṭṭār cultivated and expanded this language of infidelity for future poets.

One of Aṭṭār's most famous narratives centers on places of infidelity and a Christian beloved. The story of the fall of the Shaykh of Ṣanʿān appears at the most pivotal part of *The Speech of the Birds*. The birds' leader, the hoopoe (*hudhud*) needs to inspire this ragtag bunch to get serious about undertaking the arduous journey to the Sīmurgh—that divine and majestic phoenixlike bird upon the mysterious and distant Mount Qāf. After hearing of the shaykh's falling in love, his embrace of infidelity, and his return to Islam, the birds finally resolve to make the trip. Thus, the story of the shaykh stands as the most significant micronarrative in ʿAṭṭār's most celebrated poem. The story also displays perfectly that love and symbolic infidelity are two sides of the same coin because of the loss of ego that both entail.

Christian Spaces: A Prelude

Christianity, as a symbol, holds an important place in ʿAṭṭār's poetry. One should not, however, expect this to mean interreligious appreciation. A man of his times—times that included the Crusades—ʿAṭṭār often describes Christians as infectiously lascivious, sexually desirable, inclined to drink, and, in some poems, hostile toward Islam and Muslims. The late Persian literary scholar Franklin Lewis has traced the theme of the "Christian child" (*tarsā-bachcha*) in ʿAṭṭār's poetry, wherein the young Christian represents a source of beauty, sexual longing, and hence the loss of one's reputation. The "Christian child" theme, along with its related subtopics, is frequent enough to qualify as a subgenre.[2] The word for "Christian" here, namely, *tarsā*, comes from a Persian word meaning "fear" and hence has a close relationship to the Arabic word for monk, *rāhib*, which bears the markings of a verbal root indicating fear, perhaps the reverent fear of God.[3] The term carries both positive and negative shades of meaning, but it certainly seems to fixate in an erotic way on Christians who, in this context, were subjects within Muslim-ruled areas.

Centuries before ʿAṭṭār, aristocrats and the poets they chose to support took interest in Arabic and Persian verses about infatuation with pubescent or postpubescent boys and girls, whether Christian or not, often in compromised social positions. These poems relished in ribald and sometimes—from a contemporary perspective—exploitative relationships. Yet such erotic images have a different tone in the verses of ʿAṭṭār and other Sufi-themed Persian poems. Lewis describes such classical Persian instances of the bewitching boy or girl as "of chaste expression."[4] This is because Persian Sufi poetry took interest in the symbolic power of this image, which represented a devastation of the human ego. Hence, ʿAṭṭār's version of the image of the bewitching young person came from the poetic tropes he inherited, which were native to the poetic genres in which he wrote. Using such images, ʿAṭṭār contributed to the development of a poetic vocabulary to describe the soul's travails and developments as it tried to reach God.

Nevertheless, such imaginings might very well qualify as what one author calls a "Muslim imperial fantasy," since the Christians described often lived under Muslim rule.[5] It is not unlike the way contemporary European and American writers and artists have fantasized about an exotic Middle East, which becomes an imaginary place filled with imaginary people, despised, backward, subjugated, and yet also eroticized. Fantasy certainly seems to apply in ʿAṭṭār's case, even though his interests were more literary than imperial. Some other Persian poets had firsthand knowledge of Christians. Afḍal al-Dīn Khāqānī Shirwānī (d. 595/1199), or simply "Khāqānī," had a Christian mother, who was enslaved and converted from Nestorian Christianity to Islam.[6] He, like Rūmī, had a cordial relationship with Christian royalty and dignitaries that included Byzantines, Armenians, and Georgians.[7] ʿAṭṭār is clearly much more removed. He seems not to have had much interaction with the Christians of Nishapur, or, at least, was willing to ignore those real-life interactions, relying instead on tropes and narratives that he inherited from the writings of Muslim authors.

One of those writings that influenced ʿAṭṭār was a small treatise attributed to Abū Ḥāmid al-Ghazālī but certainly not by al-Ghazālī. The treatise belongs to the "mirror for princes" genre of writing, which offers advice for aristocrats that is ethical, spiritual, and even at times political. It is titled *The Gift to Kings* (*Tuḥfat al-Mulūk*). While he reverentially borrows from al-Ghazālī's writings, as well as passages from al-Ghazālī's brother Aḥmad, the author was mostly likely ʿAlī ibn Abī Ḥafṣ ibn Faqīh Maḥmūd al-Iṣfahānī, who penned it toward the end of the twelfth century CE.[8]

The story that ʿAṭṭār borrows and versifies from *The Gift to Kings* is that of a pious shaykh who loses his faith when he crosses into Byzantium and falls in love with a Christian girl. In *The Gift to Kings*, the story is placed immediately before a rousing call to the writer's audience to reclaim sacred spaces from the invading Crusaders. "Today in our time," the writer proclaims, "the disbelievers have occupied the Lands of Islam, taken Muslim pulpits, and turned the Garden of God's Friend [Abraham], peace be upon him, into a sty for hogs, and the prayer niche of Zacharias and the cradle of Jesus, peace be upon him, into a wine cellar for disbelievers."[9]

Byzantium, as a setting, would have mattered to the audience of *The Gift to Kings*. After all, Byzantium, especially Constantinople, represented the seat of Christian power to those in western and central Asia. Thus, while the Crusaders originated in western Europe, Constantinople appeared to be the center of anti-Muslim hostility for Muslims such as ʿAṭṭār. In fact, cementing Constantinople as a seat of Christian antagonism, the Crusaders sacked Constantinople in April 1204, during ʿAṭṭār's lifetime, and ruled that area for almost sixty years. Even well before that, Muslim-led militaries had long aspired to conquer it.[10] Byzantium was at Islam's frontiers, after all. Of the two empires—Byzantine and Persian—that surrounded Muslims in Islam's earliest days, Byzantium represented the one remaining nearby imperial force. The Persians had already been conquered.

Muslim writers imagined the city to be populated by women both beautiful and promiscuous.[11] Like the tavern and the ruins, Byzantium endangered the reputation of any Muslim who entered. In *The Gift to Kings*, even the Prophet Muhammad, appearing there only in the dreamworld, feels compelled to explain his presence there.[12] ʿAṭṭār imagined Constantinople as a sort of anti-Kaaba: a place of temptations that include wine and sins like idolatry. It was the capital of infidelity, one might say. Perhaps this is why ʿAṭṭār and so many others took interest in stories of the men psychologically conquered by Christians, often Christians in Byzantium, such as the story of the enamored shaykh.

This story of the enamored shaykh also results from a long tradition in Arabic and Persian writings of describing pious men who became entrapped by the love of a Christian. One story is quite similar to that which ʿAṭṭār adopts, and it clearly belongs to the same genre of the enamored shaykh tale. In it, a renunciant falls in love with a young Christian girl. The enraptured man dies while enduring beatings for that love and marries her beyond the grave, acquainting her with her place in Paradise, leading to the conversion of the whole Christian town, ʿAmmūriyya, as well as its monastery.[13] Hellmut Ritter has located many others. An early account, attributed to the famous Sufi teacher Abū Bakr al-Shiblī, concerns a Spanish shaykh in Baghdad who falls for a Christian.[14] In like manner, ʿAṭṭār's later compatriot ʿUmar ibn al-Ḥasan al-Nīsābūrī (ca. 807/1404) describes two historical incidents in which men left Islam for the Christian women with whom they fell in love, one taken prisoner by the Byzantines, the other rerouted while in Armenia on his way to the Kaaba for the Hajj.[15]

One final source is especially important for this version of the enamored shaykh tale. It is an account narrated by Abū Bakr ʿAbd al-Razzāq al-Ṣanʿānī (d. 211/827), which eventually evolved to make him the protagonist of the story.[16] The original version, which was actually a ḥadīth narrated by al-Ṣanʿānī, tells of a renunciant who, for three hundred years, occupied his time worshiping God by the side of the sea, spending his days hungry in fasts and his nights busy in prayer. He jeopardized his salvation when he fell in love with a woman and renounced his righteous habits, yet in the end God saved him by inspiring the formerly pious man to repent.[17] The name of the narrator, al-Ṣanʿānī, referencing Yemen's urban center, ends up becoming the name of the protagonist of the enamored shaykh story in *The Gift to Kings*. Thus, since ʿAṭṭār adopts this story incredibly faithfully from *The Gift to Kings*, the name of that narrator becomes the name of the protagonist of his most famous story: The Shaykh of Ṣanʿān (*Shaykh-i Ṣanʿān*).

The Case of the Shaykh of Ṣanʿān

The story of the Shaykh of Ṣanʿān brings together all the themes we have explored earlier: Christian spaces, the Kaaba, the ruins, love, and infidelity. The story in itself is quite captivating. The shaykh is, according to ʿAṭṭār and his source, a miracle worker, numbering among the most pious and spiritually perfected men of his age, indeed, "the foremost master of his time."[18] At the Kaaba in Mecca for much of the year, the shaykh engages in worship and teaching, having acquired a large following. Internally, however, things are not perfect. He has been suffering from an ongoing dream in which he worships an idol in Byzantium. He sees little choice but to travel to Byzantium, to Constantinople itself, taking a group of his devoted pupils along with him. Previously, the shaykh had made "fifty Ḥajj pilgrimages" to Mecca, which involved circuits around the Kaaba. Now, his circuits are not around the Kaaba but around the capital of infidelity, Constantinople, which they find themselves "circumambulating . . . from end to end" (*ṭawf mīkardand*). That is, the shaykh's center of orientation is already beginning to shift:

> Four hundred men, his trustworthy disciples,
> followed him devotedly on this expedition.
> They went from the Kaaba to the furthest ends of
>   Byzantium,
> circumambulating that place from end to end.

By the decree of God, they saw a balcony up high,
and at the forepart of the balcony was sitting a girl,
a girl, both Christian and Christlike in her immateriality,
one hundred points of true knowledge could be found
  on her path as Spirit of God.
In comeliness's heaven and in beauty's constellation
she was a sun—but one that would never set.[19]

As these lines describe, the shaykh espies a beautiful Christian girl on her terrace. With one glance, he falls so deeply in love that he cannot bring himself to leave the city. Like Christ, known as God's "spirit" (*rūḥallāh*) in Islamic writings, the Christian girl's beauty serves as a conduit, through which the spiritual, otherworldly, and indeed heavenly enters the domain of that which is physically visible.[20] Despite the protests of his pupils, he insists on staying, adopting the alley outside the Christian girl's home as his new abode.

His students finally leave him there, having lost hope in his redemption. He is old, poor, and Muslim, none of which interests the young, beautiful Christian girl. She constantly rejects him. He will not and, indeed, cannot quit. Finally, she caves, deciding that this might be an opportunity to turn him away from Islam. She makes four demands upon him if he is to marry her. The first is that he must worship an idol—which seems to be ʿAṭṭār's ecumenically ungenerous interpretation either of the crucifix or the icons inside Christian churches.[21] The second condition is that he must burn the Qurʾān. The third is that he must drink wine. And the fourth is that he must renounce Islam entirely.

Eventually, he capitulates, engaging in four of Islam's greatest sins. His new communal allegiance is not so much a conversion to Christianity as it is one away from Islam. His real object of worship is clearly the Christian girl. For reasons worthy of discussion, the shaykh describes his apostacy as a liberation. He lacks a bridal gift for the girl, so the shaykh agrees to her demand that he tend to her pigs for a year—an act both sinful and degrading. Yet, despite all these sins, God ends up saving him. The pupils who left him consult with a friend of his, who chastises them for abandoning the shaykh. The friend advises a forty-day vigil, focused on praying for the shaykh's redemption. The Prophet Muhammad appears as the answer to their prayers. The Prophet announces that he has cured the shaykh, whom they find in Byzantium, among the pigs, repentant, tearing off his Christian *zunnār*. He begins to return to Mecca. The Christian girl sees in a dream that a beam of sunlight directs her to find and follow the shaykh, to adopt his spiritual way and religion. Overwhelmed, she runs out to him. Significantly, she must leave the city—which represents infidelity—to search for him in the "desert fields and wild plains."[22] While the shaykh cannot hear her cries to him, God inspires him to realize her change and turn back to be reunited with his "idol."[23] At his hands, finally, she makes a formal conversion to Islam. Her longing to be reunited with God becomes so intense that she dies immediately after her conversion.

The shaykh's story is the perfect way to wrap up this discussion of love and infidelity. On one hand, we have Mecca and its heart, the Kaaba. There the shaykh is pious, but his piety suffers from a hidden sickness. On the other hand, we have Byzantium and its heart, the Christian girl. There the shaykh loses his religion but—and this is the entire point of the story—gains something much more valuable in exchange.

The shaykh needed a major jolt. While before his fall he enjoyed a sort of proximity to God, an obstacle still stood in his way. Falling in love was the last step, allowing him to move beyond his final spiritual obstacle. We might call this jolt a paradigm shift. He needed to fall in love in order to become liberated from that which remained of an achievement-centered and hence self-centered piety. Put differently, he needed to fall in love to rediscover God through a selfless mode of being. In this, ʿAṭṭār comments on the sort of piety that thrives on the approbation of others. The pious person, the beloved of many, has much to lose. The lover's focus is entirely on one beloved—not many. He has nothing to lose. In this sense, he is free, as the shaykh tries to explain to his pupils, pleading with him to repent:

> Another [disciple] said, "O elderly master!
> If there's been moral error, repent as soon as possible!"
> The shaykh said: "I've repented of acclaim and concern
> with spiritual states—
> I'm reformed from being a 'master,' from awaiting ecstasy,
> and other hopeless things."

Another said, "O keeper of divine secrets,
arise and collect yourself in the prescribed prayer."
He said: "Where is the prayer niche (*miḥrāb*) of the face of that painted image,
to leave me occupied in nothing but prayer?"
Another said, "For how long will you speak like this?
Arise and, in devotional retreat, fall prostrate!"
He said: "If my idol were here before me
prostration before her face would be something beautiful indeed."
Another said, "Don't you have any sense of regret?
Don't you miss, even for a moment, your having been Muslim?"
He said: "No one has ever been as regretful as I
that I had not earlier than now been a passionate lover."[24]

Above and beyond the pupils' devotional "Islam" is a reality—the reality of love. Without doubt, that reality lies at the very core of what Islam truly is. But "Islam" here refers not to the reality of Islam as a timeless submission to God; it refers to a set of practices and communal ties that can become frozen, and in which one can become ethically static. God's love for humans, His love for Himself, human love for God, and human love for other humans transcends all that. In love, selfishness implodes. In love, barriers—including right and wrong—fall away, because love is a mode of being without beginning or end that cannot be contained. Hence, remorse for sin disappears for the shaykh. In its place is remorse for not having known love earlier. Prayer, that firm pillar of Islam, disappears. In its place is contemplating beauty, the beautiful face of a human beloved, because it enkindles the flames of love. The prayer niche, facing the Kaaba in Mecca, is replaced by a face that allows the shaykh to come face-to-face with his beloved, which is the closest one can be to standing face-to-face with love itself. Knowing love, one can then return to devotional Islam with renewed clarity of intention.

With this transformative process in mind, ʿAṭṭār wants to communicate that this way of love resembles a religion of its own. In one way, he presents falling in love as an inverted counterpart to Islam. Love also involves inversions of Sufi practices:

> The shaykh took a retreat at the alley of his beloved,
> becoming chummy with the dogs of her alley;
> he sat, having undertaken a devotional withdrawal at
> the dirt of her path,
> turning as thin as a hair for that moonlike face.
> For nearly a month, night and day, he was in her alley,
> patiently awaiting the sunshine of her face.[25]

References in this passage to retreats and withdrawals are meant as a reversal. Thus, for example, a shaykh of this stature once practiced Sufi "retreat" (*khalwat*), which was usually a forty-day period of isolation, sensory deprivation, and remembrance of God. It was often applied to early initiates into a Sufi course of ethical training, though sometimes adopted as an ongoing practice. In this case, the shaykh practices a retreat for love. In Sufi retreat or *khalwat*, seclusion was meant to stimulate a "separation from reprehensible character traits." By persisting in this practice, a seeker would eventually find "intimacy with God."[26] The shaykh's retreat, aimed at intimacy with the Christian girl, strips him of all the traits of self-concern. Haunting the beloved's alleyway (*kūy*) was, in Persian literature even before ʿAṭṭār, more than just a sign of devotion to that beloved. Waiting outside the beloved's home also meant a lack of concern for one's reputation. After all, everyone in the neighborhood could see the lover waiting there.[27] Our shaykh is in an alleyway in Constantinople, among the city's stray dogs, rendering his actions even bolder. ʿAṭṭār describes the shaykh as undertaking another type of retreat as well: the poet uses the term *muʿtakif*, which means one who performs a devotional withdrawal inside a mosque. Seen from an Islamic legal context, such a withdrawal can obligate the worshiper to eschew all worldly interactions, spending the intended time confined to the mosque and focused on worship, exiting the mosque only for calls of nature.[28] Our shaykh, however, has confined himself to the girl's doorstep, growing thin not from worship and asceticism but from longing for her.

These references are indeed meant to be shocking and subversive. Yet ʿAṭṭār also wants us to make a connection between retreats, withdrawals, and other Islamic and Sufi practices and love-centered practices. Ideally, they should be one and the same:

one ought to approach prayer with the sort of focus that a head-over-heels lover has when encountering his beloved. One ought to approach retreat and withdrawal with the sort of contended and wholesale resignation of selfhood that a lover has when waiting outside his beloved's door. Just as the shaykh finds liberation in love for the Christian girl, we, too, can find liberation in love—ideally in the love for God.

This sense of liberation from selfishness explains the shaykh's brazen reply to his pupils when they try to bring him back to Mecca:

> Another pupil said, "Reconcile yourself to the company of your friends
> so that we can return, tonight, to the Kaaba."
> The shaykh said: "If there's no Kaaba here, there's a monastery;
> I am sober at the Kaaba, but drunk at the monastery."[29]

The problem was not the Kaaba—it was the sobriety. "Sobriety" signifies spiritual complacency. The Kaaba can and should bestow upon a seeker a new sense of humility, freeing a person from egoism. Returning to the case of Rābiʿa, for example, ʿAṭṭār tells us that the divine voice explains to her the wisdom of the Kaaba: "The first station [of those seeking union with God] is for them to belly-crawl for seven years just to visit a lump of dried earth for My sake."[30] That is, by enduring hardships to seek a sacred site made of earth, the human being should be jolted out of an ego state. Yet when the Kaaba cannot arouse such selflessness, more drastic measures are necessary. Enter the monastery, which ʿAṭṭār imagines as flowing with wine and busy with idolatry. Here a man can become drunk (*mast*), which means much more than physical intoxication.

The shaykh's drunkenness means surrendering one's sense of self, losing one's footing, and being plunged instead in the ocean of love. Earlier Sufi figures also described drunkenness (or, perhaps better translated, "besottedness") in such a way. It meant being so overcome by God's presence that one was unable to discern pleasure from pain.[31] The monastery, the tavern, the idol temple, and the ruins allude to states of being wherein one loses oneself in drunkenness. ʿAṭṭār, therefore, prescribes drunkenness for those who, like the shaykh, find themselves trapped not by sin but by piety. People of the highest spiritual ambition are ʿAṭṭār's primary audience; those who need to lose themselves even more than others, because there is much more "self" to lose. This is in fact why love is best described as a religion and the ultimate religion as the way of love: whether worshipers become lovers, or lovers become worshipers, one must know both worship and love to make it to the end of the journey to the majestic Sīmurgh, that is, to God.

Part III

Union

13

ʿAṭṭār and Mystical Experience

Union with the beloved is the full achievement of love for ʿAṭṭār, as for many other Sufi writers. In a general sense, "union" is when a person realizes they are one with their beloved. Lover and beloved might be one in terms of what they desire or will. They might, also, be one in terms of identity, in which case the lover realizes that the beloved is their ultimate reality.

Specific terms differentiating grades and kinds of union abound in Sufi writings, including in ʿAṭṭār's. In *The Speech of the Birds*, ʿAṭṭār describes the seven valleys on the path to the Sīmurgh as having various hints of union.[1] At one point, for example, the soul shifts its focus from interest in variety and multiplicity to the oneness undergirding multiplicity. This shift represents "recognizing oneness" (*tawḥīd*).[2] As things progress, the lover becomes confused about separations, leading to perplexity (*ḥayrat*). The lover feels lost, keeping inside them all sorts of contradictions, including sensing simultaneously their own existence and lack of existence. The most advanced union occurs beyond the valley of "poverty (*faqr*) and annihilation (*fanā*)." ʿAṭṭār compares this to being incinerated. All things acquire a sameness when they are ash, he says, or when they become dissolved in the ocean, sharing in the water's qualities.[3] Like ash or sea foam, having undergone annihilation, the lover does remain, but only through the traits of the beloved. This remaining in the traits of the beloved is called *baqā*.[4] Descriptions of the path to union with the Sīmurgh in *The Speech of the Birds* tend to follow the language of "spiritual states and stations" (*aḥwāl* and *maqāmāt*) in Sufism.[5]

In *The Book of Affliction*, which is our main concern in this last part, ʿAṭṭār presents union from the perspective of psychology: that is, he focuses on the faculties of the soul. ʿAṭṭār's theory of union describes a building of experience from basic components, including a series of symbolic entities. The wayfarer eventually goes beyond those symbols. Drawing closer to the spirit within each human being, the wayfarer simultaneously draws closer to the Real, who is beyond all symbols. Yet even if union lies beyond symbols, one must understand and remember such union through the symbolic language of Islam.

Before ʿAṭṭār's own words can guide us through this third and final part on the topic, it makes sense to consider the poet's perspective on union theoretically, within the larger context of studies of religious experience. For the sake of the coming discussion, we can define religious experience as encounters, perceptions, realizations, and firsthand events that matter within a person's religious or spiritual-philosophical framework. The awkwardness of this definition reflects a sentiment in the field that it might be impossible to differentiate between "religious" experiences and "nonreligious" ones. "Mystical" experience usually describes especially significant or intense religious experiences, such as those that are beyond words, undo or expand one's sense of self, or establish contact with sacred or otherworldly beings. Union, which I will explore in the context of ʿAṭṭār, is one type of mystical experience. Comparing contemporary studies to the thought of ʿAṭṭār helps us appreciate that the questions asked today about mystical experience seem to go back millennia. They are probably as timeless as the experiences they try to understand, even as the rise of the modern sciences might have altered the way we answer them. Indeed, in many ways, ʿAṭṭār's observations mirror the reports of experience shared by many seekers, world-renouncers, and lovers of some reality beyond the human self. Yet the specifics of ʿAṭṭār's writings, within their Islamic context, matter as well, as we will see.

Within religious studies, the word "experience" is considered laden with bias. There was, after all, a tendency among early European and American scholars to assume that the "essence" of religion was internal—that an encounter with the "sacred" or some transcendental presence tied together all religions. The psychologist William James, for example, had a more contemporary perspective, in that he did not believe religion to have any one essence. Nevertheless, he did see religions as tied together by experience and hence made experience the focal point of his studies of religion. He famously inhaled nitrous oxide or "laughing gas" to alter his mind in such a way that he might know religious experience firsthand. For James, mystical experience was the most intense realization of religious experience. He described mystical experience as "intuitive" as opposed to "discursive," because it relied on "immediate feeling" and not "proposition" or "judgment."[6]

The problem for James, however, appeared in the fact that "mystics may emphatically deny that the senses play any part in the very highest type of knowledge which their transports yield." He noticed that mystical experience was somehow both immediate, like sensory experience, and yet also disconnected from the senses. Interestingly enough, ʿAṭṭār addresses the gap that James notices between the senses and supersensory experience, as we will see.

James clearly felt empowered enough by his scientific approach to try to have a universal theory of mystical experience, one that would explain the common denominators in Christian, Jewish, Muslim, Hindu, Buddhist, and Neoplatonic accounts of that experience. Today's scholars of religion, over a century removed from James, are more hesitant to make such generalizations. In fact, the complexities behind a phrase like "religious experience" extend not just to vast differences in "experience" but also to difficulties in having a coherent conception of "religion," as I mentioned earlier in this book.

Ann Taves has offered a very compelling response to the problem of "religious experience." Taves studies experience in a way that is both humanistic and scientific, making use of religious studies and neuroscience. Her interest is in why we see some things, actions, or points of view, as "special," which brings her to replace the murky term "religious experience" with "special things." Setting things apart as special, it turns out, is a practice common to other primates and mammals.[7] Taves explains that science might even offer an evolutionary purpose to perceiving the world around us as alive, instilled with spirits and the like—an important part of mystical experience. Over the course of our evolution, humans benefited from having minds that perceived agency in everything, assuming everything around them to be alive. This helped them avoid failing to notice a predator.[8] In general, Taves offers a data-driven study of modes of consciousness that people generally acknowledge as distinct from the ordinary, that is, as special. Taves's work has resemblances to that of ʿAṭṭār, however limited those might be, considering their different lifeworlds. Both approach experience as something generated from within but not distinct from the perceptible world.

Of those recent thinkers who have offered theories of experience perhaps none is more pertinent to this discussion of ʿAṭṭār than Steven Katz. Steven Katz's theory of mystical experience is *contextual* and thus quite different from William James and most who followed him. James and others offered *universal* views of religious experience, and that includes the most well-known theorists of mystical experience: Rudolf Otto, Walter Stace, Robert Charles Zaehner, Mircea Eliade, and Ninian Smart.[9] The difference is that universal theories search for some unifying quality behind all the various accounts of mystical experience. Contextual theories see experience as shaped by each person's individual knowledge. Katz argued that the particulars of one's own situation form mystical experiences, and, thus, each religious tradition would have its own distinct variety of mystical experience. "There are," Katz said, "no pure experiences," explaining that the word "pure" here means "unmediated."[10]

Experience must, in other words, emerge through a set of "patterns and symbols," which usually come from one's religious community.[11] Through the course of our lives, we acquire an understanding of the world around us through the symbols, stories, and values of our cultural circumstances. For those lacking any formal religious commitments, their experience would still be shaped by their own understanding of the world, an understanding resulting from the social and symbolic contexts in which they lived. Each of us belongs to a symbolic world. According to Katz, that symbolic world shapes our experiences. We might say that our religious or cultural traditions give us a language not only with which we understand experience but with which we create it.

Katz argues that "patterns and symbols of established religious communities" are formative in anything that might be labeled a mystical experience, "at work before, during, and after the experience."[12] By this, he means that—at every stage of a mystical experience, even before it can exist—a person's particular frame of perception comes into play. One might mistakenly interpret this as if Katz were claiming that many or even all mystics perceive a common reality through the various lenses of their respective traditions. Rather, using a comparative analysis of Buddhist, Jewish, Muslim, and Christian aspirants, Katz illustrates ways in which the reported experience that results from such training relies in every way on the symbol system and outlook formed by that tradition. To use his phrasing, experiences are contextually "over-determined." That is, an entire "world of concepts, images, symbols, and values" that we acquire throughout life provides the most basic code for any experience.[13]

Katz argues that differences in religious or philosophical traditions affect the way we perceive and undergo mystical experiences. He claims that, though some might see similarities between the Islamic-Sufi idea of *fanāʾ* (annihilation) and the Buddhist idea of *sūnyatā* (emptiness), there is one important difference: annihilation in Sufism always assumes remaining (*baqāʾ*) in God, whereas traditional Buddhism has no counterpart to this—no deity in which to remain. That is, according to Katz, without a conception of God, the mystic only experiences a loss of false selfhood, not a union with God.[14]

As we move forward to consider ʿAṭṭār's view of union, then, there are two important matters to take away from Katz. First, Katz helps us think about the necessity of having a system of symbols for the construction and memory of mystical experience. We might call this a "language of experience." This shines a new light on the way ʿAṭṭār presents the process of achieving union, which involves the wayfarer's exploration of the major symbols in the universe, as well as an exploration of the faculties of perception within himself.

Second, ʿAṭṭār offers us some clarity about a matter that remains, at least in Katz's thought, clouded by ambiguity, namely, the objective reality behind mystical experience. When a person has such an experience, we can appreciate how that experience has been shaped and understood through their individual cultural or religious tradition. Still, is there anything "real" about it? Katz himself neither confirms nor denies that there is an objective reality at the core of mystical experience.[15] Taves, too, acknowledges the difficulty in answering this question.[16] ʿAṭṭār, however, offers a model in which the limits of human intelligence form the bedrock of his thought. What happens in union does have an objective reality, and yet it is a reality unknowable by human thought. The experience of union is both universal and contextual at once, a point that would be deliberated by later Sufi figures.[17] The symbolic language of experience that ʿAṭṭār's wayfarer encounters results from the reality that ʿAṭṭār knew—Islam and the sciences of his day. Yet ʿAṭṭār acknowledges that the sum total of the experience of union transcends that language of experience, without ever invalidating it.

ʿAṭṭār presents his ideas on union in multiple ways that include poetic metaphors and Sufi terminology. Yet his focus on the psychological workings of the soul—the role of the inner faculties in achieving union—renders his account in *The Book of Affliction* especially gripping and thought-provoking. Before we consider that, the coming two chapters will uncover the religious and literary sources that made ʿAṭṭār's perspective on union possible. This begins with the most celebrated encounter in all of Islam, the encounter between Muhammad and God on a certain special night.

14

Ascents to the Real

Among the symbols and narratives in Islam most associated with what might be called "mystical experience" is a journey that the Prophet Muhammad took on a certain night. A famous Qur'ānic verse describes the Prophet's celestial journey, during which he is reported to have met other prophets, ascended into the heavens, and engaged in intimate discourse with God: "Glory be to the One Who took His servant on a night journey from the Sacred Mosque to the Farthest Mosque, the area of which We have blessed, so that We would show him some of Our signs! Certainly, He is the Hearing, the Seeing."[1] This nightly ascent or *mi'rāj* captured the devotional imaginations of Muslims. The *mi'rāj* narrative mattered especially to those who, like the Prophet, sought direct encounters with God. Some described their own encounters in ways that resembled the Prophet's. Bāyazīd Basṭāmī, whom Sufis considered a major predecessor, had such a narrative. The celestial journey motif also appeared in Arabic and Persian literature, often as a prelude to other poetic narratives.

In each of his long narrative poems, 'Aṭṭār includes either a section on the Prophet's nightly ascent (*mi'rāj*) or a description of it embedded in praise of the Prophet.[2] This practice was later adopted by other Persian poets too. Reference to the *mi'rāj* would usually be placed after a discussion of recognizing God's oneness (*tawḥīd*). The first Persian poet who made this convention popular was Sanā'ī, who was then followed by 'Aṭṭār, Khāqānī, Niẓāmī, and then others.[3] It was not restricted to Sufi, philosophical, or devotional poetry but rather became a practice shared by many narrative poets.

For ʿAṭṭār, the Prophet's experience is the archetype of self-annihilation and union, as illustrated in *The Book of the Divine*:

> A call came from the Universal Essence: "Hurry and come here!
> Abandon body and soul! Bodyless and soulless, come here!
> Enter! O you who are Our destination and Our intended one!
> Gaze upon Our essence, through this intimate encounter."[4]
> His tongue—in the perplexity of the moment—stopped working:
> Muhammad became separated from Muhammad.
> Muhammad saw not himself. Instead, he saw the Spirit of all spirits.
> He beheld an encounter with the Creator of being and place.
> It was not Ahmad anymore. It was God Himself who was there.[5]
> An eyewitnessing through the eye of direct encounter was there.[6]

The ascent or *miʿrāj* shows us the Prophet's exalted status with God. Yet ʿAṭṭār sees it as much more than that. The *miʿrāj* functions as a model for God's knowers and friends. It is a framework for other human encounters with the divine. In this, ʿAṭṭār draws from a long tradition of interest in the saintly ability to encounter God as Muhammad did.

After the Prophet, no saintly ascent was as famous as that of Bāyazīd Basṭāmī, whose utterances gave later generations pages upon pages to ponder. Indeed, ʿAṭṭār dedicates a long section of *The Memorial of God's Friends* to Basṭāmī's famous encounter with the Real, his saintly *miʿrāj*.[7] ʿAṭṭār devotes this large section to Basṭāmī's ascent because the lives of the saints represent the peak of human potential. ʿAṭṭār relays Basṭāmī's own account of drawing nearer to God, meeting Him and being enveloped by His love, unity, and conversation. He lets Basṭāmī speak, as the saint describes the discovery of his true self and the disappearance of every other form of selfhood that might obscure that discovery:

> When He saw the purity of the secret place within my heart, and when my heart heard the call of satisfaction from the Real, He inscribed gratification upon me, and He rendered me luminous. He brought me out of the darkness of the self and its impurity. I knew then that I am alive through Him. And I knew that it was through His grace that I opened up the wide expanse of jubilance in my heart.
>
> He said, "Whatever you want, just ask."
>
> I said, "I want you."[8]

ʿAṭṭār makes it clear that Basṭāmī's journey culminates in a realization of oneness in which Basṭāmī must shed more and more of himself: "Once I arrived at Unity (*waḥdāniyyat*), which was my first glimpse of Oneness (*tawḥīd*), I spent many years running in that valley on the feet of different types of understanding. I did that until I became a bird whose eyes were uniqueness and whose wings were foreverness. I would flutter in the air of howness. After I became hidden from all creatures, I said, 'I have arrived at the Creator.' "[9] Trying to know things through human understanding (*fahm*) is like walking: it will not get you very far, nor will it give you panoramic vision. Walking is a prelude to becoming a bird, one that can soar far away from selfhood until arriving at the true self.

ʿAṭṭār's account of Basṭāmī is about the firsthand achievements and experiences of a saint, richer in subjective detail than in theoretical abstractions, so it does not directly convey the complexities that we find in ʿAṭṭār's poetic works. In more technical discussions, especially in *The Speech of the Birds* and *The Book of Affliction*, the wayfarer's search for union appears as a journey to the spirit (*rūḥ*). That journey to the spirit is actually a journey to the purest sense of self, the self that reflects God. As ʿAṭṭār emphasizes repeatedly, the spirit is unlike other human faculties; its identity is divine. Here ʿAṭṭār maintains the immediacy of Basṭāmī's earnest first-person account without adding any specialized Sufi language about psychology.

Nevertheless, there is one subtle way in which we see Basṭāmī's arrival as one that takes place at his own spirit. Early in the account, matters are about the lower soul, that is, the *nafs*. Basṭāmī describes himself as saved from the "darkness of the self (*nafs*) and its impurity."[10] Toward the end of his account, however, as he witnesses Paradise and Hell, greeting the various prophets, Basṭāmī identifies himself with the spirit (*rūḥ*). Moreover, we learn that Basṭāmī's destination lies in a mode of being that describes the spirit, namely, a reflection of divinity. His human attributes come to reflect attributes of divinity: "When He became aware that my attributes had finally met His, He named me after His own Presence and honored me in the selfness of Himself, so that at that moment duality left. Then it became like so: 'Your satisfaction is Our satisfaction. Your speech will admit no contamination. And people will see in you that which you have of My I-ness.'"[11] This is precisely the model that we see in ʿAṭṭār's poetic writings, as well. The spirit is Godlike. The seeker becomes Godlike as well, once they convene with their spirit, which occurs for Basṭāmī after spending hundreds of thousands of years at various stages of divine proximity.[12] It is then that this change for Basṭāmī occurs at the place of his very identity: "Now, by necessity, my tongue speaks from the kindness of divine needlessness. My heart shines with the light of Lordliness. My eye sees by means of the crafting of Godliness. By His aid, I speak. By His strength, I grasp. Because I live through Him, I will never die."[13]

A special ḥadīth valued by generations of Sufi authors confirms this process of losing oneself in God, so that God acts through His servant. In this narration, the Prophet Muhammad quotes God's direct speech. God declares that His servant approaches Him, first and foremost, through obligatory acts. Then the servant goes beyond that, doing more than what is required, worshiping and serving God simply because the servant wants to. These "supererogatory acts" (*nawāfil*) lead to God's love for the servant. At that stage, once God loves the servant, the servant's perception and actions become God's: "Once I love him, I am his hearing by which he listens, his vision by which he sees, his hand by which he seizes, and his foot by which he walks."[14] It is at this lofty destination that Basṭāmī has arrived.

15

Celestial Journey Literature

ʿAṭṭār's stories of union belong to what I call the "celestial journey genre" of literature. A "genre" is a category or type of literature that carries certain expectations about content. In this case, celestial journey literature comprises narratives about some movement or flight to a distant or otherworldly goal—a journey that awakens sensibilities, unveils realities, and reveals the soul's true nature. As we have discovered, this genre took its initial inspiration from one narrative in particular, the celestial journey of Muhammad. Yet the celestial journey genre did more than simply recount the Prophet's ascent: it converted it into a universal narrative of the soul's return to its origins. In that way, this genre resembled a Neoplatonic tradition preceding Islam.[1] It became a means by which poets, Sufi thinkers, and philosophers could explore the maturation of the human soul, what we might call "human completion," in an allegorical way. Using his predecessors' models and adopting the celestial journey genre of literature, ʿAṭṭār composed *The Book of Affliction* and *The Speech of the Birds,* which were both extended deliberations on union.

Many classical treatises in Persian and Arabic can be classified as celestial journey narratives. Among them are those described in the following paragraphs by Ibn Sīnā and Sanāʾī, namely, Ibn Sīnā's *Living, Son of Awake* (*Ḥayy ibn Yaqẓān*) and *The Book of Celestial Ascent* (*Miʿrāj-nāma*), as well as Sanāʾī's *The Journey of God's Servants to the Return* (*Sayr al-ʿibād ilā al-maʿād*). Also in this category is *The Lantern of Spirits* (*Miṣbāḥ al-arwāḥ*) by Shams al-Dīn Muḥammad

Bardsīrī Kirmānī (d. before 618/1221)—a lesser known but beautiful Persian poem in the *mathnawī* style of rhyming couplets. In its form and themes, *The Lantern of Spirits* resembles ʿAṭṭār's *The Book of Affliction*. Like ʿAṭṭār's book, and like Sanāʾī's before him, *The Lantern of Spirits* blends Ibn Sīnā's understanding of the soul with those of the Sufis. It describes a progression through the soul's stages and through cities that represent virtues such as renunciation and wisdom. An old man—who is both spirit and intellect—guides the soul until it reaches its final stage, "the soul in love" (*al-nafs al-ʿāshiqa*). The poem references the Prophet's *miʿrāj*, and the Prophet himself appears at the soul's final stages, where the soul recognizes that it, the elderly guide, and the Prophet are indeed one. Worthy of mention, as well, is a portion of Najm al-Dīn Kubrā's *The Proprieties of Wayfaring* (*Ādāb al-sulūk*). While not as allegorical as the other narratives mentioned, Kubrā's account describes the soul's journey through virtues and vices, light and darkness, until the soul travels through God's names and attributes, cultivating saintlike intimacy with God. Finally, Ibn ʿArabī has two passages concerning his own celestial ascent to the innermost human reality in his *The Openings in Mecca* (*al-Futūḥāt al-makkiyya*), as well as one treatise that mentions the topic and another devoted entirely to it.[2] That latter treatise is titled *The Book of the Night Journey to the Highest Station* (*Kitāb al-isrāʾ ilā al-maqām al-asrā*).

One major variation on celestial journey narratives made use of bird allegories. The most famous of these is ʿAṭṭār's *The Speech of the Birds*. Before ʿAṭṭār, however, Ibn Sīnā also had a *Treatise on Birds* (*Risālat al-ṭayr*). Ibn Sīnā's version was about a caged bird who—along with other feathered companions—traveled beyond eight mountains to meet a king who possessed perfection and absolute beauty.[3] ʿAyn al-Quḍāt composed a short passage in Arabic describing himself as a bird who escapes his cage to reunite with the king in the nest of his origins.[4] The philosopher Shihāb al-Dīn Yaḥyā Suhrawardī (d. 587/1191) had three Persian-language celestial narratives with bird-themed journey narratives. They include his *The Red Intellect* (*ʿAql-i surkh*), in which the narrator recounts having been in the form of a falcon who is taught spiritual mysteries by a luminous old man. The young-looking old man comes from a place farther than Mount Qāf and includes in his lesson mention of the Sīmurgh. *Treatise on Birds* (*Risālat al-ṭayr*) was Suhrawardī's

Persian translation of Ibn Sīnā's narrative of the same title. His *The Screech of the Sīmurgh* (*Risāla-yi ṣafīr-i sīmurgh*) has a short account of a hoopoe who migrates to Mount Qāf to morph into the Sīmurgh. Finally, Rūmī uses the metaphor of the soul as a bird seeking liberation from its cage in his lyrical poems, as well as a short section on the soul's propensity for birdlike spiritual flight in his *Mathnawī*.

Reviewing the history of this celestial journey genre helps clarify why it tended to include certain topics, especially the soul's maturation and its faculties. The philosopher Ibn Sīnā contributed to the connection between such journey narratives and the study of the soul. Two of Ibn Sīnā's texts in particular matter to the genre as it was received by ʿAṭṭār. The first text, *Living, Son of Awake*, in Arabic, describes the philosopher's encounter with an old man who gives him advice on becoming virtuous, which appears in the guise of a discussion about his companions. The old man—the titular Ḥayy—then recounts his journeys through the various climes, which becomes an allegorical contemplation on the place of the human soul in the universe. The old man offers to lead Ibn Sīnā to a sunlike King, representing the intellect's potential to deliver the soul to God. The second treatise that mattered to ʿAṭṭār's predecessors, in Persian, *The Book of Celestial Ascent*, might or might not be Ibn Sīnā's. Nevertheless, the psychology it presents, the terminology it uses, and the universe it describes reflect Ibn Sīnā's philosophy closely.[5]

Ibn Sīnā's *The Book of Celestial Ascent* begins with a recounting of his view of the soul, its relationship to the body and its humors, as well as the means by which the soul takes flight to become an intellect. Following that, the author comments on the *miʿrāj* narrative, wherein the author interprets the ḥadīth of the *miʿrāj* in the terms and hierarchies of Ibn Sīnā's psychology. In this way, *The Book of Celestial Ascent* is both a recounting of the Prophet's *miʿrāj* as well as a more theoretical story of the soul's journey to union. This is a case of a celestial journey narrative emerging directly from an account of the *miʿrāj*.

The author—who is either Ibn Sīnā or an admirer of his—sees a correspondence between the Prophet's instance of direct contact with God and the final maturation of the human ability to know. The Prophet's declaration of intimacy becomes a philosophical statement about the soul's encounter with the intellect. The Prophet is reported to have said, "From being in awe of God, I forgot everything that I had seen and known. Such unveiling, grandeur, and pleasure from proximity was produced that you would say that I was intoxicated."[6] The author rephrases the Prophet's words, interpreting them as a complete absorption in universals: "I was no longer engaged in perceiving and preserving particulars. The rational soul achieved so much pleasure from this knowledge that all the faculties of the natural and animal (souls) stopped working. I was so immersed in unity that I was no longer engaged in the world of substances and bodies."[7] The realm of what might be called "ideas," that is, universal concepts, now rules over the Prophet's entire being, in the same way that the intellect rules over the human soul when it reaches completion. Academic discussions of Islamic philosophy often ignore "mystical experience," focusing instead on terms, arguments, and history. Yet the author here assumes that the soul's experience of union matters greatly to Islamic philosophy.

ʿAṭṭār's understanding of the place of the intellect among the faculties differs.[8] For him, the intellect is exalted, but not the most exalted faculty. This parallels the celestial narrative that impacted ʿAṭṭār most directly, that of Sanāʾī. Sanāʾī wrote a celestial journey narrative called *The Journey of God's Servants to the Return* that became admired and imitated by later Persian poets, including ʿAṭṭār. Sanāʾī himself drew heavily from the two aforementioned texts attributed to Ibn Sīnā.[9]

In Sanāʾī's narrative poem, *The Journey of God's Servants to the Return*, he describes an allegorical excursion, where animals, colors, places, numbers, and other descriptive elements all signify a philosophical or ethical point.[10] Sanāʾī's treatise, at first, follows the model and philosophy of Ibn Sīnā.[11] The treatise starts with the development of the soul. He follows this with a fascinating and detailed analysis of the negative ethical traits—associated with imbalances in the humors and their corresponding nature—that keep a soul bound to animal qualities and hence restrain the soul from successful flight.

As if in a dream, Sanāʾī then describes being led by an old man, a guide who, Sanāʾī hints, is the Active Intellect.[12] They traverse through places where jealousy takes on the form of a viper with one head, seven faces, and four mouths; rancor appears as a demon; and avarice shows itself in the form of a barren, smoky, and rocky place. The guide instructs him in saving himself from the strange and the threatening, passing these scenes safely. Most of this part of the treatise is focused on what might be called philosophical ethics: an awareness of imbalances in the body's forces that necessitate control; descriptions of the four humors, their effect on character, and their ties to astronomy; and the perfection of human becoming in union with the intellect.

What seems to have made Sanāʾī's first-person poetic treatise so appealing to readers like ʿAṭṭār, however, is that matters do not end there. The persona, having united with his guide, realizes that he is barred from where the lovers are—those affiliated with a certain light that he has seen. Here, he has reached a place where beings have no discernible forms, "Free from form and matter were they all; / above multiplicity and opposition were they all."[13] He must abandon form and selfhood to join them, and so needs a new guide:

> Your guide now is that light,
> remarkably close, and yet oh so far away!
> He will liberate you from the thinking of self.
> He will deliver you to your original nature.[14]

Sanāʾī gives us some sense as to why this new guide has abilities that the intellect did not. Those abilities lie in revelation, in uncovering truths communicated through the Qurʾān and God's commands:

> He can show you those pearls—
> the letters of the Qurʾān unveiled.
> For in this day and age, he is the Possessor;
> throughout all the world's kingdoms, the open eye
> belongs to him.[15]

Sanāʾī names this new guide, this man of pure light. He is Abū al-Mafākhir Sayf al-Dīn Muḥammad ibn Manṣūr (fl. 6th/12th c.), a Ḥanafī preacher and jurist from the city of Sarakhs who served as chief justice (*qāḍī al-quḍāt*) of Khurāsān. He had his own *khān-*

aqāh—a communal house for the pious—and was among Sanāʾī's patrons, serving as the object of the poet's praise in other poems as well. In Sanāʾī's journey, unlike Ibn Sīnā's, when the soul needs to go beyond the Universal Intellect, it can only be guided by the lover, epitomized by Ibn Manṣūr.

Unfortunately, the great scholar of Persian literature, J. T. P. de Bruijn, sees this conclusion of the poem as being "of little interest," as it is "merely a panegyric on the poet's patron."[16] De Bruijn misses the ways in which this section exists to correct Ibn Sīnā's vision of the completion of the human being and the consummation of the soul's knowledge. Beyond union with intellect, the highest levels of human existence lie in contemplating revelation and worshiping God through the law He revealed. With this in mind, Sanāʾī describes Ibn Manṣūr as "preacher to Intellect and preserver of revelation" and "blood-tied confidant to both Love and Inner Interpretation."[17] The jurist represents lived piety and profound meditation on God's words and names.[18]

According to Nicholas Boylston, Sanāʾī's praise of this patron exceeds the norms of panegyrics. Yet such exalted praise accentuates the urgency—for Sanāʾī and other Persian poets who followed in his tracks—of spiritual training informed by the Qurʾān, the way of the Prophet, and the guide's own wisdom and experience. We see this guide in ʿAṭṭār's poetry as well, in the hoopoe (*hudhud*) of *The Speech of the Birds* and throughout *The Memorial of God's Friends*. Their relationship seems to have been one where Ibn Manṣūr led Sanāʾī "beyond the limitations of selfhood," so that some of his poems indicate a "perspective shift" that occurred for him at Ibn Manṣūr's hands.[19] It is unclear whether Ibn Manṣūr was formally Sufi or not.[20] Of course, the word "Sufi" might not matter in this case, since advanced Islamic ethics often reflected themes shared by Sufis, even when the authors did not have formal connections to Sufism. Ibn Manṣūr and other Ḥanafī teachers focused on a contemplatively informed submission to God, instead of intellectual abstractions. This same style appears in the works of Rūmī's father, Bahāʾ al-Dīn Muḥammad Walad (d. 628/1231). Like Ibn Manṣūr, Rūmī's father was also a Persian Ḥanafī preacher, and Rūmī's poetry often shows his father's influence.[21]

Sanāʾī's conclusion implies that love lies beyond the cultivation of the virtues and the full development of the intellect. Even if it is clearly modeled on Ibn Sīnā's universe, Sanā'ī's narrative poem offers an alternative to it, as did al-Ghazālī, ʿAṭṭār, and Rūmī—all of whom took interest in what remained beyond the intellect's reach. They borrowed from philosophy because it provided certain tools to all well-educated individuals to understand the soul and the cosmos. For them and for all those who wrote within the celestial journey genre, such narratives were often a means to convey their version of an ordered universe, both the universe outside the soul and the universe of the soul.

16

Union in *The Book of Affliction*

In *The Book of Affliction,* ʿAṭṭār tells us of a wayfarer whose quest is for relief from the pain of existence. The entities he meets along the way all teach him something about the universe and himself, but they are not the ultimate resolution he seeks. His is, at first, a journey downward from that which is most transcendent. It begins with the angels, followed by the Divine Throne and Divine Footstool, the Tablet, the Pen, Paradise, Hell, the Heavens, the Sun, the Moon. Then, within the realm beneath the moon, the wayfarer moves from the simple to the complex. He visits fire, wind, water, earth, the mountains, the seas, minerals, vegetables, wild creatures, birds, four-legged animals, Satan, the race of jinn, the human, Adam, Noah, Abraham, Moses, David, Jesus, and then the Prophet Muhammad. The Prophet initiates the wayfarer's spiritual salvation by diverting his journey from the outer world into the inner world of the soul. This leads him to sense, imagination, intellect, heart, and, at long last, spirit, where he finds what he has sought.

Those cosmological symbols are each presented as modes of human knowing, and their speech presented as "internal-state language."[1] ʿAṭṭār explains this himself, defending the dialogue he has ascribed to sacred entities (such as the Divine Throne, angels, or the Prophet Muhammad):

> It all comes from the "tongue of the inner state" (*zafān-i ḥāl*),
> not in any way from the tongue of speech (*zafān-i qāl*).
> It would all be a lie were it meant as the tongue of speech,

> but as the inner state's tongue, it is true and good.
> If you're unfamiliar with the inner-state tongue, no worry!
> Just call it "inner thoughts put to words" and you're
> done.[2]

This apology for the act of sacred fiction tells us two things. First, that the poet does not see himself as above the need to justify his work, as it is not the only place in his writings that he apologizes.[3] He speaks to his audience as though they are peers (as they might have been) or equals, not as pupils. Hence the tale of union that he tells seems to be less often a cataloging of his own experiences for the edification of novices than it is an act of scholarship upon which he and his audience might reflect together.

Second, and more important, "internal-state language" implies the creation of a system of symbols that gives the wayfarer a "language" of union. All things, even inanimate objects, have speech in ʿAṭṭār's universe. Their speech sometimes describes their own state of being relative to humans, as if a road might say, "Upon me people walk." At other times, though, ʿAṭṭār seems to designate as "language" what is an ongoing universal discourse. This echoes a Qurʾānic imperative: "All that is in the heavens and the earth glorifies Him."[4] It is ʿAṭṭār's role, as poet and as caller to this sacred discourse, to awaken within the heart reverberations of the cosmos's act of praise. In this poem, that universal speech takes the form of a lament of the distance between all things and God.

Thus, since communication with God and awareness of Him make up the fabric of the universe, the pathway to true knowledge—the knowledge of the states of things—lies in *dhikr*, or remembrance of God in the heart. This is why the wayfarer's journey leads him from the senses and into the heart: it is there that he can become aware. In a way, ʿAṭṭār's story is the story of *dhikr*, that is, the story of remembering God through His names. Uttering the holy names takes the soul throughout the universe in an instant. Yet, when *dhikr* is truly successful, the heart settles and unites with the spirit. This is why ʿAṭṭār's story of union ends with the spirit.

The prophetic principle—the guiding power of Muhammad—initiates this union with the spirit by reining in the wayfarer's movement, causing that movement to turn into the self. This implies that the end goal of revealed knowledge and practice lies in union through self-knowledge, a self-knowledge that begins with contemplating cosmological symbols.[5] Having some human understanding of things—the names, attributes, and states of things—provides the wayfarer with a working language of reality. This language of reality then allows the wayfarer to explore the world within himself and experience union.

The Signs within Themselves

Union requires a willingness to lose one's identity, for identity is one's false sense of self. To illustrate this, let us begin with what might be called "negative example." For ʿAṭṭār, the one who sought union and failed is a lesson to us all. He is Satan, or "Iblīs," and ʿAṭṭār describes him as the most afflicted character in his *Book of Affliction*: "No one has seen more affliction (*muṣībat*) than you!"[6] Satan represents the very essence of damnation, namely, God's distancing of the besotted lover. That distancing can be as long as "one hundred thousand years," and at the end of that period, as the lover seeks water from the goblet of the beloved, he draws out "curses" to drink instead.[7] This occurs for those who, like Satan, seek union without a corresponding willingness to relinquish their own identities. His maintenance of selfhood when paired with his longing for union leads to the pain of separation represented by fire.

"I stand far, blackened inside by estrangement," Satan declares, "because I lack endurance for the proximity of such union."[8] As an ambitious failure, Satan's position resembles those bound to their reasoning capacities. The nature of intellect is to retain, to draw in, to describe—in other words, all means of knowing that acknowledge duality. The tension between duality and proximity is shared between intellect and Iblīs. Yet his predicament—for which ʿAṭṭār expands upon the sayings of Ḥallāj—is that of the scorned lover, doomed to distance. While Ḥallāj's focus was on Iblīs's noble and uncompromising declaration of God's unity, which would not allow him to prostrate before Adam, ʿAṭṭār's Iblīs is not exactly a brave hero. Rather, he gives the wayfarer an important lesson, namely, that the slightest attachment to selfhood will dash any hopes of union, with eternal and devastating results. Iblīs provides a symbol of frustration by which the wayfarer constructs his language of union. Once a celebrated worshiper, now the accursed Satan, Iblīs must listen longingly to the Prophet Muhammad's meeting with God, his *miʿrāj*, savoring a mere idea of proximity.[9]

In all his encounters, the wayfarer acquires parameters for his expectations, as various narratives color and shape his experiences. Because the entities he meets result from ʿAṭṭār's Islamic milieu, they become symbols bearing the stamp of Islamic revelation. Most revelatory of all is the thirty-sixth encounter of forty, when the wayfarer meets Muhammad. Muhammad is a representation of the fully achieved wayfarer and is in direct contrast to Satan. With the authority of his proximity to God, the Prophet redirects the wayfarer toward the inner faculties, in which he can find the "poverty and annihilation" that he seeks.[10]

The Prophet explicitly uses Qurʾānic language for this redirection: "Since the horizonal signs have been laid bare to you," he says, "gird up your loins now for the signs within yourself."[11] This refers to a Qurʾānic verse, "We will show them our signs in the horizons and in themselves until it becomes clear for them that it is the truth."[12] First, one recognizes the signs outside oneself in the horizons, and then God's signs within the soul. This indicates that a language of spiritual psychology begins with an awareness of universal symbolic value. One cannot know oneself without first learning the meanings of the world around oneself. In ʿAṭṭār's interpretation, the Qurʾān sanctions and in fact calls for a discovery of the revealed language of everything—a reading of the cosmos as if it were a series of Qurʾānic verses, or *āyāt*. Read the universe as God's revelation, the Prophet tells him, so that you can read the inner human faculties in like manner and thereby achieve union.

As we will see, when it comes to the encounter with the Real, one must let go, be lost, and give up ownership of everything, including selfhood. The Prophet Muhammad is the finest example of a guide who has achieved this selfless encounter. Thus, in characterizing the Prophet's meeting with God, ʿAṭṭār says that "the 'm' in 'Aḥmad' was erased, pure in that instant." The result of the erasure of the "m" in the Prophet Muhammad's other, celestial name is that "only 'one' (*aḥad*) remained and Aḥmad disappeared."[13] The letter that has disappeared, the "m," signifies Muhammad himself, whose name begins with that letter; its disappearance from his other name, Aḥmad, yielding the Absolute One (*aḥad*) represents the process of utter self-annihilation. The significance of this shift as something beyond words, as something that cannot be grasped, becomes clear in the lines that follow:

> Because this situation renders the tongue unable to speak,
> it must be described using the tongue of muteness:
> When it comes to such a place, which is not a place of placeness,
> our lot is nothing more than to say, Wow, wow, wow![14]

As someone with firsthand knowledge of shedding the veils of false selfhood, the Prophet gives the wayfarer just the guidance that he needs. The wayfarer's experience of union results from the movement the Prophet prescribes, that is, a movement from the "signs in the horizons" (the external universe) and toward the "signs in themselves" (the universe within). Through that union, the wayfarer acquires an awareness of the microcosm within himself, which reflects "both worlds," both the temporal cosmos and the eternal hereafter:

> O wonder! The wayfarer left the "signs in the horizons"
> to travel with the "signs in themselves" day and night.
> He saw much of what has passed and what lies ahead,
> but he saw the entirety of both worlds inside himself.
> He discovered that both worlds were the reflection of himself
> and that, compared to both worlds, his soul was greater.
> Once he became a viewer of the secret of his soul (*jān*),
> he became a truly living entity and a servant to God.[15]

This process of discovery followed by the experience of union brings the wayfarer to life. While ʿAṭṭār does not share much about what ensues beyond the stage of union, he does tell us that the wayfarer becomes a true servant, living in harmony with God's will. He also tells us that the journey does not end for the wayfarer, since "after this, the journey ahead for him was one *in* the Real."[16] That is, God's limitlessness means that the journey within God—within

His names and His attributes—is limitless for the wayfarer who has annihilated ego. Yet, before ego can be annihilated, it must be constructed. That is where sense enters the scene.

Sense and the Ego State

Other than spirit, each of the faculties has both strengths and shortcomings, beginning with sense. Sense feeds "reports" about the outer (*ẓāhir*) to the intellect so that it can transform them into insights about the inner (*bāṭin*):

> Not until you have gotten the job done in the outer
> can Intellect become—within the inner—worthy of the secret.
> Once, through wisdom, Intellect has come to possess the secret,
> It must return to your doorstep.[17]

To sense belong the "world's five courtly kettledrums," that is, the five sensory modes making constant announcements about all that enters, just as kettledrums would announce what enters a monarch's court. The six directions of forward, backward, right, left, up, and down also belong to sense.[18] Using this information, sense allows for the creation of a sense of self. That is, it is from this raw sensory material that selfhood is formed:

> Sense replied, "Because the origin of I-ness is my essence,
> hence associating false partners [with God] and innovating worship are accidental qualities of mine.[19]

Sensory existence creates "I-ness"—a sense of identity and first-person perspective that might be called the "ego state" (*man-ī*). For this reason, ʿAṭṭār associates sense with "existence" (*hastī*), by which he means the illusion of independent existence that each of us has.[20] In other words, *hastī* means "being in the world," while its opposite (*nīstī*, or "nonexistence") means "not being in the world." One should aspire to the latter.

I-ness or the ego state (whichever you prefer to call it) might seem undesirable in ʿAṭṭār's works, but it is a very necessary stage in human becoming. A person cannot move beyond the self until there is a self. Influenced by Sufi writers, however, ʿAṭṭār reminds his readers that the ego state created by the senses should not be a permanent one. It must melt away in the blaze of love, just like wax does when the candle burns—here I paraphrase ʿAṭṭār's predecessor, Sanāʾī.[21] Once it melts away, the True Self rises sunlike from the darkness of night, making candles unnecessary. In this regard, Sanāʾī says elsewhere, "Love for you snatched from me the very basis of we-ness (*māʾī*) and I-ness (*man-ī*)," leaving the soul compelled to latch on to the divine self-identity: "The self had no choice but your selfhood, when faced with selflessness."[22] ʿAṭṭār disparages "I-ness" in order to encourage the process of replacement, where the divine identity mirrored in the human spirit replaces the false identity (the ego state) constructed by sense.

Faced with a multiplicity of experiences, all the input it receives, sense helps the soul form a conception of its own oneness in contradistinction to that multiplicity: the world outside the self is multiple perceived entities, while the world inside is one perceiving entity, the ego. In its interactions, therefore, sense continuously encounters multiplicities and becomes distracted by them, even worshiping those multiplicities and the variety they display:

> When oh when will that pure wine of my declaration
> of absolute oneness arrive?
> If it arrives, then a scent of my unquestioning yielding
> to God's revealed command will also arrive.
> I'm on one hundred thousand different branches at once,
> coming from all directions:
> When oh when will I have one *qibla*-prayer-direction
> and one face?
> When oh when will I be freed from my multiplicities,
> stacked along my neck, one upon the other?[23]

This leaves sense longing for the ability to declare God's oneness (*tawḥīd*) and to be able to obey the divine command. Yet the multiplicity of sensory experience has rendered sense a worshiper of the forms or externalities of things. Many Sufi practices teach a person how to control the multiplicity of sensory stimuli. These include vocal and silent repetition of God's names, seclusion, silence, volitional hunger, and reflection on the senses themselves. These allow a person to collect their faculties and direct them toward one center of orientation (*qibla*), namely, the remembrance of God. ʿAṭṭār has a word for directing the soul's focus beyond the senses, toward the highest and most unitary form of knowledge: namely, "the bringing of things together" (*jamʿiyyat*).[24] Bringing things together is real knowledge, as we will see.

Without such intentional control of the senses, a person becomes subject to the ongoing distractions of the external world and deprived of hidden realities. Sense, after all, has no access to the inner meanings of things:

> I do not have even an atom of awareness of meaning,
> besides the life of the outer and the worldly, I have
> nothing.
> It's an anomaly for a whiff of the inner to strike
> the person whose life is one of the outer.
> If nothing of the scent of meaning's secret is for me,
> it's because Sense belongs to associating partners and
> isn't fit for that alleyway.
> How can Sense, so imperfect, give perfection to anyone,
> since, then, it can offer you no cure, you have no choice
> but to Imagination.[25]

Sense is the origin of a certain kind of affliction—the affliction of distraction and meaninglessness, which is ultimately the affliction of the ego state. As the wayfarer's guide warns him and us: "Sense is I-ness within I-ness."[26] That is, sense places a person deep within a certain perception of the world in which each of us stands distinct and surrounded by multiplicities that are also distinct. This position is one of distance from God.[27] To see beyond such multiplicities and perceive unity is "eternal fortune" for ʿAṭṭār.[28] Since sense cannot hope to do this, sense directs the wayfarer to the higher faculty of imagination.

A technical explanation is necessary here. Sense—for ʿAṭṭār—refers to the five senses and not what Ibn Sīnā dubbed "the common sense" (*al-ḥiss al-mushtarak*), a sorter and synthesizer of all sensory information.[29] In this omission, ʿAṭṭār's model of the soul's faculties represents that found in a section of al-Ghazālī's *Revival* on the armies of the heart, which is a simplified version of Ibn Sīnā's psychology. Like al-Ghazālī, the poet makes it clear that the five senses become one through the imagination (*khayāl*), which is where al-Ghazālī locates the common sense that brings the five together.[30] Also like al-Ghazālī, ʿAṭṭār leaves out estimation (*al-wahm*), which Ibn Sīnā described as perceiving "meaning" (*maʿnā*), by which he meant the nonsensory features that might matter to the perceiver. Finally, in both books, the heart appears superior to the intellect and the apex of human knowing. The other interior faculties exist to serve it. This predominance of the heart is perhaps the most important feature shared by al-Ghazālī and ʿAṭṭār. The heart, as a faculty of perception, does not appear in Ibn Sīnā's intellect-focused psychology. Rather, the heart belongs to a different variety of studies of the soul, namely, Sufi treatises. Sufi thinkers centered the heart, its states, and its amorous relationship with the Real, drawing from the Qurʾān's focus on the heart. Of course, ʿAṭṭār's presentation is full of original insights, especially in being much more emphatic and explicit than al-Ghazālī that the spirit is the point of union between the soul and the Real.[31]

Imagination's Many Forms

With sense's shortcomings in mind, the wayfarer now leaves sense and turns to imagination. Imagination lends form and unity to all that is variegated and dissimilar by organizing the flood of input into comprehensible forms. In this way, imagination resolves the problem of multiplicity. This leads the wayfarer to hope for salvation from disunion, seeking from imagination a way to the "Valley of Love," as well as a "nearness" that will resolve his state of being "estranged."[32] Yet, as imagination declares, it is unable to deliver: it receives the speech of inspiration only in sleep, and never while awake.[33] This is a reference to the prophetic verisimilitude of dreams, an inspired application of imagination much different from what imagination offers while awake. Moreover, imagination declares:

> Not a form, nor a meaning, nor an act
> becomes evident to me except through a veil
> how can that which cries for help within the veil
> show another the pathway into the veil?[34]

Imagination receives a veiled sort of knowledge and cannot know things as they are. Moreover, it cannot construct knowledge with the forms it receives, for it is the tool of another. For that reason, imagination directs the wayfarer to the intellect.[35]

Intellect, the Stranger to Love

More than any other in *The Book of Affliction*, ʿAṭṭār's passage on intellect echoes Abū Ḥāmid al-Ghazālī's thought, that is, al-Ghazālī's rebuttal to the arguments of Ibn Sīnā and the philosophers.[36] ʿAṭṭār begins by praising the intellect using a ḥadīth.[37] The full text of this ḥadīth can be found in the *Revival*, where al-Ghazālī uses it to begin his section on the "honor of the intellect": "The first thing God created was the Intellect, and so He said to it, 'Draw near,' and it drew near. Then He said, 'Go back,' and it went back. Thereupon, God—the mighty and majestic—declared, 'By my might and by my majesty, I have not created anything as noble in my view as you. By means of you, I take. By means of you, I give. By you, I reward. And by you, I punish.' "[38] The intellect is without doubt a wonder of God's creation. It makes use of a process of multiplication, according to ʿAṭṭār, converting what is received from the five senses and then from the imagination into one hundred thousand different notions.[39] Yet it is this complexity that causes it to respond diffidently and irately to the wayfarer's praise: "The Intellect responded: Don't you yourself have an intellect? / Can't you see all the contortions in the Intellect?"[40]

The intellect leads to contradicting arguments, confusion, and errors, some of which are fatal for one's commitment to God, one's *dīn*.[41] From intellect, all denials—like all confessions—arise.[42] What is one to do? ʿAṭṭār's resolution resembles that of Sanāʾī before him:

> The Intellect is perfect when it comes to knowing the
> Truth (*ḥaqq*)
> but more perfect than it are the Spirit (*jān*) and the
> Heart (*dil*).
> If you must have the perfection of Love,
> the curtain will not open for you, except through the
> Heart.[43]

In other words, the truth known by the intellect seems perfect and complete. The intellect comes away from its knowledge satiated and self-assured. This is because, in its own domain, it knows its own truth completely. It knows what it was suited to know. Yet there is something far more complete that can only be known by the heart. Often those unbound by the fetters of intellectualism, logical thinking, and the forms of egoisms attached to all this have greater access to the realm of the heart than the intellectually brilliant. This is the significance of the "religion of old women" for ʿAṭṭār, as mentioned earlier.

This advice, given to the wayfarer from the intellect itself, becomes elaborated by the wayfarer's master, the sage or *pīr*. Yes, the sage concedes, the intellect is the "judge of what is just on earth and in the sky," and the intellect's determinations reverberate throughout creation, determinations that are the "keys to all difficulties."[44] Nevertheless, the sun does not shine on every branch of the "tree of Intellect."[45] There are those who brag about their intelligence, while uttering nothing but lies and vanities, for, the master declares, "When has a man ever reached, merely from dialectics, / perfection in the domain of his own intellect?"[46] The process takes years, perhaps a lifetime, and even then does not lead to the final destination.

> In illustrating the limited role of the intellect and its dangers, the master declares:
> You need Intellect only inasmuch to keep you sound,
> free both from praise and from the censure of others;
> if you've acquired a simple intellect for yourself,
> yours outweighs one hundred guileful intellects.
> Though your intellect is simple, disarranged,
> Still, your aim will have been completely reached.
> Such an intellect is further from danger,
> and—wonder of wonders—it reaches its objective more quickly![47]

Here ʿAṭṭār refers to the sincere lover whose wisdom stems from their simplicity and earnest love of God. Elsewhere that simple but wise lover is often Rābiʿā, while here in *The Book of Affliction* it is the insightful madman.

Judging by previous chapters, you might have come to the very correct conclusion that overcoming the intellect is a major theme in ʿAṭṭār's poetry, beyond just *The Book of Affliction*. In *The Speech of the Birds*, also, ʿAṭṭār prescribes a journey that begins with the intellect but moves beyond it:

> Whenever you commence escaping from the self,
> you'll discover a path from intelligence toward meaning.
> Once intelligence points you toward meanings,
> Khiḍr will bring to you the water of life.[48]

The intellect (here "intelligence," *khirad*) must point you in the right direction at first. But once one encounters spiritual realities ("meanings") that remain beyond intellect, only God and His elect spokespeople—the prophets and saints—can guide the soul. In these lines, taken from *The Speech of the Birds*, that guide is the mysterious sage sought by Moses named Khiḍr.[49] The soul must migrate from intelligence to pure meaning in order to delve into the depths of recognizing God's absolute oneness (*tawḥīd*, here "the water of life"). This movement beyond selfhood brings the soul to the valley of contra-rational perplexity (*ḥayrat*). It leaves each wayfarer with a new self, one purged by a fire that incinerates, among other things, the intellect.[50]

Premodern Muslim philosophers assumed that the intellect represented the highest human realization. As such, intellect was the way one knew God, or, at least, what was closest to Him. The intellect was the furthest point from the sublunary realm—the realm beneath the sphere of the moon, mainly what we know of as "earth." This lowest level of the cosmos was a place of death and decay, where physical substances only lasted as long as their four major natures could remain in balance. That highest level of being—that of the intellect—was pure insofar as, like spirits, angels, and even God, it was not composed of lower substances temporarily in harmony.

For ʿAṭṭār, however, the intellect represented a human ability to understand the order of the universe, in a very human way. The intellect was not something from beyond, or from as far beyond as some philosophers thought, but rather a heightened ability to grasp the realities that surround us, as well as some realities that are beyond us. In ʿAṭṭār's version of things, the human intellect was something more developed from what animals knew, but not wholly different—just more advanced. As such, the intellect allowed humans to monitor themselves, so that they could conform to what makes sense in their physical world, taking care of their bodies and societies, creating social laws and understanding universal ones, and drawing conclusions about how to live. The intellect would also, in ʿAṭṭār's view, allow us to conform to what God has ordained: studying His scripture, His commands, and His ways.

Spirit, and not intellect, corresponded to something higher than the universe, something well beyond us, for ʿAṭṭār. Whether we are intelligent or not, glimmers of the light of this spirit would shine upon us as sudden realizations. The truth of weeping in prayer, or the truth of being overcome by some feeling of God's presence, would be temporary portals to something beyond the universe that surrounds us. In this, the intellect would not be all that helpful. While it might give us an outline of what these experiences *do not* mean, keeping us from complete confusion, the intellect too is merely an observer in the contact that we have with reality.

What I have presented as the view of unnamed "philosophers" is somewhat more of a caricature than the complex reality one might find in their writings. In the thought of Ibn Sīnā, the intellect was in some ways similar to what ʿAṭṭār imagined for the spirit. Moreover, moments of sudden inspiration, as well as acts of worship and remembrance of God, do have a place in Ibn Sīnā's system. This caricature of the worship of reasoning, though, seems to have influenced many Muslim thinkers in eastern Iran, thinkers like ʿAṭṭār. They, like ʿAṭṭār, responded unapprovingly to a more simplified version of monotheistic rationalism—a rationalism associated with Ibn Sīnā and the philosophers.

ʿAṭṭār hints that the intellect's limitations stem from the nature of knowledge itself. As described in his sections on sense and imagination, the wayfarer must make his way to a knowledge beyond multiplicity. Throughout their lives, human beings come to learn the world around them by means of multiplicity. The intellect functions well in this world of variety and multiplicity; it compares things and relates them to one another to draw conclusions. True knowledge, however, is one transcendent reality:

Anything that becomes manifest from the Absolute One's
proximity,
once sent down, appears multiple in number;
the Qur'ān is—in reality—one utterance.
It became innumerable once its descent was complete.
One hundred thousand droplets are one Sea of Oman;
making its way beyond that sea, the water becomes rain.
All things that were named and have come into
existence—
they're all one dew, from the sea of munificence.
You will attain what belongs to your recognition ability
(*ʿirfānat*)
when that which you've called "Intellect" loses its validity.
Intellect must carry [you] to servitude.[51]
Your soul (*jānat*) must carry [you] to Lordliness.[52]

All knowledge resembles the Qur'ān, which descended from one divine utterance to its multiple verses. In fact, since God's speech engendered the entire cosmos, through the command "be," we can say that one divine utterance descended to become an infinite variety of created things.[53] We can become attuned to the faculty endowed with the ability to trace knowledge back to its one transcendent origin. That faculty, the spirit, awaits beyond the heart. Yet the process demands, first, that the intellect cease its interferences.

The Drama of the Heart

Now the wayfarer has left the intellect for the heart. The heart is a faculty of direct vision, able to engage with Love. This makes it superior to the intellect, for, as the poet says elsewhere, in *The Book of Secrets*: "When Love's army comes from its place of ambush, / the Intellect has no direction in which to escape."[54] The heart, however, was made for love. The heart is a subtle organ, meaning that it has access to another, unseen world, a world that evades the faculties mentioned earlier.

With this concept in mind, the wayfarer of *The Book of Affliction* addresses the heart. The wayfarer salutes the heart, describing it as a "buffer between body and soul," telling it that "the universe's atoms are but a mirror image of your secrets."[55] He proclaims to the heart that "all secrets of existence and nonexistence, in truth / come from your essence and are yours to harvest into perpetuity."[56] Sense belongs entirely to existence. The spirit belongs entirely to nonexistence. The heart is between the two. Yet the heart responds by humbly acknowledging, "I am only a reflection of the sun that is the Spirit."[57]

Little does the wayfarer know, however, that the heart's exalted status as a vessel of love also makes it constantly susceptible to what might be called the "drama of the heart." The heart's location between body and spirit, between existence and nonexistence, qualifies it for occupying a place between the "two fingers" of the All-Merciful, referring to the ḥadīth appearing in *Ṣaḥīḥ Muslim*, among other collections:[58] "The hearts of the children of Adam are between two of the fingers of the All-Merciful. He turns them, as if they were one heart, howsoever He wills."[59] The heart's strengths lie in its position as intermediary between two contrasting realms. Conversely, the heart's shortcomings also lie in its in-betweenness. That in-betweenness results in the heart's constantly changing nature, its fluctuations between God's two fingers.

The heart shifts and vacillates continuously, longing for a breeze "from the Spirit," a mere greeting or *salām*, or even merely a waft of its fragrance.[60] The heart becomes "drunk without wine," suffering from its awareness that the inner, the *bāṭin*, is the home of the spirit.[61] The heart's outward qualities keep it from the inner, that is, keep it from its beloved spirit. This renders the heart in a perpetual state of pain:

> If you must come near me, even for the duration of a breath,
> you'll find your forever homeland will be [here] in the midst of blood.
> If you cannot, then abandon blood and relinquish earth—
> become purified and set out purely on the path of Spirit.[62]

The wayfarer's master clarifies that the endlessness of love renders the heart "a hundred worlds in a hundred worlds in a hundred worlds."[63] This leaves the seeker without resolution, thus bringing no end to the wayfarer's affliction.

Drowning in Spirit

So, the wayfarer makes his way to the spirit. The wayfarer's meeting with the spirit is a commentary on mystical union and a statement of denial regarding alterity. The wayfarer realizes that there is no Other, just as there is no Self. The core of human existence and the essence of the cosmos is an entity lacking both essence and attributes. His encounter with the spirit is a discovery of the Self in the Other and the Other in the Self. The Qurʾān gives readers a clue to the mystery of Self and Other when God creates Adam. God forms Adam from clay and breathes into him "of My Spirit."[64] So the human spirit is indeed divine in origin. And since the Other, the spirit, is a breath from the transcendent God, it is also a meeting place between human and divine, or immanence and transcendence.

This presents the wayfarer with a solution to the problem of human existential suffering, or affliction, an apt ending for this *Book of Affliction*. To see this, we must turn to the meeting between the wayfarer and the spirit, whose sublimity is on bold display. The wayfarer hails him:

> He said, "O mirror image of the sun of majesty
> a shaft from never-ending sunlight!
> Whatever has been relayed about absolute *tawḥīd*,
> all of it has been verified in you.
> Since you are outside the reach of Intellect and
> immediate knowledge,
> you cannot be described, whether through commentary
> or description.
> Because you are always without essence and without
> attribute,
> both your essence and your eternal attribute are perfect.
> Tracelessness pure and namelessness are yours alone;
> 'Hidden of the Hidden' indeed suits your stature.
> No created thing is more sublime than you.
> No beloved exists other than you."[65]

The wayfarer recognizes that this universal spirit is "both spirit and the cosmos in absolute form," yet it is also the origin of his own eternal spirit: "My spirit," he says, "is a stream from your ocean."[66] This metaphor of the spirit as ocean and the wayfarer's individual spirit as a portion thereof, often as a drop of water, carries ʿAṭṭār's discussion of union through to its end. Indeed, the spirit responds to the wayfarer, encouraging him to dive in, swim, and even drown himself:

> Now that you've arrived here, be a man.
> Become drowned in my ocean—be singular!
> Since I appear like an infinite ocean
> I'll be forever without limit and without end.
> Here at the shore of my sea walk away from separations (*farq*);
> throw aside your love of life and drown yourself.[67]

The spirit has been aware of the wayfarer's suffering. The spirit has seen the separation that he and all of creation endure, as well as his attempts to find an answer. Summarizing the wayfarer's tortured journey succinctly, the spirit says:

> You searched through one hundred worlds in your longing for me,
> until you came to the bank of my ocean;
> if you really want to draw near to every atom [of what you seek],
> the way doesn't need to be from the moon on high to the deep-sea fish.
> That which you've lost, if indeed you've lost it,
> exists within you. You are your own veil.[68]

The spirit is both ultimate other and ultimate self: it is simultaneously the apogee of all that the wayfarer desires, as well as the deepest and truest part of the wayfarer's self. The spirit lies so deep within the wayfarer's self, so veiled by layers of false selfhood, that the wayfarer has not been able to locate it. To get there, the wayfarer traversed the cosmos, in the process learning how to move beyond the veil of selfhood.

Removing the veil of selfhood represents the completion of knowledge, which is a movement away from human knowledge and into an awareness beyond that which is learned or taught. To get there, of course, the wayfarer had to begin his journey by encountering the major symbols in a universe shaped by the branches of learning that ʿAṭṭār valued. Then, before he could arrive at the spirit, the wayfarer also had to traverse layer upon layer of selfhood. That is, before the wayfarer could go beyond the heart and its fluctuations, he had to arrive at the station of the heart. This represents the years, even decades, that seekers spend in an enamored, albeit in-between state—sometimes feeling close to God, and sometimes feeling distant. Similarly, before the wayfarer could arrive at the heart, he needed to engage with the intellect. He employed the intellect to have a basic knowledge of everything from theology to the management of one's life. Before doing that, he had to come to know both the external forms and the raw data of the things around him, employing imagination and sense. He had to have an awareness of the cosmos from which to work before he could move beyond it.

Now union will make the wayfarer's focus so singular that the knowledge of things will no longer matter. As the spirit informs him:

> Yet once that drop is in the river neither why, nor what,
> nor how will exist;
> once you're here, whyness disappears, meddling in
> happenings disappears.[69]

The spirit explains that a process of purification has occurred, whereby the wayfarer will no longer return to the "dirt" of concern for such things.[70] This ocean of union precipitates a process of erasure, so that it is not just pain and affliction that disappear, but even comfort and longing for eternal Paradise. The spirit informs the wayfarer of this new psychological orientation of absolute tranquility:

> One by one, things disappear from one's imagination,
> whether old or young, they all pass into oblivion;
> comforts and trials are removed from here.
> Hellfire and Paradise join them from here too.[71]

Once "the worship of an imagined self" disappears, with it goes concern for that which passes, indeed concern for everything.[72]

It seems, therefore, that there is a possibility of transcending the language of existence that the wayfarer once needed.

Deliverance from Egocentricity

Liberation from selfhood is not peculiar to ʿAṭṭār, Sufism, or even Islam. As mentioned, it is an ambition common to many world traditions, expressed in a variety of ways. This commonality has led the contemporary German philosopher Ernst Tugendhat to attempt to integrate such ancient wisdom about the self with contemporary European deliberations on selfhood.

For Tugendhat, mysticism, especially Eastern mysticism, is a remedy to the pains of our centeredness around a sense of self or ego, that is, the affliction called "egocentricity."[73] Despite his interest in the world's mystical traditions, Tugendhat seems completely unaware of Islam's own mystical traditions. Nevertheless, like ʿAṭṭār, Tugendhat sees this affliction as the core pain of human existence, such that "egocentricity is . . . hard to endure for life."[74] Tugendhat argues that our discovery of self-consciousness is a grammatical one, that it comes to the fore in our use of the pronoun "I." As infants, we learned to identify with that "I" until it became an embedded part of our consciousness. Here, too, we see that acquisition of symbols, language, and a sense of multiplicity forces us to carve out a space for ourselves: each of us becomes an "I," or an "ego," and then becomes trapped by that understanding of the world.[75]

You might recall that sense is, for ʿAṭṭār, "the origin of I-ness." That ego or "self" created by sense, and then maintained by imagination, intellect, and heart, is saturated with the turmoil of lacking proximity and imperfect knowledge. This is finally followed by a discovery of the true self and union with that self, transcending difference. Spirit, one might say, begins where human selfhood ends; it is the divine side of the human faculties. Thus, in spirit, the wayfarer finally sheds the veil that caused him suffering. The irony of this is that Tugendhat sees religion and mysticism as at odds, two diverging solutions to the problem of egocentricity. Religion, according to Tugendhat, aims to transform the world, while mysticism aims to transform the self. It is perhaps a noteworthy rebuttal to Tugendhat, then, that ʿAṭṭār's solution to the problem of egocentricity is a transformation of the self that occurs through a symbolic transformation of the world, that is, through religion. That transformation of the world must be followed by an undoing of such symbolic knowledge as one transcends it, a falling away of the bridges that one has used to cross over into the true self. ʿAṭṭār's model speaks, then, not only to a metaphysical reality beyond such symbols but also to the absolute necessity of those symbols. Without religious symbols, the mystic has no language through which to build and understand a relationship with the divine, and thus no language to transcend, and thus no language through which to achieve union.

17

The Source of Affliction

Life, for ʿAṭṭār, is itself a kind of suffering. So long as we remain disjoined from our spirit, we suffer the affliction named in the title of his book—an affliction of angst, longing, and dissatisfaction. In his justifiably celebrated study, *The Terror of God: Attar, Job and the Metaphysical Revolt,* Navid Kermani sets his sights on this very theme in ʿAṭṭār's *The Book of Affliction*. His analysis is a vivid case of the ways in which one text can lend itself to varied and even opposing interpretations. Kermani sees behind *The Book of Affliction* an almost nihilistic message, a reflection on a sense of gloom and despondence borne by a poet who lived during catastrophically difficult times. For Kermani, the poem's "utopian" resolution—the scene of union between the wayfarer and his own spirit—seems "strangely forced," such that a reader might mistakenly see it as existing "to conceal its provocation."[1] It is only when ʿAṭṭār resumes his descriptions of suffering and declares the near impossibility of achieving union that we can see, according to Kermani, this narrative poem for what it is: a work of radical "metaphysical wretchedness," "religious furore," "rebellion," "righteous anger," and "desperate heresy."[2]

Kermani sees in ʿAṭṭār resonances of the German philosopher Arthur Schopenhauer (d. 1860), as well as the Dublin-born playwright Samuel Barclay Beckett (d. 1989). Both are relatively contemporary figures who embraced the hopelessness, irony, and unending pain of human existence. If one were introduced to Kermani's book before having read *The Book of Affliction*, one would expect to see a darker poet who would lean more heavily on the absurdity of life than on the resolution offered in Islamic ethics and the Sufi path. What the reader will find instead is largely the ʿAṭṭār we know from other texts, certainly treating the topic of existential angst, but doing so within the framework of a treasure hunt for the Real that is full of revealed clues and natural signposts. Much of ʿAṭṭār's lament is not over the fixed and wretched condition of humanity, but rather over the human failure to cling to the clues and signposts and refusal to ignore the detours.

ʿAṭṭār complains that a person can go through life without once stopping to reflect on reality, and many indeed are doing just that. His protagonist, the wayfarer, doubts the very ability of humanity to know the Real, an objective for which they have been created.[3] Human earthly life, which begins from the fertilizing powers of a sperm-drop, should culminate in a recognition of God and His authority.[4] That is, it should culminate in a return to the life that preceded earthly life, the life of the purest spirit within. Yet this project of human maturation seems in peril:

> The human is not a sperm-drop of water and earth;
> the human is the sanctified secret and a soul so pure.
> A hundred worlds filled with angels in existence,
> but when will the sperm-drop finally fall prostrate?
> They have such hopes for you, you handful of earth—
> that the handful of earth might become a pure soul.[5]

The problem is that there is a deep sense of moral loss in the world around him. Even the divine knowers (*ʿārifān*), Sufis (*ṣūfīyān*), ascetics (*zāhidān*), and worshipers (*ʿābidān*) fail to meet ʿAṭṭār's expectations.[6] The means that should lead to felicity are not working:

> Neither was spiritual counsel able to change anyone,
> nor did divine law (*sharīʿat*) appear to him as anything
>   but a way for people to fall short.
> Everyone stuck in the heedlessness of commotions,
> everyone diseased by the effects of causes.[7]

The reasoning for their failure is due in part to the sectarianism of the day, a sectarianism that had contributed to the destruction of much of ʿAṭṭār's home city in his own lifetime.[8] Schools of thought, denominations of Islam, and branches of the religious sciences are all roads that should end at the Real. Yet, instead, their practitioners use them to serve the ego:

> Everyone following a different school or way,
> every heart because of some doubt in a different borehole;
> the philosophizing one stuck in questions of "quality" and "quantity,"
> the sophist stuck denying the whole world.
> All with their heads to the sky, with the rings of imitation on their necks,
> imagining the founders of their schools to be like themselves:
> One might very well call this "partisanship."
> Doubtful matters are being named "secrets" and "learning."
> This one has learned dogmatic theology for the sake of arguing,
> while that one has pursued logic for trickery.
> This one's studied the Sunni-Khilāfī legal dialectic out of zealotry (*ghuluww*),[9]
> while that one's become an astronomer out of arrogance.
> Each ignoble person is drowned in learning—
> but not learning! Rather, being better than others.
> One hundred thousand vile appetites have besieged the soul,
> standing on its roof and before its door.
> The bewildered wayfarer, having lost intellect and focus,
> was perceiving the hundred worlds like an ocean boiling.
> He saw that, atom by atom, the seekers of the truth
> have fallen into the whirlpool of the Real.[10]

This brings the "wayfarer of contemplation" to be afflicted by bafflement (*taḥayyur*), as he reflects on the lack of direction around him.[11] The wayfarer himself tarries at a place where it seems no one can help him. He is engulfed by an overwhelming sense of futility in everything around him, in large part because he does not know how to proceed:

He neither thought of himself as any better than a dog,
nor could he find anyone more of a dervish than himself.
Neither all nor naught, neither part nor whole,
neither bad nor good, neither dignified nor base.[12]

What does one do in such a state of confusion? The Prophet's solution is the solution of the poem: seek God's signs within the human self. Modes of realization within the human self will give the wayfarer the certainty he needs. In fact, all those seeking refuge from mass confusion, doubt, and errancy can find it in interior knowledge. In this way, while we might find union with the Real elusive and difficult, we should not mistake it for something impossible. It is not merely an unattainable fix attached to a pessimistic poem; rather, it is the only ending that suits the tales of futility and suffering that precede it.

It is certainly not farfetched to wonder if this inward turn was related to the dire situation in Nishapur at the time: "In affliction," ʿAṭṭār says about his book, "I put together this theatrical scene; / I decided to name it *The Book of Affliction*."[13] Some have surmised that—beyond just ʿAṭṭār—much of the Persian-speaking world, and even the larger Muslim-occupied areas surrounding it, embraced the interior dimensions of Islam on account of the devastation wrought by the Mongol and then Timurid conquerors toward the end of ʿAṭṭār's long life. Supporting this theory, the Soviet Orientalist Ilya Pavlovich Petrushevsky (d. 1977) held that the turbulence and suffering of those times created a popular affinity for "the pessimism associated with the Ṣūfī outlook on this perishable world, and heighten the appeal of self-abnegation and retirement from the social scene, voluntary poverty, and the like."[14]

An objection that might be raised to this theory is that Sufism, as well as ʿAṭṭār's worldview, cannot be reduced to "pessimism," "self-abnegation," or "retirement from the social scene." Throughout this book we have seen ʿAṭṭār's celebrations of life and love in poetry. Concerning the social scene, on a day-to-day basis, a Sufi aspirant's focus would be largely on external matters, from service to one's community, to acts of worship, to politics.[15]

ʿAṭṭār's solution to the problem of suffering is a turn inward. The cure lies within the deepest awareness of selfhood, as one makes one's way to the divine core of human selfhood. Even there, suffering does not cease—at least not until the journey's very end. The pains of love and separation continue to besiege the soul in love with God. Explaining these ongoing pains, ʿAṭṭār says, "Your soul is an ocean. Its water is melted gold. / It will doubtless have both its saltiness and gems."[16] One might also translate the word for the seawater's "saltiness" as "burning" (*shūr*). To get to the ocean's coral, pearls, and other treasures, one must endure the ocean's harsh and unpleasant salinity. Likewise, to acquire dross-free gold, one must endure the pains of purifying fire.

ʿAṭṭār implies that the burning most worth enduring is the affliction of human-divine separation, for meeting God is the most valuable prize of all. God is, after all, the hidden treasure, as ʿAṭṭār declares in *The Book of Secrets*:

> Even by a hair, You cannot be weighed in any place
> nor in existence.
> The whole cosmos is a talisman, and You are a treasure.
> You are the treasure concealed in the soul and in the heart.
> You said, "I am a treasure," and You know it to be true.
> The two worlds appear through You. And You, within
> the soul,
> each moment keep speaking hidden secrets.[17]

Here he references a saying that did not meet the criteria of Sunni Ḥadīth specialists for authenticity but was cited frequently by Sufi writers, many of whom confirmed it by a mystical experience called "unveiling" (*kashf*). In it, God replies to a query made by the Biblical king David, who asks Him why He created all things. God replies, "I was a hidden treasure, so I loved to be known. Thus I created the creatures that they might know Me."[18] One of ʿAṭṭār's Persian predecessors, ʿAyn al-Quḍāt Hamadānī, cites this saying.[19] He clarifies, though, that most people have been spared from the trials and pains involved in this divine declaration. To uncover this hidden treasure involves too much suffering for most. Indeed, for ʿAṭṭār, we only discover the treasure when all we once knew and valued is lost, when human selfhood disappears, leaving us with the spirit that He first breathed into us.

Conclusion

Nishapur has long been famous for having the finest turquoise in the world, which forms through a process that takes tens of millions of years. Water flows over minerals, especially copper, aluminum, and phosphorous, which collect in one place, often in the veins of a mountain. This collection of minerals solidifies over time and becomes the enchanting baby blue color that we know so well—the color of the sky. Similarly, ʿAṭṭār's prescribed pathway begins with being earthlike in humility. One must shed all pretense in order to become the simple, grateful, and love-filled creature that God once formed out of earth.[1] Patience, mixed with following the examples of generation after generation of prophets and saints, carries a person through a transformative process. Wisdom percolates through the receptive soul. Finally, in this earth of the self-effacing person, in the end, one finds the sky itself. The soul takes on the color of the heavens. The two become aligned as one, by means of something that always resided in the soul itself, like those minerals that always resided in the earth. When the conditions are right, this formation is less of a miracle than an inevitability, an operation of nature impervious to almost everything but the obstinance of the human will. Removing that obstacle was ʿAṭṭār's primary ambition as a thinker and writer.

Love initiates this transformation, the removal of the barriers of selfishness, ego, and obstinance before God. Because it can transmute the soul, bringing it to its goal, love is the most exalted state of being. Love is a complete relinquishing of selfhood in order to seek, serve, and find the Other. In its finest and ultimate expression, love means uniting with the Other in every way possible. Among the learned and the pious, many in ʿAṭṭār's time did not speak of love. ʿAṭṭār was aware of them and their branches of religious learning, and he admired those sciences as variations of truth-seeking. Yet he took issue with any science that made claims beyond its own reaches. Philosophers were guilty of just that. They made a claim about ultimate realities that escaped their modes of learning. The tool that they used—reasoning—was certainly powerful. Nevertheless, no matter how powerful one's eyes are, they cannot hear. No matter how powerful one's ears are, they cannot see. What ʿAṭṭār's audience needed to see, according to him, resided in the domain of the spirit. Its message could be heard only by the heart.

For ʿAṭṭār, the spirit was an ever-mysterious entity whose mode of knowledge was direct presence. Thus, humans could know the spirit only through the experience of presence. Once known, the spirit would reveal itself as the core of divinity within each of us. The heart longs for that divinity. The heart goes through decades of painful and joyous maneuverings just to be close to it. Because of the relationship between heart and spirit, love was ʿAṭṭār's pathway of choice to the ultimate truth that everyone sought. Outside of love, there was no way toward the spirit, for it remained outside the reach of reasoning.

ʿAṭṭār also saw himself as a conveyer of a tradition that knew the heart and had mapped out a homecoming to the primordial spirit. The tradition that he valued above others had mastered the art of self-transformation, a tradition that had laid out the steps and stages one needed to proceed from selfishness to selfless love. We often call that tradition "Sufism," but for ʿAṭṭār it was "the Way" (*ṭarīqat*). It stemmed from the earliest revealed sources, namely, God's revelation of Himself and of His biddings to the Prophet Muhammad in the form of the Qurʾān and the Ḥadīth. "Once you have studied the Qurʾān and Ḥadīth," ʿAṭṭār declared on this topic, "no discourse is superior to that of the masters of the Way, may God be pleased with them, for their discourse is the result of striving and inner states, not the fruit of memorization and verbal transmission."[2] These masters had immediate, experiential knowledge (*ʿilm-i ladunnī*), as opposed to acquired learning.[3]

The entire history of religion in all its manifestations, as known to ʿAṭṭār, came to fruition in the teachings of these masters, the saints of the Way. In fact, the multifariousness of their teachings meant that they offered a path suited for every different soul. That is, the Way was as diverse as the diversity of souls undertaking the journey. The masters of the Way themselves had differences that came from variations in spiritual predisposition, which they inherited from the prophets. "Some corresponded to the heart of Adam," ʿAṭṭār explained, "some corresponded to the heart of Abraham; some to the heart of Moses; some to the heart of Jesus; some to the heart of Muhammad, God's blessings on them all!"[4] Their Way was one, because their goal was one: to chart a path back to God. In the language of the Way, this meant to find one's direction from self-centeredness to spirit, from I-ness to the true self. We must make that return by learning from one another, helping one another, and complementing one another in our strengths and shortcomings. In other words, we must make that return as a community, just as thirty birds flew to meet the great Thirty-Bird, the Sīmurgh. Multiplicity is our lived reality, even if our origins lie in unity. Everyone and everything in creation is on a journey from multiplicity back to unity.

The reality of the Way is what I have called the "religion of love." We cannot reduce this "religion of love" to the "Islam" known by all. As we saw, metaphorical infidelity and moving beyond the symbols of Islam is an essential part of ʿAṭṭār's path for those seeking the Real. Yet it doubtless requires Islam: in almost every major narrative the poet offers, the intercession of the Prophet Muhammad plays an essential role in directing the wayfarer from a raw and bewildering love to an encounter with the divine within oneself. The religion of love is not Islam as a historical religion but rather Islam as an eternal cosmic paradigm. The journey that ʿAṭṭār describes is the core reality from which historical Islam emanates, the truth behind the message, the meaning behind the form. One cannot have one without the other, for ʿAṭṭār. The kernel cannot exist without the shell, nor can the hidden secrets be uttered without first learning to speak the principal language of piety and devotion.

ʿAṭṭār's literary expressions of Persianate Sufism matter deeply to the world around us today. The "religion of love" doubtless applies to contemporary audiences, even as they live hundreds of years and thousands of miles from ʿAṭṭār. I have hinted throughout that many of us can feel trapped inside a worldview shaped by positivism, that is, a sense that only science and reasoning convey truth and that everything beyond that is speculation at best, and superstition at worst. Many of us can feel as though the standard of truth does not include the metaphysical (that which pertains to the transcendent nature of existence) or the spiritual (that which pertains to the human spirit). Taking science and reasoning as our only standards of truth confines the realm of religion, so that religion corresponds to that which is personal or emotional, and nothing more.

ʿAṭṭār flips that scenario. He makes the standard of truth the spiritual realities that remain out of reach for those whose center of orientation is reasoning, sensoria, or the material world in general. Yet, aside from that, he also provides a model for thinking outside of dogma (or what some might call "religion") while adhering closely to it. Many see spirituality and religion as being at odds with each other. ʿAṭṭār, however, shows us how the two can be closely connected. He offers example after example of God's servants who took their outward commitments seriously to reap the rewards of inward illumination. He repeatedly reminds his audience to cultivate a love-based relationship with God, which demands obedience and contemplation of His beauty, as opposed to an empty intellectual relationship with Him. Profundity can come from simplicity, and the gift of spiritual flight can belong to those blessed with the wings of humility and selflessness. In this receptive approach to God's revelations, one can go so far beyond the external dimensions of religion that belief becomes infidelity. Praiseworthy or blameful appearances cease to matter. The absoluteness of love—as a presence and as an end—contradicts what others assume to be proper actions and beliefs.

Often, as we have seen throughout this book, ʿAṭṭār takes for granted that his audience appreciates the relationship between religion's outer and inner dimensions. On rare occasion, however, he uses the classical threefold Sufi model of Sharīʿa, Way, and Reality (*sharīʿat, ṭarīqat,* and *ḥaqīqat*) to explain the interconnectedness of the various stages of awareness. The most basic is God's law, or Sharīʿa, a set of commands that allows one to serve God and become liberated from the base animal nature that plagues all human beings. Then comes the Way, which demands an even greater awareness of the Real and even more stringent ethical standards than what Islam has made obligatory. Finally, there is Reality: the encounter with the human secret. He describes them as three paths, each more exclusive and difficult than the one before it:

> The first path is to proceed upon the Sharīʿa,
> which means to engage in worship free from base nature (*ṭabīʿat*).
> Then, your second path is the Way (*ṭarīqat*).
> And if the third you seek, there awaits Reality (*ḥaqīqat*).
> If you wish to walk into Reality,
> you're erased by the time you've taken your first breath!
> Anyone who takes two steps on the path of Reality,
> will become nonexistent forever—and that's that.
> With the first step, the self's secret becomes unqualified,
> then, with the second step, one becomes erased in the Real.
> Anyone who retains the slightest scent of that rank
> will cease to occupy even a hair of measurable space.[5]

As a poet, ʿAṭṭār's role was to expand the scope of his audience's imaginations, so that they could hope for that third path, the walk into Reality. To bring them there, he had at his disposal images and symbols from the Islam-centric culture of Nishapur, which shaped his view of Sharīʿa. He also had in his quiver the lives and sayings of saints, that is, the stories and teachings of pious men and women that constituted his understanding of the Way.

As for that third route, the route leading to Reality, we cannot know for certain what ʿAṭṭār experienced. Judging by his poetry, however, his experiential knowledge was vast—so vast that generations of Persian poets, from Rūmī to Jāmī and beyond, drew from his well and found meaning and inspiration in his written legacy. ʿAṭṭār's experiential knowledge gave him a sense of spiritual confidence and lasting wisdom that percolated throughout his writings, bringing them to be preserved in libraries and hearts, from the period of classical Persian literature until today, as this book sits before your eyes.

His message for us all about that Reality might be designated, in simplest terms, as "the theme of return." The end is the beginning. We return to the spirit first breathed into us. We dive into the ocean of oneness that we first learned as Islam's most basic doctrine, recognizing oneness (*tawḥīd*): the declaration that there is no god but God. There, in the Reality of oneness, we depart from selfhood "like a snake leaves its skin," ʿAṭṭār informs us, using the words of Bāyazīd. There we see "love, lover, and beloved as one," Bāyazīd continues, "for in the Realm of Recognizing Oneness (*tawḥīd*), everything can be seen as one."[6] A lifelong tension that brought both joy and pain to the lover finally collapses into one Reality. What had once been a wild display of fire and tears now becomes the realization that the lover has always been at home with the Beloved. They have both—lover and Beloved—been characters in a narrative told by Love.

Notes

Introduction: The Religion of Love

1. Navid Kermani offers an illuminating discussion of the reception in Persian poetry of ʿAṭṭār, who was largely overlooked until the latter years of the Timurid dynasty, in the ninth/fifteenth century, when he had a sudden surge in popularity. The poet has sometimes been neglected by contemporary Persian literati because of his "unadorned" and "immediate" style focused—for some—too heavily on "inwardness." See Navid Kermani, *The Terror of God: Attar, Job and the Metaphysical Revolt* (Cambridge: Polity Press, 2011), 27 and 31–32.

2. It is difficult to compare the number of lines in a poem with the number of *bayts*. The *bayt* is a kind of distich, with two halves, though each half will often end in a rhyming word. From another perspective, while couplets are usually written one line above the other, the two halves of a *bayt* are written side by side. That a poet such as ʿAṭṭār would see each hemistich (*miṣrāʿ*) as an equivalent to a unit of verse or "line" can be seen in his use of the word "quatrain" (*rubāʿī*) to describe four hemistiches, that is, two *bayts*.

3. See Austin O'Malley, *The Poetics of Spiritual Instruction: Farid al-Din ʿAttar and Persian Sufi Didacticism* (Edinburgh: Edinburgh University Press, 2023), 23. These included Shahīd-i Balhkī (d. 315/927 or ca. 325/37), Abū al-Qāsim Firdawsī (d. 411/1020 or 416/1025), and Sanāʾī (mentioned later and at length in this book).

4. For example, Aḥmad al-Ghazālī's *Inspirations of the Lovers* (*Sawāniḥ al-ʿushshāq*) describes the soul's fraught relationship with Love in a way that is certainly meant to stimulate the heart and even the imagination, much more than the intellect. Granted, his prose is often interspersed with poetry. One might also mention *The Book of Ṭawāsīn* (*Kitāb al-ṭawāsīn*) of al-Ḥallāj, which shares with much of ʿAṭṭār's poetry the goal of inspiring wonder: awakening the reader, as opposed to convincing him or her.

5. Benjamin Boysen, *The Ethics of Love: An Essay on James Joyce* (Odense: University of Southern Denmark, 2013).

Chapter 1. Who Was ʿAṭṭār?

1. As O'Malley discusses, the editor and ʿAṭṭār critic Muḥammad-Riḍā Shafīʿī-Kadkanī raises the possibility that the poet inherited the name from his father, without actually being a professional apothecary, but this seems to be mostly a technical point: Shafīʿī-Kadkanī intends to say that there is no certain textual evidence that ʿAṭṭār ever actually worked as an apothecary. To me, ʿAṭṭār's allusions to his line of work (as O'Malley references)—as well as a lack of any evidence that ʿAṭṭār held some other profession—makes it highly unlikely that ʿAṭṭār was not a professional apothecary. O'Malley, *The Poetics of Spiritual Instruction*, 121 n. 21, as well as 90–99. Also, see Farīd al-Dīn ʿAṭṭār, *Mukhtār-nāma* (*MKH*), ed. Muḥammad-Riḍā Shafīʿī-Kadkanī (Tehran: Sukhan, 1996), 28–29, as also cited by O'Malley.

2. Farīd al-Dīn ʿAṭṭār, *Mantiq al-tayr* (*MT*), ed. Muḥammad-Riḍā Shafīʿī-Kadkanī (Tehran: Sukhan, 2012), 31. Editorial commentary on the text, such as this, will henceforth be signified by "(ed.)" following the author's name.

3. Dawlatshāh reports that Ḥaydar's death was either in 597/1200–1201 or 602/1205–1206. See Amīr Dawlatshāh b. Amīr ʿAlāʾ al-Dawla Bukhtīsha al-Ghāzī al-Samarqandī, *Kitāb-i tadhkirat al-shuʿarāʾ*, ed. Edward G. Brown (Leiden: Brill, 1901), 192. From this point forward, dates will be offered with the Hijrī or Anno Hegirae year (AH) followed by the Common Era (CE) year.

4. Ahmed T. Karamustafa, *God's Unruly Friends: Dervish Groups in the Islamic Middle Period, 1200–1550* (Salt Lake City: University of Utah Press, 1994), 93.

5. Dawlatshāh admits that the poem "does not resemble the shaykh's style" yet dismisses claims that it was a forgery of Ḥaydar's followers, who falsely attributed it to ʿAṭṭār. After all, the poet was young and as yet unpolished in his abilities. See Dawlatshāh, *Kitāb-i tadhkirat al-shuʿarāʾ*, 192.

6. Badīʿ al-Zamān Furūzānfar, *Sharḥ-i aḥwāl wa naqd wa taḥlīl-i āthār-i Shaykh Farīd al-Dīn ʿAṭṭār-i Nīshābūrī* (Tehran: Dihkhudā, 1975), 31. See also B. Reinert, "ʿAṭṭār, Farīd al-Dīn," *EIr* 3, fasc. 1 (1989): 20–25.

7. Farīd al-Dīn ʿAṭṭār, *Asrār-nāma* (*AN*), ed. Muḥammad-Riḍā Shafīʿī-Kadkanī (Tehran: Sukhan, 2007), 233, ll. 3288–3290.

8. ʿAṭṭār, *AN*, 233–234, ll. 3293, 3301, 3294.

9. Hellmut Ritter, *The Ocean of the Soul: Man, the World and God in the Stories of Farīd al-Dīn ʿAṭṭār*, trans. John O'Kane (Leiden: Brill, 2003), 157.

10. Farīd al-Dīn ʿAṭṭār, *Tadhkirat al-awliyāʾ* (*TA*), ed. Muḥammad-Riḍā Shafīʿī-Kadkanī (Tehran: Sukhan, 2018), vol. 1, 6.

11. ʿAṭṭār, *TA*, vol. 1, 8.

12. ʿAṭṭār (ed.), TA, vol. 1, xxvii. "Ibn," sometimes abbreviated as "b.," translates to "son of."

13. Rkia Elaroui Cornell, *Rabiʿa from Narrative to Myth: The Many Faces of Islam's Most Famous Woman Saint, Rabiʿa al-ʿAdawiyya* (London: Oneworld, 2019), 297.

14. Cornell, *Rabiʿa from Narrative to Myth*, 297.

15. ʿAṭṭār (ed.), *TA*, vol. 2, 1173, n. 9:2.

16. ʿAṭṭār (ed.), *TA*, vol. 1, vii.

17. ʿAṭṭār (ed.), *TA*, vol. 1, iv.

18. Dawlatshāh, *Kitāb-i tadhkirat al-shuʿarāʾ*, 187.

19. ʿAṭṭār (ed.), *TA*, vol. 1, iv–v.

20. Farīd al-Dīn ʿAṭṭār, *MKH*, 70.

21. Richard W. Bulliet, "The Age Structure of Medieval Islamic Education," *Studia Islamica* no. 57 (1983): 112, 114–115.

22. ʿAṭṭār (ed.), *TA*, vol. 1, xxvi.

23. Of course, the significance lost in translation is that, in ʿAṭṭār's words, it is the letter *kāf* that begins the word *kufr* (disbelief) that he praises as superior to *falsafa*'s (philosophy's) letter *fā*. Sufi cosmological interpretations sometimes focus on the Qurʾānic word for God's command to engender the world, *kun*, beginning with the letter *kāf*. This gives to the letter *kāf* a sense of implying God's timeless love, preexisting creation, a sort of truth that would be beyond the reaches (for ʿAṭṭār) of philosophy's rational methods, but not beyond the reaches of the earnest, enamored, but condemned disbeliever. ʿAṭṭār, *MT*, 439, l. 4563.

24. Those are Discourse 10, Story 10 (243) and Discourse 15, Story 3 (307) for Abū Ḥāmid, and Discourse 22, Story 6 (392) for Aḥmad. See Farīd al-Dīn ʿAṭṭār, *Ilāhī-nāma* (*IN*), ed. Muḥammad-Riḍā Shafīʿī-Kadkanī (Tehran: Sukhan, 2008). The account of al-Ghāzālī's assassination belongs to Discourse 10, Story 10 (243).

25. A possibility, raised by Hellmut Ritter, is that Kūshahd is an alternative name of a village of Nishapur, Bushtanaqān, also known as Būshataḥqān, the birthplace of al-Juwaynī. Ritter's suggestion is discussed by Shafīʿī-Kadkanī in his notes to this passage. Shafīʿī-Kadkanī favors the possibility that the reference is to a certain Abūshahd Aḥmad b. Muḥammad b. ʿAbdallāh b. Ziyāf al-Qaṭṭās of the fourth/tenth century. See ʿAṭṭār, *IN*, 607, n. 2,961. See Ritter's comment in Farīd al-Dīn ʿAṭṭār, *Ilāhī-nāma*, ed. Hellmut Ritter (Istanbul: Maʿārif, 1940), 399.

26. These were the renowned Sufi author, Abū al-Qāsim ʿAbd al-Karīm ibn Hawāzin al-Qushayrī (d. 465/1072); the young head of the Shāfiʿī school, Abū Sahl Muḥammad ibn al-Muwaffaq (d. 456/1064); and the prominent "leader" or *raʾīs* of the city, Abū al-Faḍl Aḥmad al-Furātī (d. 446/1054). See Martin Nguyen, *Sufi Master and Qurʾan Scholar: Abūʾl-Qāsim al-Qushayrī and the Laṭāʾif al-Ishārāt* (Oxford: Oxford University Press, 2012), 36–42. The title of *raʾīs* placed a person as an intermediary between the city's ruler and its powerful men and families; see Richard W. Bulliet, *The Patricians of Nishapur: A Study in Medieval Islamic Social History* (Cambridge, MA: Harvard University Press, 1972), 68, and, for its relevance to the life of al-Furātī, 136.

27. For example, in *The Memorial of God's Friends*, ʿAṭṭār took pains to show great respect to the "imams" (eponymous foundational figures) of all three major schools of Sunni law in his region: Abū Ḥanīfa Nuʿmān ibn Thābit (d. 150/767), Muḥammad ibn Idrīs al-Shāfiʿī (d. 204/820), and Aḥmad ibn Ḥanbal (d. 241/855). On one hand, he seems to hint at associations between Shāfiʿī and the most salient themes of his writings: the spiritual way (*ṭarīqat*), love for God (*maḥabbat*), the quest for reality (*ḥaqīqat*), and the discovery of secrets (*asrār*). On the other hand, his praise for Abū Ḥanīfa and Ibn Ḥanbal, especially the former, obscures any sense of his denominational preferences. See ʿAṭṭār, *TA*, vol. 1, 245.

Chapter 2. ʿAṭṭār's Writings

1. ʿAṭṭār names his work on two separate occasions in this introduction, first, *MKH*, 70–71, and second, *MKH*, 72. His seeming ranking of them as two categories occurs on 72.

2. See ʿAṭṭār, *MKH*, 70. See also ʿAṭṭār (ed.), *MT*, 22–23. Paul Losensky mentions two others referenced by ʿAṭṭār in his introduction to *The Memorial of God's Friends*, namely, *The Unveiling of Secrets* (*Kashf al-asrār*) and *On Knowing the Self* (*Maʿrifat al-nafs*). See Farīd al-Dīn ʿAṭṭār, *Farid ad-Din ʿAttār's Memorial of God's Friends: Lives and Sayings of Sufis*, trans. and introduced by Paul Losensky (New York: Paulist Press, 2009), 15.

3. ʿAṭṭār, *MKH*, 70. There is another lost poem that he mentions, "The Two Potpourris" (*dū muthallath*), referring to a combination of three fragrant substances that apothecaries would give to patients. See ʿAṭṭār (ed.), *MT*, 23. He had also planned to compose another "Potpourri," in prose, describing the lives of the prophets, including Muhammad, as well as the lives of the Prophet Muhammad's family and companions. He seems not to have completed that task, or, at the very least, whatever was written has been lost.

4. ʿAṭṭār, *MKH,* 71.

5. ʿAṭṭār (ed.), *IN,* 50–51.

6. See *al-Qurʾān al-karīm* (Q), 33:4, signifying chapter followed by verse number.

7. All lengths mentioned correspond to the versions used here, those edited by Muḥammad-Riḍā Shafīʿī-Kadkanī.

8. For a discussion of the history of the reception of this text, see Christopher Shackle, "Representations of ʿAṭṭār in the West and in the East: Translations of the *Manṭiq al-ṭayr* and the Tale of Shaykh Ṣanʿān," in *ʿAṭṭār and the Persian Sufi Tradition: The Art of Spiritual Flight,* ed. Leonard Lewisohn and Christopher Shackle (London: I. B. Tauris, 2006), 165–193.

9. ʿAṭṭār, *MKH,* 70 and 72.

10. François de Blois, "Dīvān, iii. Collected Works of a Poet," *EIr* 7, fasc. 4 (1995): 432–438.

11. Sīrūs Shamīsā, *Sayr-i ghazal dar shiʿr fārsī: az āghāz tā imrūz* (Tehran: Firdawsī, 1983).

12. J. T. P. de Bruijn, *Persian Sufi Poetry: An Introduction to the Mystical Use of Classical Poems* (Surrey, UK: Curzon Press, 1997), 64–65.

13. Again, it was not new especially because Sanāʾī had explored this exciting ribald-spiritual combination before. See Franklin D. Lewis, "Reading, Writing and Recitation: Sanāʾī and the Origins of the Persian Ghazal," PhD dissertation, University of Chicago, 1995, 559–560.

14. That version alluded to is Farīd al-Dīn ʿAṭṭār, *Dīwān-i Farīd al-Dīn ʿAṭṭār Nīshābūrī,* ed. Saʿīd Nafīsī (Tehran: Sanāʾī, 1960). The edition preferred here, edited by Mahdī Madāyinī and Mihrān Afshārī, and supervised by ʿAlī-riḍā Imāmī, does not number its lines of poetry. It has 661 poems, divided as follows: 503 *ghazal*s and twenty-three longer *qaṣīdas*, followed by poems that might be ʿAṭṭār's, or might not, that is, 130 *ghazals*, four *qaṣīdas*, and one *tarkīb-band* poem in six stanzas. For comparison's sake, the edition by Badīʿ al-Zamān Furūzānfar includes 902 separate poems (thirty longer *qaṣīda* poems; 852 *ghazal* poems; and twenty *tarjīʿāt* poems). My preference for the edition in question is because of the editors' use of the earliest manuscript and exclusion of poems that do not appear therein.

15. ʿAṭṭār, *MKH,* ch. 12, no. 542, 144.

16. ʿAṭṭār, Farid ad-Din *ʿAttār's Memorial of God's Friends,* 15–18.

17. ʿAṭṭār (ed.), *TA,* vol. 1, lxxx. The version used here has twenty-five accounts after al-Ḥallāj, but the editor expresses enough uncertainty about this that he has placed those twenty-five biographies in a separate section. Interestingly, though, there is still symbolic significance in the book's ending, which, in Shafīʿī-Kadkanī's edition, ends with a short account of Muḥammad al-Bāqīr (d. 114/733), father to Jaʿfar al-Ṣādiq, with

whose mention ʿAṭṭār begins the *Memorial*. His reasoning is that "just as the beginning of this Sufi band was with Jaʿfar al-Ṣādiq, who is one of Muṣṭafā's [the Prophet Muhammad's] children, peace be upon him, so too is this book concluded with their mention." ʿAṭṭār, *TA*, vol. 1, 929.

18. I will notify the reader in those rare instances when a passage was rendered by another translator, though that never applies to ʿAṭṭār's writings.

Chapter 3. The City and the Saint

1. ʿAṭṭār (ed.), *MT*, 32. I have also relied on an unpublished article by Richard W. Bulliet, titled "The Druggist of Nishapur," for some information on Shādyākh and its history. For mention of his origins in Kadkan, see Dawlatshāh, *Kitāb-i tadhkirat al-shuʿarāʾ*, 187.

2. Dawlatshāh, *Kitāb-i tadhkirat al-shuʿarāʾ*, 189.

3. Charles Melville, "Earthquakes in the History of Nishapur," *Iran* 18 (1980): 109.

4. Richard W. Bulliet, "Medieval Nishapur: A Topographic and Demographic Reconstruction," *Studia Iranica* no. 5 (1976): 67–89, here 88, as cited in Jens Kröger, *Nishapur: Glass of the Early Islamic Period* (New York: Metropolitan Museum of Art, 1995), 10.

5. Bulliet, *The Patricians of Nishapur*, 9–11.

6. Mostafa Vaziri, *Iran as Imagined Nation: The Construction of National Identity* (New York: Paragon House, 1993), 91. The historian Walī al-Dīn ʿAbd al-Raḥmān ibn Khaldūn (d. 808/1406) describes those areas traditionally associated with the former Persian empire, which includes ʿAṭṭār's native Khorasan, in which is Nishapur. See ʿAbd al-Raḥmān Ibn Khaldūn, *al-Muqaddima*, vol. 1, ed. ʿAbd al-Salām al-Shaddādī (Casablanca: Khizānat Ibn Khaldūn, Bayt al-Funūn wa al-ʿUlūm wa al-Ādāb, 2005), 14–15.

7. C. Edmund Bosworth, s.v. "Nishapur i. Historical Geography and History to the Beginning of the 20th Century," *EIr* (2010), https://iranicaonline.org/articles/nishapur-i.

8. Bulliet, *The Patricians of Nishapur*, 10.

9. That is, 490–511 AH. He reigned as Seljuk sultan proper during the years 511–552/1118–1157. For a description of this raid on Nishapur, as well as the details offered here, see Bulliet, *The Patricians of Nishapur*, 76–79. See also Kermani, *The Terror of God*, 66–67.

10. Bulliet, *The Patricians of Nishapur*, 78.

11. Melville, "Earthquakes in the History of Nishapur," 106.

12. Bulliet, *The Patricians of Nishapur*, 80.

13. Melville, "Earthquakes in the History of Nishapur," 111.

14. Melville, "Earthquakes in the History of Nishapur," 109.

15. Pūrān Shajīʿī, *Jahān bīnī-i ʿAṭṭār* (Tehran: Wīrāyish, 1995), 17.

16. Margaret Malamud, "The Politics of Heresy in Medieval Khurasan: The Karramiyya in Nishapur," *Iranian Studies* 27, no. 1/4 (1994): 41.

17. Bulliet, *The Patricians of Nishapur*, 13.

18. Aron Zysow, "Karrāmiya," *EIr* 15, fasc. 6 (2011): 590–601.

19. See Muḥammad-ʿAlī Kāẓim-Baygī, "Akhlāq-i ḥirfa-ī wa bāwar-hā-yi dīnī dar bāzārhā-yi īrānī, sadahā-yi 8–12 hijrī-qamarī," *Akhlāq-i ḥirfa-ī dar tamaddun-i īrān wa islām*, ed. Aḥad-Farāmarz Qarāmalikī (Tehran: Pizhūhishkada-i Muṭālaʿāt-i Farhangī wa Ijtimāʿī, 2008), 491–513.

20. Sara Sviri, "Ḥakīm Tirmidhī and the *Malāmatī* Movement in Early Sufism," in *The Heritage of Sufism*, vol. 1, *Classical Persian Sufism from Its Origins to Rumi (700–1300)*, ed. Leonard Lewisohn (Oxford: Oneworld, 1999), 583–613. Also, J. Chabbi, "Abū Ḥafṣ Ḥaddād," *EIr* 1, fasc. 3 (1985): 293–294.

21. Sviri, "Ḥakīm Tirmidhī and the *Malāmatī* Movement in Early Sufism," 585.

22. Fritz Meier, *Essays on Islamic Piety and Mysticism*, trans. John O'Kane (Leiden: Brill, 1999), 189–192.

23. Meier, *Essays on Islamic Piety and Mysticism*, 214.

24. See Omid Safi, "Bargaining with *Baraka*: Persian Sufism, 'Mysticism,' and Pre-modern Politics," *Muslim World* 90 (Fall 2000): 259–287.

25. ʿAṭṭār, *TA*, vol. 1, 524.

26. ʿAṭṭār, *IN*, 152–153, ll. 964–991.

27. See Hamid Algar, *Jami* (New Delhi: Oxford University Press, 2013), 104–107.

28. Nūr al-Dīn ʿAbd al-Raḥmān Jāmī, *Nafaḥāt al-uns min ḥaḍarāt al-quds*, ed. Maḥmūd ʿĀbidī (Tehran: Sukhan, 2007), 597.

29. ʿAṭṭār, *TA*, vol. 1, 8.

30. ʿAṭṭār, *TA*, vol. 2, 1144 n. 25.

31. The grammarian in question is Abū Muḥammad Qāsim b. al-Ḥusayn al-Khwārazmī Ṣadr al-Afāḍil (d. 617/1220). These possibilities are reviewed by Paul Losensky in ʿAṭṭār, *Farid ad-Din ʿAttār's Memorial of God's Friends*, 409–410 n. 12. As Losensky notes, the reference to an "Imām Aḥmad Khwārī" that appears in "other manuscripts of *The Memorial of God's Friends*" occurs in Muḥammad-Riḍā Shafīʿī-Kadkanī, *Zabūr-i pārsī: nigāhī bi zindigī wa ghazal-hā-yi ʿAṭṭār* (*ZP*) (Tehran: Āgāh, 1999), 71.

32. Shafīʿī-Kadkanī, *ZP*, 597.

33. Shafīʿī-Kadkanī, *ZP*, 597.

34. Dhabīḥallāh Ṣafā, "Dawlatšāh Samarqandī," *EIr* 7, fasc. 2 (1994): 149–150. See also Brown's preface in Dawlatshāh, *Kitāb-i tadhkirat al-shuʿarāʾ*, 5–16.

35. Dawlatshāh, *Kitāb-i tadhkirat al-shuʿarāʾ*, 192.

36. Dawlatshāh, *Kitāb-i tadhkirat al-shuʿarāʾ*, 188. The name is "Akkāf," beginning with a *hamza*, probably refers to the profession of making saddles stuffed with straw.

37. Dawlatshāh, *Kitāb-i tadhkirat al-shuʿarāʾ*, 188.

38. Dawlatshāh, *Kitāb-i tadhkirat al-shuʿarāʾ*, 191.

39. Jāmī, *Nafaḥāt al-uns min ḥaḍarāt al-quds*, 597.

40. Dawlatshāh, *Kitāb-i tadhkirat al-shuʿarāʾ*, 187–188.

41. Furūzānfar, *Sharḥ-i aḥwāl wa naqd wa taḥlīl-i āthār-i Shaykh Farīd al-Dīn ʿAṭṭār-i Nīshābūrī*, 65.

42. Furūzānfar, *Sharḥ-i aḥwāl wa naqd wa taḥlīl-i āthār-i Shaykh Farīd al-Dīn ʿAṭṭār-i Nīshābūrī*, 65–66.

43. Reinert, "ʿAṭṭār, Farīd al-Dīn," 20–25.

44. Dawlatshāh, *Kitāb-i tadhkirat al-shuʿarāʾ*, 191.

45. Melville, "Earthquakes in the History of Nishapur," 110. See also Furūzānfar, *Sharḥ-i aḥwāl wa naqd wa taḥlīl-i āthār-i Shaykh Farīd al-Dīn ʿAṭṭār-i Nīshābūrī*, 91.

46. Shafīʿī-Kadkanī, *ZP*, 62–69. For Brown's comment, see also Dawlatshāh, *Kitāb-i tadhkirat al-shuʿarāʾ*, 6.

47. Shafīʿī-Kadkanī, *ZP*, 65.

48. Bosworth, "Nishapur i. Historical Geography and History to the Beginning of the 20th Century."

Chapter 4. Religion, Then and Now

1. Brent Nongbri, *Before Religion: A History of a Modern Concept* (New Haven, CT: Yale University Press, 2013), 17–18, 20.

2. ʿAṭṭār, *MKH*, 131, no. 449.

3. See Joseph Norment Bell, *Love Theory in Later Ḥanbalite Islam* (Albany: State University of New York Press, 1979).

4. Carlin A. Barton and Daniel Boyarin, *Imagine No Religion: How Modern Abstractions Hide Ancient Realities* (New York: Fordham University Press, 2016), 47 and 212. In ancient Rome, the term *religiones* signified a loose collection of moral guidelines that governed social relations. As Romans began to develop institutions, *religiones* became what the stateman Cicero (d. 43 BCE) called *religio*, a structured system placing gods at its apex, regulated by state officials and priests. The Greek *thrēskeia* referred—before the spread of Christianity—to taboos, often the taboos of outsiders and, in Biblical literature, to an unreasonable and immoderate adherence to Jewish practice. See Barton and Boyarin, *Imagine No Religion*, 124, 132, and 149–150.

5. Daniel Boyarin, "Rethinking Jewish Christianity: An Argument for Dismantling a Dubious Category (to which is appended a correction of my *Border Lines*)," *Jewish Quarterly Review* 99, no. 1 (2009): 30.

6. Bruno Latour, *We Have Never Been Modern*, trans. Catherine Porter (Cambridge, MA: Harvard University Press, 1993), 74.

7. Jason Ā. Josephson-Storm, *The Myth of Disenchantment: Magic, Modernity, and the Birth of the Human Sciences* (Chicago: University of Chicago Press, 2017), 308–309.

8. Josephson-Storm, *The Myth of Disenchantment*, 316.

Chapter 5. *Dīn, Dunyā,* and the Pious Life

1. Especially in *The Book of Secrets*, ʿAṭṭār extols a *dīn* that privileges love above intellect and intelligence.

2. For such examples, see Rushain Abbasi, "Did Premodern Muslims Distinguish the Religious and Secular? The *Dīn-Dunyā* Binary in Medieval Islamic Thought," *Journal of Islamic Studies* 31, no. 2 (2020): 185–225.

3. Q 2:86.

4. ʿAṭṭār, *AN*, 185, l. 2199.

5. Nor in fact do these distinctions hold in the case of contemporary Persian poetry, as Fatemeh Keshavarz argues, illustrating ways in which twentieth-century Persian poets cannot be called "secular." These poets locate the sacred in nature and not in traditional Islamic rituals. See Fatemeh Keshavarz, *Recite in the Name of the Red Rose: Poetic Sacred Making in Twentieth-Century Iran* (Columbia: University of South Carolina Press, 2006), 19–28.

6. Or, as Talal Asad labels them, each is a "Siamese twin" to the other, from the modern perspective. Talal Asad, "Reading a Modern Classic: W. C. Smith's 'The Meaning and End of Religion,'" *History of Religions* 40, no. 3 (2001): 221.

7. Farīd al-Dīn ʿAṭṭār, *Muṣībat-nāma* (*MN*), ed. Muḥammad-Riḍā Shafīʿī-Kadkanī (Tehran: Sukhan, 2007), 219, ll. 2200–2210.

8. ʿAṭṭār, *TA*, vol. 1, 41.

9. ʿAṭṭār, *AN*, 185, l. 2209.

10. ʿAṭṭār, *MN*, 356, l. 5128.

11. By this, ʿAṭṭār means that the "material world" (one of the many meanings of *dunyā*) is composed of four basic elements, which are always in opposition to each other and hence necessarily subject to decay.

12. ʿAṭṭār, *AN*, 160–161, l. 1662, ll. 1670–1675. The ḥadīth attributes to the Prophet the saying, "The worst of humanity are those with two faces, those who show one face to some and a different face to others."

See Muḥammad ibn Ismāʿīl al-Bukhārī, *Ṣaḥīḥ al-Bukhārī* (Damascus: Dār Ibn Kathīr, 2002), 1774, no. 7179.

13. Q 43:35.

14. ʿAṭṭār, *MT*, 325, ll. 2091–2097.

15. Q 5:54.

16. ʿAṭṭār, *AN*, 200, l. 2547.

17. ʿAṭṭār, *AN*, 200, ll. 2555–2556.

18. ʿAṭṭār, *AN*, 200, ll. 2557–2558.

19. In fact, this narrative of the Jewish man who gambles away his eye provides O'Malley with an opportunity to analyze ʿAṭṭār's method of using surprising language—"sudden cognitive reframings"—to awaken his audience. See O'Malley, *The Poetics of Spiritual Instruction*, 225 and 227–229.

Chapter 6. Sciences of Empty Reasoning

1. The Prophet Muhammad belonged to the Banū Hāshim tribe and was hence a "Hāshimī." ʿAṭṭār's emphasis on his Arabian lineage here intimates a contrast between the Arab origins of revelation and the Greek origins of philosophy.

2. ʿAṭṭār here generalizes, extending his perception of "philosophers" to the Muʿtazilī theologians, known among Ashʿarīs for embracing rational arguments that affirmed the concept of human free will. For Ashʿarīs (and here for ʿAṭṭār) those rationalist arguments contradicted the Qurʾān and Ḥadīth, making them akin to philosophers, who often interpreted scripture allegorically. Human free will presents a duality of wills (God's will and human will) that, to ʿAṭṭār and those who agreed with him, resembled Zoroastrian theological dualism. Thus, ʿAṭṭār refers to a ḥadīth usually applied to the Muʿtazilīs but here extended to philosophers thought to resemble them: "The free-willers (*al-Qadariyya*) are the Magians (Zoroastrians) of this nation (*al-umma*). Do not visit them when they are sick. When they die, do not attend their funerals." See Sulaymān ibn Ashʿath Abū Dāwūd al-Sijistānī (d. 275/889), *Sunan Abī Dāwūd*, vol. 5, ed. Ibrāhīm Sayyid (Cairo: Dār al-Ḥadīth, 1999), ch. 17, 2003, no. 4691. A similar ḥadīth follows. For more on this see ʿAṭṭār (ed.), *MN*, 532 n. 854.

3. ʿAṭṭār, *MN*, 156, ll. 851–857.

4. In Ibn Sīnā's philosophy, *al-ʿaql al-kullī* (the Universal Intellect) refers to a conception of all human intellects as one, that is, not a real entity, but the way we might imagine the human intellect in a universal way. On the other hand, *ʿaql al-kull* (the intellect of the "whole") can refer to all immaterial things, or the first intellect, namely, the sublime intellect

closest to God. ʿAṭṭār's Persian construction (*ʿaql-i kull*) would imply the latter, that is, *ʿaql al-kull*. See Michael E. Marmura, "Some Questions Regarding Avicenna's Theory of the Temporal Origination of the Human Rational Soul," *Arabic Sciences and Philosophy* 18 (2008): 130–131. Ibn Sīnā also attributes the "whole" or the "ultimate universal" to the first intellect in *al-Shifāʾ*. See Abū ʿAlī Ḥusayn ibn Sīnā, *The Metaphysics of* The Healing (*al-Shifāʾ: al-Ilāhīyāt*), trans. Michael E. Marmura (Provo, UT: Brigham Young University Press, 2005), 291.

5. For Persian poetic perspectives on the intellect, see William C. Chittick, "ʿĀql ii. In Persian Literature," *EIr* 2, fasc. 2 (1986): 195–198.

6. It is a descent, for ʿAṭṭār, from unity to multiplicity, but unity leads to spirit, not intellect, as we will see in part 3.

7. Q 112:1.

8. As a poet, ʿAṭṭār often concerns himself with descriptions that avoid technical language. For that reason, there is not one word in his corpus that corresponds to the reasoning that he sees as limited in its access to the highest realities. We have seen him use *ʿaql* or intellect, in both a positive and negative sense. He describes excessive reliance on reasoning in one instance as "intellect without limit (*bī-ḥadd*) and analogical reasoning (*qiyas*)" that must be silenced in order to attain wisdom. See ʿAṭṭār, *MN*, 453, l. 7207.

9. That is, exchanging human attributes for divine ones.

10. The phrase "no benefit" comes from a prayer of the Prophet Muhammad, part of which states, "I seek refuge in You from knowledge that has no benefit." See Muslim ibn al-Ḥajjāj, *Ṣaḥīḥ Muslim* (Riyadh: Dār al-Mughnī, 1998), 1457, no. 2722. This poetic passage corresponds to ʿAṭṭār, *MN*, 156–157, ll. 865–869.

11. ʿAṭṭār, *MN*, 157, l. 871.

12. ʿAṭṭār, *MKH*, 99, no. 193.

Chapter 7. Beyond the Limits of Intelligence

1. David Hume, *A Treatise of Human Nature: Volume I*, ed. David Fate Norton and Mary J. Norton (Oxford: Oxford University Press, Clarendon Press, 2007), 175.

2. Dimitri Gutas, *Avicenna and the Aristotelian Tradition: Introduction to Reading Avicenna's Philosophical Works*, 2nd ed. (Leiden: Brill, 2014), 201–202.

3. Ibn Sīnā, *The Metaphysics of* The Healing, 288. I have used Marmura's translations for these passages from Ibn Sīnā's *al-Shifāʾ*.

4. Ibn Sīnā, *The Metaphysics of* The Healing, 359.

5. Ibn Sīnā, *The Metaphysics of* The Healing, 366.

6. See Paul E. Walker, "Philosophy of Religion in al-Fārābī, Ibn Sīnā, and Ibn Ṭufayl," in *Reason and Inspiration in Islam: Theology, Philosophy and Mysticism in Muslim Thought, Essays in Honour of Hermann Landolt*, ed. Todd Lawson (London: I. B. Tauris, 2005), 91.

7. Abū Naṣr Muḥammad al-Fārābī, *Kitāb ārā ahl al-madīna al-fāḍila*, ed. Albayr Naṣrī Nādir (Beirut: Dār al-Mashriq, 1986), 115.

8. According to Griffel, Ibn Sīnā's philosophical system presented "the most potent challenge to the various theological schools of Islam." Frank Griffel, "Al-Ghazālī's (d. 1111) *Incoherence of the Philosophers*," in *The Oxford Handbook of Islamic Philosophy*, ed. Khaled El-Rouayheb and Sabine Schmidtke (New York: Oxford University Press, 2017), 192.

9. Sohaira Z. M. Siddiqui, *Law and Politics under the Abbasids: An Intellectual Portrait of al-Juwayni* (Cambridge: Cambridge University Press, 2019), 32. See also Ovamir Anjum, *Politics, Law, and Community in Islamic Thought* (New York: Cambridge University Press, 2012), 154. My gratitude goes to Shankar Nair for suggesting these sources.

10. Muḥammad ibn Ṭāhir al-Maqdisī ibn al-Qaysarānī, *Maʿrifat al-tadhkira fī al-aḥādīth al-mawḍūʿa*, ed. ʿImād al-Dīn Aḥmad Ḥaydar (Beirut: Muʾassasat al-Kitāb al-Thiqāfiyya, 1985), 166, no. 511.

11. Anjum, *Politics, Law, and Community in Islamic Thought*, 155.

12. Anjum, *Politics, Law, and Community in Islamic Thought*, 155–157.

13. Specifically, this concerns the Qurʾānic terms "tablet" (*al-lawḥ*) and "pen" (*al-qalam*) as they appear in Avicennan cosmological psychology. He mentions elsewhere that saints and prophets know secrets of the realm of the heavens (*asrār malakūt al-samāwāt*) through inspiration (*ilhām*), as opposed to reasoning (*istidlāl*), hence why the philosophers' attempts to explain such topics fail. See Abū Ḥāmid al-Ghazālī, *The Incoherence of the Philosophers (Tahāfut al-falāsifa)*, trans. Michael E. Marmura (Provo, UT: Brigham Young University Press, 2000), 155–157, as well as 151–152. See also Griffel, "Al-Ghazālī's (d. 1111) *Incoherence of the Philosophers*," 198. Finally, for unveiling as a mode of knowledge, see Abū Ḥāmid al-Ghazālī, *The Marvels of the Heart: Book Twenty-One of the Iḥyāʾ ʿUlūm al-Dīn* (*Kitāb Sharḥ ʿAjāʾib al-Qalb*), trans. Walter James Skellie, ed. T. J. Winter (Louisville, KY: Fons Vitae, 2010), 59.

14. While Griffel argues that al-Ghazālī downplayed his longstanding interest in philosophy, al-Ghazālī's later writings—especially the treatise called *Restraining the Common from the Science of Theology* (*Iljām al-ʿawāmm ʿan ʿilm al-kalām*)—do show his increasing skepticism toward the abilities of the intellect. See Frank Griffel, *Al-Ghazālī's Philosophical Theology* (New York: Oxford University Press, 2009), 30–36, as well as Wilferd Madelung, "Al-Ghazālī's Changing Attitude to Philosophy," in *Islam and Rationality:*

The Impact of al-Ghazālī, Papers Collected on His 900th Anniversary, vol. 1, ed. Georges Tamer (Leiden: Brill, 2015), 31–32.

15. ʿAṭṭār, *AN*, 121, l. 795.

16. ʿAṭṭār, *AN*, 121, l. 799.

17. Cyrus Ali Zargar, *The Polished Mirror: Storytelling and the Pursuit of Virtue in Islamic Philosophy and Sufism* (London: Oneworld, 2017), 175 n. 68.

18. Al-Muṣṭafā, or "the Chosen One," is one of the epithets of the Prophet Muhammad.

19. ʿAṭṭār, *AN*, 121, ll. 801–805.

20. The term *wahm* can also refer to a faculty that perceives meanings or intentions in the information the soul receives, in the psychology of Ibn Sīnā, a psychology that left its mark on almost all Muslim intellectuals following the philosopher.

21. For this saying, attributed to the Prophet in multiple renderings, see Badīʿ al-Zamān Furūzānfar, *Aḥādīth wa qiṣaṣ-i mathnawī: talfīqī az du kitāb-i* Aḥādīth-i mathnawī *wa* Maʾākhidh-i qiṣaṣ wa tamthīlāt-i mathnawī, 5th ed., ed. Ḥusayn Dāwūdī (Tehran: Amīr Kabīr, 2011), 167, no. 272.

22. ʿAṭṭār, *AN*, 135–136, ll. 1116–1122.

23. Abū Ḥāmid Muḥammad al-Ghazālī, *Deliverance from Error: An Annotated Translation of* al-Munqidh min al-Ḍalāl *and Other Relevant Works of al-Ghazālī*, trans. Richard Joseph McCarthy (Louisville, KY: Fons Vitae, 1999), 56.

24. al-Ghazālī, *Deliverance from Error*, 57.

25. ʿAṭṭār, *AN*, 114, l. 641.

Chapter 8. The Religion of Old Women

1. Shams al-Dīn b. Qayyim al-Jawziyya, *Madārij al-sālikīn bayn manāzil iyyāka naʿbud wa iyyāka nastaʿīn*, ed. Muḥammad al-Muʿtaṣim bi-llāh al-Baghdādī, 3 vols. (Beirut: Dār al-Kitāb al-ʿArabī, 2003), vol. 1, 272.

2. ʿAṭṭār, *AN*, 120, ll. 786–787.

3. ʿAṭṭār, *AN*, 120, ll. 789–793.

4. Shafīʿī-Kadkanī traces a citation of this ḥadīth to *Kanz al-ʿummāl fī sunan al-aqwāl wa-l-afʿāl* by ʿAlāʾ al-Dīn ʿAlī ibn ʿAbd al-Malik Ḥusām al-Dīn al-Muttaqī al-Hindī (d. 975/1567), which is a reworking of the *Jāmiʿ al-kabīr* of Jalāl al-Dīn al-Suyūṭī (d. 911/1505), as well as the *Ḥilyat al-awliyāʾ wa ṭabaqāt al-aṣfiyāʾ* of Abū Nuʿaym al-Iṣfahānī (d. 430/1038). See ʿAṭṭār (ed.), *TA*, vol. 2, 1174 n. 9:2.

5. Shafīʿī-Kadkanī traces this to a similar ḥadīth, "Take one-third of your *dīn* from the home of that rosy-cheeked woman [*al-ḥumayrāʾ*, that is, ʿĀʾisha]." Its authenticity has been rejected by experts in Ḥadīth, but

ʿAṭṭār refers to it here and once in *The Book of Affliction*, but with two-thirds in place of one-third. See ʿAṭṭār (ed.), *TA*, vol. 2, 1174 n. 9:2. For the reference in *The Book of Affliction*, see ʿAṭṭār, *MN*, 133, l. 348, as well as ʿAṭṭār, *MN* (ed.), 505 n. 348.

6. This refers to the preacher and author Abū Muḥammad ʿAbbās ibn Muḥammad ibn Abī Manṣūr ʿAṣṣārī Ṭābirānī Ṭūsī, who died in a mosque fire during the Ghuzz raids of Nishapur at the age of seventy in Shawwāl of 549 AH, that is, December 1154 or January 1155. ʿAṭṭār cites him often and some have proposed that he was ʿAṭṭār's teacher. See Ritter, *The Ocean of the Soul*, 703, as well as ʿAṭṭār (ed.), *TA*, vol. 2, 1173 n. 9:2.

7. ʿAṭṭār, *TA*, vol. 1, 77.

8. Cornell, *Rabiʿa from Narrative to Myth*, 266.

9. Cornell, *Rabiʿa from Narrative to Myth*, 289, 51–52.

10. Cornell, *Rabiʿa from Narrative to Myth*, 315. Suleiman Ali Mourad discusses potential historical and literary reasons for anachronistic depictions of al-Ḥasan al-Baṣrī in Persian literature. See Suleiman Ali Mourad, *Early Islam between Myth and History: Al-Ḥasan al-Baṣrī (d. 110H/728CE) and the Formation of His Legacy in Classical Islamic Scholarship* (Leiden: Brill, 2006), 114–116.

11. ʿAṭṭār, *TA*, vol. 1, 82.

12. Abū ʿAbd al-Raḥmān al-Sulamī, *Majmūʿat āthār ʿAbd al-Raḥmān Sulamī*, ed. Nasrollah Pourjavady and Muḥammad Sūrī (Tehran: Iranian Institute of Philosophy and the Institute of Islamic Studies at the Free University of Berlin, 2009), vol. 3, 494.

13. Cornell, *Rabiʿa from Narrative to Myth*, 13, 44, 100–101, 277–278.

14. See Margaret Smith, *Rabiʿa: The Life and Work of Rabiʿa and Other Women Mystics in Islam* (Oxford: Oneworld, 1994), as well as *Rābiʿa the Mystic, A.D. 717–801 and Her Fellow Saints in Islam, Being the Life and Teachings of Rābiʿa al-ʿAdawiyya al-Qaysiyya of Basra, Sufi Saint ca. A.H 99–185, A.D. 717–801, Together with Some Account of the Place of the Women Saints in Islam* (Cambridge: Cambridge University Press, 1928). Smith's contribution is discussed in Cornell, *Rabiʿa from Narrative to Myth*, 18–19.

15. Michael Sells, *Early Islamic Mysticism: Sufi, Qurʾan, Miʿraj, Poetic, and Theological Writings* (New York: Paulist Press, 1996), 151–154. See also Cornell, *Rabiʿa from Narrative to Myth*, 345.

16. Sells, *Early Islamic Mysticism*, 151–170, as well as ʿAṭṭār, *Farid ad-Din ʿAttār's Memorial of God's Friends*, 97–114.

17. Claudia Yaghoobi, *Subjectivity in ʿAṭṭār, Persian Sufism, and European Mysticism* (West Lafayette, IN: Purdue University Press, 2017), 45–70.

18. See Tamara Albertini, "Meanings, Words, and Names: Rābiʿa's Mystical Dance of the Letters," in *Ineffability: An Exercise in Comparative*

Philosophy of Religion, ed. Timothy D. Knepper and Leah E. Kalmanson (Honolulu: Springer International, 2017), 219–243.

19. Rkia Elaroui Cornell, "'Soul of a Woman Was Created Below': Woman as the Lower Soul (*Nafs*) in Islam," in *World Religions and Evil: Religious and Philosophical Perspectives*, ed. Hendrik M. Vroom (New York: Rodopi, 2007), 266.

20. Zahra Ayubi, *Gendered Morality: Classical Islamic Ethics of the Self, Family, and Society* (New York: Columbia University Press, 2019).

21. ʿAṭṭār, *TA*, vol. 1, 77.

22. ʿAṭṭār, *TA*, vol. 1, 77.

23. Cornell, *Rabiʿa from Narrative to Myth*, 17.

24. Ibn al-Jawzī identifies Rābiʿa's servant as a certain ʿAbda bint Abī Shawwāl. See ʿAṭṭār (ed.), *TA*, vol. 2, 1175 n. 9:10.

25. That is, a test from God. She uses the word *makr* (trick), alluding to the "devising" or "trickery of God" (*makr Allāh*) mentioned in the Qurʾān, e.g., Q 7:99.

26. ʿAṭṭār, *TA*, vol. 1, 81–82.

27. As Cornell indicates, Moses's name comes up twice in ʿAṭṭār's entry, but there are—again, as Cornell reviews—other references to Moses. These include her being born into unjust captivity, her fingers becoming illuminated, her direct speech with God, and her lack of satisfaction with direct speech, wanting vision or immediacy instead. Interestingly, she is given onions, while Moses's people, tired of manna and quails, complain that they have not been given, among other things, onions (Q 2:61). See Cornell, *Rabiʿa from Narrative to Myth*, 290–291.

28. Ritter, *The Ocean of the Soul*, 104.

29. ʿAṭṭār, *TA*, vol. 1, 90. Shafīʿī-Kadkanī reports that another version of Rābiʿa's encounter with these two angels has been narrated by Abū al-Rajāʾ Chāchī. See ʿAṭṭār (ed.), *TA*, vol. 2, 1178 n. 9:58.

30. As one example, Muḥyī al-Dīn ibn ʿArabī (d. 638/1240) reports that God's declaration, "O human! What has beguiled you concerning your generous Lord?" (Q 82:6), is actually a subtle message teaching them to respond, "Your own generosity." That is, what beguiles humans from obeying God is that God is indeed so generous and kind that they ceased fearing Him. This will then arouse His generosity for Him to have mercy upon them. See Muhyī al-Dīn Ibn ʿArabī, *al-Futūḥāt al-makkiyya* (Beirut: Dār Ṣādir, 1968), vol. 1, 308–309.

31. ʿAṭṭār, *TA*, vol. 1, 85.

32. Ali Gorji and Maryam Khaleghi Ghadiri, "History of Headache in Medieval Persian Medicine," *Lancet Neurology* 1 (December 2002): 513.

33. Gorji and Khaleghi Ghadiri, "History of Headache in Medieval Persian Medicine," 513–514.

34. ʿAṭṭār, *TA*, vol. 1, 87. Pharaoh's statement of arrogance is quoted from Q 79:24.

35. Ghazzal Dabiri has considered ʿAṭṭār's presentation of a universalist sort of Sufism from a social-political perspective, especially in *The Book of the Divine* (*Ilāhī-nāma*). She notes astutely that it is a Sufism completely free from the differences in legal and theological schools that had "torn ʿAṭṭār's home city of Nishapur apart in the generations before he was born." See Ghazzal Dabiri, "'When a Lion Is Chided by an Ant': Everyday Saints and the Making of Sufi Kings in ʿAṭṭār's *Elāhi-nāma*," *Journal of Persianate Studies* 12, no. 1 (2019): 69.

Chapter 9. Love Beneath the Cloak of Infidelity

1. ʿAṭṭār, *AN*, 112, l. 598.

2. ʿAṭṭār, *MT*, 245, l. 308.

3. Q 21:107. William Chittick details Muhammad's status as God's beloved, as well as his light as a creative medium in Sufi cosmologies, in *Divine Love: Islamic Literature and the Path to God* (New Haven, CT: Yale University Press, 2013), 36–40.

4. ʿAṭṭār's description of blinding using a scalding iron prod is certainly a disturbing image, but as the punishment was often applied to potential political rivals, it alludes to the constant threat that reasoning poses to someone who should be committed to a love that transcends reasoning. The wording of this double line resembles and yet also reverses one by "Niẓāmī" or Ḥakīm Ilyās ibn Yūsuf Niẓāmī Ganjawī (d. 605/1209), as quoted by ʿAlī-Akbar Dihkhudā in his *Lughat-nāma*, under *dar-kashīdan*: "Blot out the eyes of all the natures, one by one; / through this good act, you can arrive at Intelligence." ʿAlī-Akbar Dihkhudā, *Lughat-nāma*, ed. Muḥammad Muʿīn and Jaʿfar Shahīdī, 2nd ed.,16 vols. (Tehran: University of Tehran Press, 1998), vol. 7, 10,369. There is no evidence that Niẓāmī and ʿAṭṭār, contemporaries (even though ʿAṭṭār was older), knew each other's works, but both had common sources of influence, especially Sanāʾī, as is probably reflected in this line. See de Bruijn, *Persian Sufi Poetry*, 99.

5. ʿAṭṭār, *AN*, 110, ll. 543–549.

6. ʿAṭṭār, *AN*, 110, ll. 550–554.

7. Interestingly, research suggests that alcohol consumption does in fact induce a sort of myopia, an exaggerated focus on one's immediate surroundings, which metaphorically might apply to the lover's commitment to the present and to any risks involved in the pursuits of love. See A.

Timur Sevincer et al., "Alcohol Affects Goal Commitment by Explicitly and Implicitly Induced Myopia," *Journal of Abnormal Psychology* 121, no. 2 (2012): 524–529. This theme reappears in this chapter's final section as well.

8. ʿAṭṭār, *MT*, 285, ll. 1173–1177.

9. ʿAṭṭār, *MT*, 285, l. 1184.

10. ʿAṭṭār, *MT*, 412, l. 3946.

11. ʿAṭṭār, *MKH*, 100, no. 203.

12. ʿAṭṭār, *MN*, 428, ll. 6671–6672.

13. ʿAṭṭār, *MKH*, 176, no. 779. The quotation is a reference to Q 4:143, a description of the hypocrites, who waver between their false commitment to the believers and their allegiance to the infidels. Scott Kugle has a helpful description of Sufi veneration of the human bodily form in *Sufis and Saints' Bodies: Mysticism, Corporeality, and Sacred Power in Islam* (Chapel Hill: University of North Carolina Press, 2007), 29–30.

Chapter 10. The School of Love in History

1. Joseph E. B. Lumbard discusses love in Aḥmad's metaphysics, and love as the divine essence, in *Aḥmad al-Ghazālī, Remembrance, and the Metaphysics of Love* (Albany: State University of New York Press, 2016), 112–116. A shared perspective in Aḥmad's and ʿAṭṭār's ethics is that, through an arduous journey to love, with love, and in love, the aspirant becomes ethically complete.

2. For the role of love in the thought of ʿAyn al-Quḍāt, see the tenth chapter of Mohammed Rustom, *Inrushes of the Heart: The Sufi Philosophy of ʿAyn al-Quḍāt* (Albany: State University of New York Press, 2023), 221–260, especially 239–248. This includes a particularly useful discussion of the relationship between love and infidelity, a major theme that ʿAṭṭār has inherited from ʿAyn al-Quḍāt, among others.

3. ʿAṭṭār, *AN*, 87, l. 15. For ʿAṭṭār, the universe is a manifestation of God, and hence the closest one can come to the essence: "Since you cannot reach His essence (*dhāt*) / be content instead with seeing the beauty of [His] construction." See ʿAṭṭār, *AN*, 88, l. 22.

4. ʿAṭṭār narrates a story about the Biblical patriarch Jacob's reunion with his son Joseph, attributing it to Aḥmad. The story's central theme—becoming one with the beautiful beloved—hints at Aḥmad's contributions to the tradition. ʿAṭṭār, *IN*, 392–393, ll. 6240–6251.

5. For the possibility that Aḥmad's text might have served as ʿAṭṭār's source text, see Lumbard, *Aḥmad al-Ghazālī, Remembrance, and the Metaphysics of Love*, 7–8. For the argument that Chāchī's is a more likely source, see ʿAṭṭār (ed.), *MT*, 125–126. It should be noted that Aḥmad's

Risālat al-ṭayr is in Persian; the Arabic version of the *Risālat al-ṭayr* is a translation of Aḥmad's treatise by his brother Abū Ḥāmid Muḥammad al-Ghazālī. See ʿAṭṭār (ed.), *MT*, 118–119.

6. The initiatic chains of Sanāʾī and Aḥmad Ghazālī intersect. Sanāʾī has been reported to have undertaken spiritual training at the hands of Abū Yaʿqūb Yūsuf Hamadānī (d. 535/1140), who was a pupil (*murīd*) of Abū ʿAlī Fārmadī (d. 477/1084). See Majdūd ibn Ādam Ghaznawī Sanāʾī, *Dīwān-i Ḥakīm Sanāʾī*, vol. 1, ed. Muḥammad-Riḍā Barzigar-Khāliqī (Tehran: Zawwār, 2015), lxxx. Fārmadī was famously a master to both Aḥmad and Abū Ḥāmid Ghazālī. See Lumbard, *Aḥmad al-Ghazālī, Remembrance, and the Metaphysics of Love*, 61. See also Hamid Algar, "Abu Yaʿqub Hamadāni," *EIr* 1, fasc. 4 (1985): 395–396.

7. Shahab Ahmed, *What Is Islam? The Importance of Being Islamic* (Princeton: Princeton University Press, 2016), 38. Ahmed reminds us that love itself, in Islamic-theoretical conceptions of it, is no mere emotion but rather "a mode of knowing, of valorizing and meaning-making." See 42.

8. Leonard Lewisohn, "Sufism's Religion of Love, from Rābiʿa to Ibn ʿArabī," in *The Cambridge Companion to Sufism*, ed. Lloyd Ridgeon (New York: Cambridge University Press, 2015), 151.

9. Q 5:54.

10. See al-Bukhārī, *Ṣaḥīḥ al-Bukhārī*, 1617, no. 6502.

11. Lewisohn, "Sufism's Religion of Love, from Rābiʿa to Ibn ʿArabī," 152.

12. Annabel Keeler, "Abū Yazīd al-Bisṭāmī and Discussions about Intoxicated Sufism," in *Routledge Handbook on Sufism*, ed. Lloyd Ridgeon (London: Routledge, 2021), 53. The name "Bāyazīd" is a popular rendering of the saint's name "Abū Yazīd," and his place of origin can be spelled either as (al-)Bisṭāmī or (al-)Basṭāmī.

13. Lewisohn, "Sufism's Religion of Love, from Rābiʿa to Ibn ʿArabī," 153–159. See 154–163 for the observations that follow.

14. Sanāʾī revised Avicennan psychology to exalt the place of love over the intellect. See Kathryn V. Johnson, "A Mystic's Response to the Claims of Philosophy: Abū'l Majd Majdūd Sanāʾī's *Sayr al-ʿIbād ilā'l-Maʿād*," *Islamic Studies* 34, no. 3 (1995): 253–295.

15. Chittick, *Divine Love*, 343 and 432; see also 369 and 396. Some modifications in spelling and capitalization have been made to correspond to the style of this book.

16. See Aḥmad Samʿānī, *The Repose of the Spirits: A Sufi Commentary on the Divine Names*, trans. William C. Chittick (Albany: State University of New York Press, 2019), 286 and 288. See also William C. Chittick, "Moses and the Religion of Love: Thoughts on Methodology in the Study of Sufism," in *Islamic Studies and the Study of Sufism in Academia: Rethinking*

Methodologies, ed. Tonaga Yasushi and Fujii Chiaki (Kyoto: Kenan Rifai Center for Sufi Studies, Kyoto University, 2018), 101–118, here 111–112, for Samʿānī's mention of the "School of Love."

17. As Chittick notes in Samʿānī, *The Repose of the Spirits*, xlvii.

18. Many of those other figures, including elaborations on those mentioned here, are included in an excellent article, Joseph E. B. Lumbard, "From Ḥubb to ʿIshq: The Development of Love in Early Sufism," *Journal of Islamic Studies* 18, no. 3 (2007): 345–385.

19. ʿAṭṭār, *DW*, 130, no. 26.

20. Abū ʿIsā Muḥammad ibn ʿĪsā al-Tirmidhī, *al-Jāmiʿ al-ṣaḥīḥ, wa huwa Sunan al-Tirmidhī*, ed. Aḥmad Muḥammad Shākir, Muḥammad Fuʾād ʿAbd al-Bāqī, and Ibrāhīm ʿAṭwa ʿAwaḍ (Cairo: Muṣṭafā al-Bābī al-Ḥalabī, 1978 [1962–1978]), vol. 5, Kitāb al-īmān, ch. 18, 25, no. 2640.

21. al-Tirmidhī, *al-Jāmiʿ al-ṣaḥīḥ*, vol. 5, Kitāb al-īmān, ch. 18, 26, no. 2641.

22. See Julie Scott Meisami, *Medieval Persian Court Poetry* (Princeton: Princeton University Press, 1987), 250. Sufi writers of the School of Love proclaimed erotic poetry and the great human lovers of human beloveds to be true in a way that often those poets, lovers, and beloveds themselves did not recognize, namely, that God is the ultimate lover and beloved.

23. The double line is as follows: "Proclaim, 'Come and adopt the School of your Lock of Hair,' / to anyone who wants to be religiously observant." While it does not appear in the *Dīwān* preferred here, that edited by Mahdī Madāyinī and Mihrān Afshārī, it can be found in Farīd al-Dīn ʿAṭṭār, *Dīwān-i ʿAṭṭār*, 5th ed., ed. Taqī Tafaḍḍulī (Tehran: Intishārāt-i ʿIlmī wa Farhangī, 1989 [1962]), 274, no. 350.

24. As mentioned, the phrase "School of Love" serves a rhetorical purpose, in that it describes an ethical orientation within Islam, not a formal commitment.

25. ʿAṭṭār, *MKH*, 112, no. 302.

Chapter 11. Metaphorical Spaces of Love and Infidelity

1. This phrase, which might also be translated as "dry renunciant," is common to ʿAṭṭār. In the preceding poem ("We, the School of Love . . ."), it occurs in the eighth line, which was not included in the translated passage.

2. ʿAṭṭār, *DW*, 407, no. 274.

3. Muḥammad-Riḍā Shafīʿī-Kadkanī, *Qalandariyya dar tārīkh: digardīsīhā-yi yik īdiʾūlūzhī* (Tehran: Sukhan, 2007), 307. Matthew Thomas Miller offers an in-depth analysis of culturally subversive characters

("rogue" figures, as feature in poems about the *qalandar*) in the poetry of ʿAṭṭār, as well as Sanāʾī and Fakhr al-Dīn ʿIrāqī (d. 688/1289). See Miller, "Poetics of the Sufi Carnival: The 'Rogue Lyrics' (Qalandariyāt) of Sanāʾi, ʿAttār, and ʿErāqi," PhD dissertation, Washington University in St. Louis, 2016, especially 55–65.

4. Fatemeh Keshavarz, "Flight of the Birds: The Poetic Animating the Spiritual in ʿAṭṭār's *Manṭiq al-ṭayr*," in *ʿAṭṭār and the Persian Sufi Tradition: The Art of Spiritual Flight*, ed Leonard Lewisohn and Christopher Shackle (London: I. B. Tauris, 2006), 127 and 129.

5. ʿAṭṭār, *TA*, vol. 1, 79.

6. See Ritter, *The Ocean of the Soul*, 539.

7. For the Qurʾānic quotation mentioned, see Q 2:125.

8. For this and the previous example, see also Ritter, *The Ocean of the Soul*, 539.

9. ʿAṭṭār, *TA*, vol. 1, 80.

10. ʿAṭṭār, *TA*, vol. 1, 80.

11. ʿAṭṭār, *DW*, 438, no. 302.

12. Q 2:219.

13. Q 5:54.

14. Q 5:54.

15. ʿAṭṭār, *MKH*, 299, no. 1720.

16. Here the poet refers to flint, which, in its seeming coolness and stasis, is able to create fire when struck against iron or steel. Similarly, within the static exterior of the wayfarer exists the potential fires of divine love, if and when struck by divine inspiration or human love.

17. As Shafīʿī-Kadkanī mentions, the prayer rug over one's shoulder was a common practice among Muslim ascetics and Sufis, perhaps to guard the rug from wrinkles, but definitely a mark of humility. See ʿAṭṭār (ed.), *AN*, 409 n. 1925.

18. ʿAṭṭār, *AN*, 172, ll. 1922–1925.

19. ʿAṭṭār, *AN*, 166, l. 1788. See Q 21:58.

20. Mohamed Tahar Mansouri, *Du Voile et du Zunnār* (Tunis: l'Or du Temps, 2007), 128.

21. Mansouri, *Du Voile et du Zunnār*, 128–129, 136, and 170.

22. Of course, there are also times of sobriety and renunciation, and those, too, have their symbols and places, as discussed in this book's previous part on religion.

23. See Ghazālī's *Sawāniḥ* as in Aḥmad Ghazālī, *Majmūʿa-yi āthār-i fārsī-i Aḥmad Ghazālī*, 3rd ed., ed. Aḥmad Mujāhid (Tehran: University of Tehran Press, 1997), 164. See ʿAyn al-Quḍāt Hamadānī, *Tamhīdāt*, 4th ed., ed. ʿAfīf ʿUsayrān (Tehran: Manūchihrī, 2004 [1994]), 120, 228, 341,

among others. For more on the *kharābāt* in ʿAyn al-Quḍāt's widely read Sufi writings, see also Rustom, *Inrushes of the Heart*, 305 n. 32.

24. Sanāʾī, *Dīwān-i Ḥakīm Sanāʾī*, vol. 1, 632, no. 325.

25. Shafīʿī-Kadkanī, *ZP*, 253.

26. Shafīʿī-Kadkanī, *ZP*, 253.

27. ʿAṭṭār (ed.), *MT*, 613–614 n. 1924. Mithra was associated with the sun, justice, and contracts. The Greeks and Romans also worshiped this deity in a tradition called "Mithraism."

28. Here the historian Najm al-Dīn Abū al-Rajāʾ Qummī (d. 6th/12th century) describes the *kharābāt* as a "half-incinerated house" that serves the purpose of quartering minstrel girls, some of whom were selected to be courtesans. See Qummī, *Tārīkh al-wuzarāʾ*, ed. Muḥammad-Taqī Dānish-pazhūh (Tehran: Muʾassasa-yi Muṭālaʿāt wa Taḥqīqāt-i Farhangī, 1984), 5.

29. He describes the decree of Ögedei Khan (called "Qāʾān"), the successor to Genghis Khan, whose subjects of a certain tribe (probably the Oirat) defied the marriages he had arranged for their daughters. In retaliation, he had four thousand of their daughters above the age of seven taken into the service of men, prostitution, or sexual slavery. While some of them were dispatched to "envoy houses" (*rasūl-khāna*), places of repose for traveling emissaries, others were sent to the *kharābāt*, here clearly "brothels." See Juwaynī (d. 681/1283), *Tārīkh-i jahāngushāy-i Juwaynī*, ed. Muḥammad Qazwīnī and Sayyid Shāhrukh Mūsawīyān (Tehran: Dastān, 2006), 285–286. For the identification of the tribe, see Juwaynī, *Genghis Khan: The History of the World Conqueror*, trans. John Andrew Boyle (Manchester: Manchester University Press, 1997), 235 n. 66.

30. In a passage about the sale of slave girls in the city, Ṭabīb refers to the *kharābāt*, in more than one instance, as a place of prostitution. See Rashīd al-Dīn Faḍlallāh Hamadānī Ṭabīb, *Jāmiʿ al-tawārīkh* (*Tārīkh-i mubārak-i ghāzānī*), vol. 2, ed. Muḥammad Rawshan and Muṣṭafā Mūsawī (Tehran: Mīrāth-i Maktūb, 2015), 1372, narrative no. 40.

31. ʿAṭṭār, *DW*, 109, no. 9.

32. Q 7:143. ʿAṭṭār alludes to this verse in the line about his "rendezvous" (*mīqāt*), the very word used to describe Moses's appointed meeting with God.

33. Yaghoobi, *Subjectivity in ʿAṭṭār, Persian Sufism, and European Mysticism*, 93.

34. Yaghoobi, *Subjectivity in ʿAṭṭār, Persian Sufism, and European Mysticism*, 40–41.

35. Michel Foucault, "A Preface to Transgression," in *Language, Counter-Memory, Practice: Selected Essays and Interviews*, ed. Donald F.

Bouchard, trans. Donald F. Bouchard and Sherry Simon (Ithaca, NY: Cornell University Press, 1977), 35.

Chapter 12. Finding the Real in Byzantium

1. These forms are discussed in chapter 2, "ʿAṭṭār's Writings."

2. Franklin D. Lewis, "Sexual Occidentation: The Politics of Conversion, Christian-Love and Boy-Love in ʿAṭṭār," *Iranian Studies* 42, no. 5 (2009): 717.

3. Lewis, "Sexual Occidentation," 714.

4. Lewis, "Sexual Occidentation," 708.

5. Thomas Sizgorich, "Monks and Their Daughters: Monasteries as Muslim-Christian Boundaries," in *Muslims and Others in Sacred Space*, ed. Margaret Cormack (Oxford: Oxford University Press, 2013), 199.

6. Lewis, "Sexual Occidentation," 713. See also Anna Livia Beelaert, "Ḵāqāni Šervāni i. Life," *EIr* 15, fasc. 5 (2011): 522–523.

7. Lewis, "Sexual Occidentation," 713.

8. ʿAṭṭār's use of *The Gift to Kings* for his story of the Shaykh of Ṣanʿān is discussed in Fāṭima Ṣanʿatī-Nīā, *Maʾākhidh-i qiṣaṣ wa tamthīlāt-i mathnawī-hā-yi ʿAṭṭār-i Nīshābūrī* (Tehran: Zawwār, 1990), 137. See also Lewis, "Sexual Occidentation" 697 n. 12. A discussion of the authorship of *The Gift to Kings*, as undertaken by an admirer of al-Ghazālī, and the identification of passages borrowed from al-Ghazālī and his brother Aḥmad appear in Nasrollah Pourjavady, "'Tuḥfat al-mulūk' wa dāstān-i Shaykh-i Ṣanʿān," *Maʿārif* 17, no. 1 (2000): 3–20. The author's identity as ʿAlī ibn Abī Ḥafṣ is asserted by ʿAlī-Akbar Aḥmadī-Dārānī, "Darbāra-yi 'Tuḥfat al-mulūk': ba bahāna-yi taṣḥīḥ wa chāp-i mujaddad," *Āyina-yi mīrāth* 4, no. 3 (2001 Winter): 60–64.

9. Abū Ḥāmid Muḥammad al-Ghazālī (attributed), *Tuḥfat al-mulūk-i Imām Abū Ḥāmid Muḥammad Ghazālī*, ed. with an introduction by Muḥammad-Taqī Dānish-pazhūh, *Majalla-yi dānishkada-yi adabīyāt-i Mashhad* 1, no. 2–3 (1965): 296.

10. Nadia Maria El Cheikh, *Byzantium Viewed by the Arabs* (Cambridge, MA: Harvard University Press, 2004), 70.

11. El Cheikh, *Byzantium Viewed by the Arabs*, 123–129. While El Cheikh focuses on early Arabic travel literature, writings such as *The Gift to Kings* show the existence of these tropes in Persian contexts as well, often with striking similarities.

12. The Prophet initially asks the shaykh's friend, who has come to save him, "What are you doing in Byzantium?" The friend's response is perhaps intentionally humorous: "O Messenger of God, what are *you* doing in the land of infidelity?" To this the Prophet replies, "I have come because a

blameful thing has befallen the master, and I will resolve it." See al-Ghazālī (attributed), *Tuḥfat al-mulūk-i Imām Abū Ḥāmid Muḥammad Ghazālī*, 296.

13. Sizgorich, "Monks and Their Daughters: Monasteries as Muslim-Christian Boundaries," 201–204. For an expanded consideration of the themes of infidelity, Byzantium, and sacred space in ʿAṭṭār's narrative of the shaykh, see Zargar, "Sober in Mecca, Drunk in Byzantium: Antinomian Space in the Poetry of ʿAṭṭār," *Journal of the American Academy of Religion* 89, no. 1 (2021): 272–297.

14. Ritter, *The Ocean of the Soul*, 399–402.

15. Ritter, *The Ocean of the Soul*, 401.

16. ʿAbd al-Ḥusayn Zarrīn-kūb, *Na sharqī, na gharbī, insānī: majmūʿa-yi maqālāt, taḥqīqāt, naqd-hā, wa namāyishwāra-hā* (Tehran: Amīr Kabīr, 1974), 268–276.

17. Abū Bakr ʿAbd al-Razzāq al-Ṣanʿānī, *al-Muṣannaf*, vol. 6, ed. Ḥabīb al-Raḥmān al-Aʿẓamī (Beirut: al-Maktaba al-Islāmī, 1983), no. 10387, 171–172.

18. al-Ghazālī (attributed), *Tuḥfat al-mulūk-i Imām Abū Ḥāmid Muḥammad Ghazālī*, 295. ʿAṭṭār, *MT*, 286, l. 1191.

19. ʿAṭṭār, *MT*, 286–287, ll. 1211–1215.

20. It is significant that the shaykh's change occurs through a glance at this beauty, as the eyes are thought to be the most direct portal to the heart. This is why Abū Ḥāmid al-Ghazālī advises caution when it comes to the forbidden glance, expanding on a Qurʾānic command to lower one's gaze when encountering the opposite sex (Q 24:30). See al-Ghazālī, *Iḥyāʾ ʿulūm al-dīn*, vol. 3, ed. Badawī Ṭabāna (Cairo: Dār Iḥyāʾ al-Kutub al-ʿArabiyya, 1957), 98–99. The story of the shaykh's glance does have an interesting parallel to that of al-Ḥallāj who deemed his own execution to have become his fate when he glanced at a woman on a terrace. See John Renard, *Friends of God: Islamic Images of Piety, Commitment, and Servanthood* (Berkeley: University of California Press, 2008), 63.

21. Conversely, ʿAṭṭār does sometimes imply that those outside the fold of Islam might achieve salvation, such as in his portrayal of a Christian in a monastery worshiping an "idol" to whose prayers God responds. Again, the word "idol" (*but*) seems to indicate either an icon or a crucifix. See ʿAṭṭār, *MT*, 313–314, ll. 1851–1870.

22. ʿAṭṭār, *MT*, 301, l. 1563.

23. ʿAṭṭār, *MT*, 301, l. 1572.

24. ʿAṭṭār, *MT*, 289, ll. 1280–1288.

25. ʿAṭṭār, *MT*, 290, ll. 1310–1312.

26. This is how Abū al-Qāsim al-Qushayrī characterizes *khalwa* in *Al-Qushayrī's Epistle on Sufism*, trans. Alexander D. Knysh (Reading: Garnet, 2007), 122–123.

27. For example, Abū al-Ḥasan ʿAlī b. ʿUthmān Hujwīrī describes the intrepid lover, unfazed by any sense of reputation, as waiting at the alleyway of the beloved in his *Kashf al-maḥjūb*, ed. Valentin Alekseevich Zhukovskiĭ (Tehran: Ṭahūrī, 2008 [1926]), 75.

28. See al-Bukhārī, *Ṣaḥīḥ al-Bukhārī*, 488, ch. 33, no. 2029.

29. ʿAṭṭār, *MT*, 290, ll. 1294–1295.

30. ʿAṭṭār, *TA*, vol. 1, 80.

31. This is the definition given by Abū Bakr Muḥammad ibn Isḥāq al-Kalābādhī (d. ca. 380/990) in his *al-Taʿarruf li-madhhab ahl al-taṣawwuf*, ed. ʿAbd al-Ḥalīm Maḥmūd Ṭāhā ʿAbd al-Bāqī Surūr (Tehran: Asāṭīr, 1992), 116.

Chapter 13. ʿAṭṭār and Mystical Experience

1. Those are the valleys of seeking (*ṭalab*), love (*ʿishq*), intimate knowledge (*maʿrifat*), needlessness (*istighnā*), recognizing oneness (*tawḥīd*), perplexity (*ḥayrat*), and poverty and annihilation (*faqr* and *fanā*).

2. With *tawḥīd* also come some of the most perplexing changes in the wayfarer's perception, since—ʿAṭṭār tells us—it is the "waystation of *tafrīd* and *tajrīd*." (See ʿAṭṭār, *MT*, 402, l. 3720.) *Tafrīd* and *tajrīd* are terms used to describe the knower's ability to segregate oneness from multiplicity or the eternal from the temporal. While *tawḥīd* applies to both common and elite, albeit in very different ways, *tafrīd* applies only to those who remove all temporality and createdness from their perception of God and His effects. They singularize the singular. *Tajrīd* allows for *tafrīd* by isolating one's concern and focus on the Real. The knower must become overwhelmed to undergo *tajrīd*. In *tajrīd* the wayfarer removes everything other than God from the heart. Thus, *tajrīd* is an isolation that must occur in the heart before one's *tawḥīd* becomes *tafrīd*. One begins to see all as one and then becomes perplexed: Is it gathering together (*jamʿ*), that is, is everything one? (See ʿAṭṭār, *MT*, 423, l. 4185.) Or is there any sense of dispersion (*farq*), that is, a separation between creation and the Real, separation needed to observe proper boundaries between created and Creator? In Sufi terms, to move beyond these oscillations and enter in pure unified vision is the "gathering together of the gathering together" (*jamʿ al-jamʿ* or *jamʿ-i jamʿ*). Since ʿAṭṭār's poetic language on the topic usually relies on intimations and allusions, see a fairly standard model presented by Abū Naṣr ʿAbdallāh ibn al-Sarrāj al-Ṭūsī, *Kitāb al-lumaʿ fī al-taṣawwuf*, ed. Reynold Alleyne Nicholson (Leiden: Brill, 1914), 348–349, and 113 for al-Sarrāj's definition of *tajrīd* specifically.

3. For both "ash" and "ocean" examples, see ʿAṭṭār, *MT*, 414, ll. 3979–3981.

4. These two terms ("annihilation" and "remaining") are spelled with a hamza (ʾ) at the end in Arabic, *fanāʾ* and *baqāʾ*, but without the concluding hamza in Persian.

5. I have offered a chapter-length analysis of annihilation (*fanā*) in *The Speech of the Birds* and ʿAṭṭār's ethics in *The Polished Mirror*, 237–262.

6. William James, *The Varieties of Religious Experience: A Study in Human Nature (The Gifford Lectures on Natural Religion Delivered at Edinburgh in 1901–1902)* (London: Longmans, Green, 1902), 405–406. This applies to the next quotation as well.

7. Ann Taves, *Religious Experience Reconsidered: A Building-Block Approach to the Study of Religion and Other Special Things* (Princeton: Princeton University Press, 2009), 35.

8. Taves, *Religious Experience Reconsidered*, 43–44.

9. Torben Hammersholt, "Steven T. Katz's Philosophy of Mysticism Revisited," *Journal of the American Academy of Religion* 81, no. 2 (2013): 468.

10. Steven T. Katz, "Language, Epistemology, and Mysticism," in *Mysticism and Philosophical Analysis*, ed. Steven T. Katz (New York: Oxford University Press, 1978), 26.

11. Katz, "Language, Epistemology, and Mysticism," 26.

12. Katz, "Language, Epistemology, and Mysticism," 27.

13. Katz, "Language, Epistemology, and Mysticism," 46.

14. Katz, "Language, Epistemology, and Mysticism," 53–54.

15. Hammersholt explores Katz's agnostic position about the reality of mystical experience. See "Steven T. Katz's Philosophy of Mysticism Revisited," 481–482.

16. Taves's approach to investigating "specialness," for example, might lead to discoveries about the scientific causes of what we call mystical experience.

17. Oludamini Ogunnaike offers this point of view as a critical analysis of Katz's position, using the philosophical Sufi thought of Ibn ʿArabī. His solution lies in Ibn ʿArabī's theory of the Real's awareness of Himself via the constructed belief of each person knowing Him. See Ogunnaike, "'Shining of the Lights and the Veil of the Sights in the Secret Bright': An Akbarī Approach to the Problem of Pure Consciousness," *Journal of the Muhyiddin Ibn ʿArabi Society* 61 (2017): 17–42. Also applying the views of Ibn ʿArabī (among others) to Katz is Reza Shah-Kazemi, who points to the "vantage point" that mystics themselves have claimed frees them from completely contextual perspectives, the very vantage point that Katz admits he lacks. See Shah-Kazemi, *Paths to Transcendence: According to*

Shankara, Ibn Arabi, and Meister Eckhart (Bloomington, IN: World Wisdom, 2006), 234, as well as, more broadly, 229–237.

Chapter 14. Ascents to the Real

1. Q 17:1.

2. As a reminder, ʿAṭṭār's four long narrative poems—each of which has a section describing the *miʿrāj*—are (1) *The Book of the Divine* (*Ilāhī-nāma*); (2) *The Book of Secrets* (*Asrār-nāma*); (3) *The Speech of the Birds* (*Manṭiq al-ṭayr*), where it is included briefly in a longer panegyrical description of the Prophet; and (4) *The Book of Affliction* (*Muṣībat-nāma*). ʿAṭṭār's version of choice for the Prophet's celestial ascent, as Najīb Māyil-Hirawī establishes, is that narrated by Abū Saʿīd al-Khudrī (d. 74/693), a version used by many historians and exegetes. See Abū ʿAlī ibn Sīnā, *Miʿrāj-nāma*, 2nd ed., ed. Najīb Māyil-Hirawī (Mashhad: Āstān-i Quds-i Raḍawī, 1987 [1986]), 59. For more on al-Khudrī's version of the narration, see Frederick S. Colby, *Narrating Muhammad's Night Journey: Tracing the Development of the Ibn ʿAbbās Ascension Discourse* (Albany: State University of New York Press, 2008), 55–56.

3. See Najīb Māyil-Hirawī's introduction to Ibn Sīnā, *Miʿrāj-nāma*, 58. Sanāʾī had a tremendous influence on Persian literature, especially the spiritual-erotic *ghazal* that ʿAṭṭār advanced. See Julie Scott Meisami, *Structure and Meaning in Medieval Arabic and Persian Poetry: Orient Pearls* (London: RoutledgeCurzon, 2003), 46–48.

4. ʿAṭṭār here draws a parallel between the Prophet's meeting with God and the divine call to the human soul invited into Paradise, as in Q 89:27–30.

5. The name "Aḥmad," or the "most praised," is the Prophet Muhammad's name most often associated with his reaching the divine proximity during the *miʿrāj*.

6. ʿAṭṭār, *IN*, 121, ll. 249–253.

7. "The shaykh had a *miʿrāj*," ʿAṭṭār plainly says about Basṭāmī. See ʿAṭṭār, *TA*, vol. 1, 198.

8. ʿAṭṭār, *TA*, vol. 1, 199.

9. ʿAṭṭār, *TA*, vol. 1, 200.

10. ʿAṭṭār, *TA*, vol. 1, 199.

11. ʿAṭṭār, *TA*, vol. 1, 199.

12. ʿAṭṭār, *TA*, vol. 1, 200–201.

13. ʿAṭṭār, *TA*, vol. 1, 200.

14. See al-Bukhārī, *Ṣaḥīḥ al-Bukhārī*, 1617, no. 6502. The significance of this ḥadīth in Sufism has been studied by Zachary Markwith in "And

When I Love Him: The *Ḥadīth al-Nawāfil* and the Formation of Sufism," PhD dissertation, Graduate Theological Union, Berkeley, 2020.

Chapter 15. Celestial Journey Literature

1. Aaron W. Hughes, *The Texture of the Divine: Imagination in Medieval Islamic and Jewish Thought* (Bloomington: Indiana University Press, 2004), 65.

2. The other treatise that makes use of *miʿrāj*-related themes and images is *The Treatise of Lights* (*Risālat al-anwār*). The two passages from *The Openings in Mecca* come from chapters 167 and 367. See James Winston Morris, "The Spiritual Ascension: Ibn ʿArabī and the Miʿrāj," *Journal of the American Oriental Society* 107 (1987): 629–652, and 108 (1988): 63–77.

3. As mentioned earlier, *The Story of the Birds* (*Dāstān-i Murghān*) by Abū al-Rajāʾ Chāchī seems to have been ʿAṭṭār's source for his bird narrative. Worthy of repeated mention as well is Aḥmad al-Ghazālī's *Treatise on Birds* (*Risālat al-Ṭayr*) in Persian, which his brother Abū Ḥāmid translated into Arabic.

4. See ʿAyn al-Quḍāt al-Hamadānī, *The Essence of Reality: A Defense of Philosophical Sufism*, trans. Mohammed Rustom (New York: New York University Press, 2022), 164–165, ch. 84.

5. See Peter Heath's analysis in his *Allegory and Philosophy in Avicenna (Ibn Sînâ), with a Translation of the Book of the Prophet Muḥammad's Ascent to Heaven* (Philadelphia: University of Pennsylvania Press, 1992), 201–206.

6. Translation from Heath, *Allegory and Philosophy in Avicenna (Ibn Sînâ)*, 136.

7. Heath, *Allegory and Philosophy in Avicenna (Ibn Sînâ)*, 136.

8. Nevertheless, Taqī Pūrnāmdārīyān discusses ʿAṭṭār's interpretation of Ibn Sīnā's philosophy, and his possible use of three allegorical treatises by the philosopher (even if through intermediaries), in *Dīdār bā Sīmurgh: shiʿr wa ʿirfān wa andīsha-hā-yi ʿAṭṭār* (Tehran: Institute for Humanities and Cultural Studies, 2011), 131–144.

9. As Franklin Lewis indicates, Sanāʾī's poem might also have drawn from the very instrumental model of Abū al-ʿAlāʾ al-Maʿarrī's (d. 449/1057) *The Epistle of Forgiveness* (*Risālat al-Ghufrān*), in which the author enters Paradise to find that the Arabic poets he has admired, including the most debauched among them, have been forgiven. See Lewis, "Reading, Writing and Recitation: Sanāʾī and the Origins of the Persian Ghazal," 123.

10. For a structural comparison of Sanāʾī's and ʿAṭṭār's poems as "dream allegories," see Bihnāz Payāmī and Fāṭima Farhūdī-Pūr, "Barrasī-i taṭbīqī-i sākhtār-i rawāʾī-i *Muṣībat-nāma*-yi ʿAṭṭār wa *Sayr al-ʿibād*-i

Sanāʾī bih mathāba-yi 'tamthīl-i ruʾyā,'" *Muṭālaʿāt-i ʿirfānī* 19, no. 1393 (2014): 55–84.

11. There is also a possibility that Sanāʾī's views on the intellect show the influence of Shiʿi Ismaʿili thought, as argued by Parisa Zahiremami in "Cosmopolitanism, Poetry, and Kingship: The Ideal Ruler in Sanāʾī's (d. 1131 or 1135) Poetry," PhD dissertation, University of Toronto, 2021. See especially 86–88 for Zahiremami's consideration of the Active Intellect in *The Journey of God's Servants to the Return*.

12. One such hint is that the guide's progenitor is the "first issue of infinite pre-existence" who illuminates nonexistence, that is, the First Intellect (*al-ʿaql al-awwal*). Majdūd ibn Ādam Ghaznawī Sanāʾī, *Sayr al-ʿibād ilā al-maʿād*, ed. Maryam al-Sādāt Ranjbar (Tehran: Mānī, 1999), 23, l. 102. This—along with other allusions described by Kathryn V. Johnson—qualifies the guide as the Active Intellect (*al-ʿaql al-faʿʿāl*). See Johnson, "A Mystic's Response to the Claims of Philosophy," 269–270.

13. Sanāʾī, *Sayr al-ʿibād ilā al-maʿād*, 49, l. 454.

14. Sanāʾī, *Sayr al-ʿibād ilā al-maʿād*, 51, ll. 482–483.

15. Sanāʾī, *Sayr al-ʿibād ilā al-maʿād*, 52, ll. 487–488.

16. De Bruijn, *Persian Sufi Poetry*, 88. William C. Chittick has detailed shortcomings in de Bruijn's approach to the study of Sanāʾī, which relies too heavily on an imposed distinction between sacred and profane and often lacks an awareness of the cultural context of his poetry. See Chittick, "Review of *Of Piety and Poetry: The Interaction of Religion and Literature in the Life and Works of Ḥakīm Sanāʾī* by J. T. P de Bruijn," *Journal of the American Oriental Society* 105, no. 2 (1985): 347–350.

17. Sanāʾī, *Sayr al-ʿibād ilā al-maʿād*, 52, l. 490.

18. Johnson seems to be making a somewhat similar point when she says that what brings the jurist to the fore at the culmination of Sanāʾī's journey is not his "legal expertise" but rather his role as a servant of God who has undertaken the journey successfully. See Johnson, "A Mystic's Response to the Claims of Philosophy," 290.

19. Nicholas Boylston, "Writing the Kaleidoscope of Reality: The Significance of Diversity in the 6th/12th Century Persian Metaphysical Literature of Sanāʾī, ʿAyn al-Quḍāt, and ʿAṭṭār," PhD dissertation, Georgetown University, 2017, 122 and 131. According to Boylston, Ibn Manṣūr becomes, in Sanāʾī's poems, the "archetype of the spiritual master," and, even beyond that, "an icon synthesizing diverse dimensions of human perfection in a single individual, much like the figure of the Prophet Muhammad." See Boylston, "Writing the Kaleidoscope of Reality," 133 and 137.

20. Nicholas Boylston addresses some of the confusion surrounding Ibn Manṣūr's identity as a "Sufi," though, in reality, to be a spiritually

enlightened guide of ethical perfection and interpretive depth is not the prerogative of initiated Sufis. See Boylston, "Writing the Kaleidoscope of Reality," 95 n. 225.

21. Zargar, *The Polished Mirror*, 271–272.

Chapter 16. Union in *The Book of Affliction*

1. Ritter, *The Ocean of the Soul*, 21.
2. ʿAṭṭār, *MN*, 158, ll. 891–893.
3. If you recall, ʿAṭṭār includes a lengthy justification for including Rābiʿa in a book about men.
4. Q 62:1.
5. Not only in Sufism but also in Islamic philosophy self-awareness is a major topic of discussion. Jari Kaukua explores how, for Ibn Sīnā, human subjectivity's origins lie in self-awareness, a self-awareness that the later philosopher Abū al-Barakāt Hibatallāh al-Baghdādī (d. 547/1152) extends as an emanation in lesser forms of awareness to the animal souls, vegetative souls, and natures. See Kaukua, "Self, Agent, Soul: Abū al-Barakāt al-Baghdādī's Critical Reception of Avicennian Psychology," *Subjectivity and Selfhood in Medieval and Early Modern Philosophy*, ed. Jari Kaukua and Tomas Ekenberg (Cham, Switzerland: Springer, 2016), 75–89.
6. ʿAṭṭār, *MN*, 333, l. 4626.
7. ʿAṭṭār, *MN*, 333, ll. 4638–4639.
8. ʿAṭṭār, *MN*, 334, l. 4661.
9. ʿAṭṭār, *MN*, 336, ll. 4710–4711.
10. ʿAṭṭār, *MN*, 398, l. 6025.
11. ʿAṭṭār, *MN*, 398, l. 6048.
12. Q 41:53.
13. ʿAṭṭār, *MN*, 137, l. 441.
14. ʿAṭṭār, *MN*, 137, ll. 441–442. Among the realities beyond the reach of the intellect is the person of the Prophet himself. In concluding his praise for Muhammad in this section, ʿAṭṭār admits the futility of trying to describe the Prophet, hinting—even in his introduction—at both the utility and limits of the intellect: "I am not the man to describe your essence / such magnitude, also, counts among your blessings; / a description is offered by my intellect, which usually arrives as a champion, / yet the intellect falls short, description itself has become incapable." See ʿAṭṭār, *MN*, 139, ll. 491–492.
15. ʿAṭṭār, *MN*, 446, ll. 7073–7076.
16. ʿAṭṭār, *MN*, 446, l. 7079.
17. ʿAṭṭār, *MN*, 407, ll. 6236–6237.

18. ʿAṭṭār, *MN*, 407, l. 6228.

19. ʿAṭṭār, *MN*, 407, l. 6239.

20. "Wherever existence (*hastī*) is, there is your essence. / Nonexistence (*nīstī*) is above and beyond what you sense." See ʿAṭṭār, *MN*, 407, l. 6230.

21. Majdūd ibn Ādam Ghaznawī Sanāʾī, *Ḥadīqat al-ḥaqīqa wa sharīʿat al-ṭārīqa*, 6th ed., ed. Muḥammad-Taqī Mudarris-Raḍawī (Tehran: University of Tehran Press, 2004), 153.

22. Sanāʾī, *Dīwān-i Ḥakīm Sanāʾī*, vol. 1, 728, no. 530.

23. ʿAṭṭār, *MN*, 407, ll. 6240–6242.

24. ʿAṭṭār, *MN*, 408, l. 6249.

25. ʿAṭṭār, *MN*, 407, ll. 6243–6246.

26. ʿAṭṭār, *MN*, 407, l. 6248. In his study of notions of selfhood in Islamic philosophy, Muhammad U. Faruque reviews the development of human subjectivity in the thought of a later philosopher, Mullā Ṣadrā (d. 1050/1640). For Ṣadrā, subjectivity also begins with the mode of the five senses. Then follows the mode of the imagination, and finally the mode of the intellect. Ṣadrā's is a modified version of Ibn Sīnā's model. See Faruque, *Sculpting the Self: Islam, Selfhood, and Human Flourishing* (Ann Arbor: University of Michigan Press, 2021), 41.

27. "Because I-ness was not compatible with Proximity, / by necessity I-ness arose in you, from a distance." See ʿAṭṭār, *MN*, 408, l. 6231. The only I-ness that suits proximity to God is God's own I-ness, which the knower freed from human I-ness can make their own, as seen in chapter 14, "Ascents to the Real."

28. ʿAṭṭār, *MN*, 408, l. 6251.

29. ʿAṭṭār, *MN*, 414–415, ll. 6390–6392.

30. See al-Ghazālī, *Iḥyāʾ*, vol. 3, 6.

31. For example, al-Ghazālī shows his hesitance to declare what ʿAṭṭār expounds in detail regarding the heart and spirit. "As for the reality of the heart (*dil*)," al-Ghazālī says, "regarding its essence and particular attributes, the divine law (*sharīʿat*) has not given us permission to venture into that topic; it is for that reason that the Messenger never elaborated on it, as the Exalted Real said, 'They ask you about the Spirit (*al-rūḥ*). Say: "The Spirit is from my Lord's command."'" See Q 17:85, as quoted in Abū Ḥāmid Muḥammad al-Ghazālī, *Kīmīyā-i saʿādat*, 9th ed., ed. Ḥusayn Khadīwjam (Tehran: Shirkat-i Intishārāt-i ʿIlmī wa Farhangī, 2001), vol. 1, 16. Drawing conclusions from this verse, al-Ghazālī comments that the spirit (here, the heart, which al-Ghazālī at times conflates in this book) is from the "World of Command . . . the created world and the World of Command are distinct." See *Kīmīyā-i saʿādat*, vol. 1, 17.

32. ʿAṭṭār, *MN*, 415, l. 6400.

33. ʿAṭṭār, *MN*, 415, l. 6403.

34. ʿAṭṭār, *MN*, 415, ll. 6404–6405.

35. Al-Ghazālī, like ʿAṭṭār, emphasizes imagination's inability to have direct sight, or witnessing (*mushāhada*) even describing—like ʿAṭṭār—the veiled state of imagination. While imagination can know only "colors and shapes," and the intellect can know the "attributes of God," both lack what direct vision offers. In the case of imagination, its veiled state is in contrast to direct witnessing (*mushāhada*), which requires a lifting of that veil and intimate knowledge (*maʿrifat*) of God. See al-Ghazālī, *Kīmīyā-i saʿādat*, vol. 2, 587.

36. The role of philosophy (based on rational arguments alone) versus Ashʿarī theology (based on rational arguments that correspond with scripture) in al-Ghazālī's thought is currently the topic of academic debate, particularly because of the thinker's seemingly contradictory views on causality. See Griffel, *Al-Ghazālī's Philosophical Theology*, especially 184–185. Also, Taneli Kukkonen offers a useful study of al-Ghazālī's notion of the self that emphasizes, as the quintessential human reality, both reason and volition. Kukkonen, "The Self as Enemy, the Self as Divine: A Crossroads in the Development of Islamic Anthropology," in *Ancient Philosophy of the Self*, ed. Pauliina Remes and Juha Sihvola (Dordrecht, Netherlands: Springer, 2008), 221.

37. ʿAṭṭār's reference to the ḥadīth is short: "*Draw near* and *go back*," the wayfarer says to the Intellect, "were said exclusively to you." See ʿAṭṭār, *MN*, 422, l. 6541.

38. al-Ghazālī, *Iḥyāʾ*, 1:83.

39. ʿAṭṭār, *MN*, 422, l. 6547.

40. ʿAṭṭār, *MN*, 423, l. 6555.

41. ʿAṭṭār, *MN*, 423, ll. 6555–6557.

42. ʿAṭṭār, *MN*, 423, l. 6558.

43. ʿAṭṭār, *MN*, 423, ll. 6560–6561.

44. ʿAṭṭār, *MN*, 423, ll. 6563 and 6564.

45. ʿAṭṭār, *MN*, 423, l. 6565.

46. ʿAṭṭār, *MN*, 423, l. 6568.

47. ʿAṭṭār, *MN*, 424, ll. 6587–6591.

48. ʿAṭṭār, *MT*, 262, ll. 670–671.

49. Q 18:65–82. Khiḍr's name comes to us from sources external to the Qurʾān.

50. See Lucian Stone, "Blessed Perplexity: The Topos of *Ḥayrat* in ʿAṭṭār's *Manṭiq al-ṭayr*," in *ʿAṭṭār and the Persian Sufi Tradition: The Art of Spiritual Flight*, ed. Leonard Lewisohn and Christopher Shackle (London: I. B. Tauris, 2006), 95–111.

51. The intellect helps to discern God's law, just as law should keep the intellect from venturing into what it cannot know and can only obscure: a unitary truth that lies beyond its comprehension. As ʿAṭṭār says, God

created a hierarchy by placing "the recalcitrant Intellect in subordination to revealed law (*shar*ʿ)," while placing "belief" or *īmān* (which is submission to an unknowable Real) as the life of the soul, just as the soul is the life of the body. See ʿAṭṭār, *MN*, 121, l. 46.

52. ʿAṭṭār, *MN*, 445, ll. 7059–7064.

53. Q 2:117, among other verses.

54. ʿAṭṭār, *AN*, 110, l. 565. Shahzad Bashir offers an excellent discussion of the heart in Sufi thought as "the most valued element in the cosmos as a whole," as well as its relationship to the body and the cosmos. See his *Sufi Bodies: Religion and Society in Medieval Islam* (New York: Columbia University Press, 2011), 43–45.

55. ʿAṭṭār, *MN*, 429, l. 6697.

56. ʿAṭṭār, *MN*, 429, l. 6698. ʿAṭṭār continues: "Those atoms," the atoms reflected in the heart, "all are spiritual (*maʿnawī*) in nature / uncontaminated always by singularity (*yikī*) or duality." See ʿAṭṭār, *MN*, 429, l. 6699.

57. ʿAṭṭār, *MN*, 430, l. 6711. For "Spirit," the poet here uses the Persian *jān*, but it clearly signifies the Arabic *rūḥ* because of the lines that follow.

58. ʿAṭṭār, *MN*, 430, l. 6706.

59. See Muslim ibn al-Ḥajjāj, *Ṣaḥīḥ Muslim*, 1427, no. 2654. Or, in a different version cited by al-Ghazālī, "He makes [the heart] *alternate* howsoever He wills." Indeed, ʿAṭṭār's understanding of the latter part of this ḥadīth seems to expand on al-Ghazālī's comments in the *Revival*. See al-Ghazālī, *Iḥyāʾ*, vol. 3, 44, as well as al-Ghazālī, *Kīmīyā-yi saʿādat*, vol. 1, 196.

60. ʿAṭṭār, *MN*, 430, ll. 6713–6715.

61. ʿAṭṭār, *MN*, 430, ll. 6716–6718.

62. ʿAṭṭār, *MN*, 430, ll. 6719–6720.

63. ʿAṭṭār, *MN*, 430, l. 6724.

64. This inbreathing of the spirit is mentioned twice in the Qurʾān. See Q 15:29 and Q 38:72.

65. ʿAṭṭār, *MN*, 437–438, ll. 6878–6882.

66. ʿAṭṭār, *MN*, 438, ll. 6891 and 6893.

67. ʿAṭṭār, *MN*, 438, ll. 6901–6903.

68. ʿAṭṭār, *MN*, 438, ll. 6896–6898.

69. ʿAṭṭār, *MN*, 439, l. 6910.

70. ʿAṭṭār, *MN*, 439, l. 6911.

71. ʿAṭṭār, *MN*, 439, ll. 6914–6915.

72. ʿAṭṭār, *MN*, 440, l. 6933.

73. See Ernst Tugendhat, *Egocentricity and Mysticism: An Anthropological Study*, trans. Alexei Procyshyn and Mario Wenning (New York: Columbia University Press, 2016).

74. Tugendhat, *Egocentricity and Mysticism*, 30.

75. See also Ernst Tugendhat, *Self-Consciousness and Self-Determination*, trans. Paul Stern (Cambridge, MA: MIT Press, 1986), 138.

Chapter 17. The Source of Affliction

1. Kermani, *The Terror of God*, 49.

2. Kermani, *The Terror of God*, 77.

3. Q 51:56.

4. ʿAṭṭār seems to be referring to the male sperm or seed (*nuṭfa*) here, but that does not mean that he or others in his time and area failed to appreciate any female role in conception. Medieval Muslim physicians, including Ibn Sīnā, inherited the discourse on reproduction that began with Hippocrates (d. ca. 375 BCE), Aristotle, and Galen (d. ca. 216). Like Hippocrates and Galen, they rejected the Aristotelian "one-seed" model, which described the male seed as a cause upon the material provided within the female body. Instead, they held the view that both male and female seeds contributed—in some way—to the conception of a child. The Qurʾān refers to conception from a seed (*nuṭfa*), but, for these premodern physicians, such references would correspond to the male seed's encounter with the female seed. See Pernilla Myrne, *Female Sexuality in the Early Medieval Islamic World: Gender and Sex in Arabic Literature* (London: I. B. Tauris, 2020), 22–23. Also see Q 20:5 and Q 23:13, among other examples. Finally, see Michael Boylen, "The Galenic and Hippocratic Challenges to Aristotle's Conception Theory," *Journal of the History of Biology* 17, no. 1 (1984): 83–112.

5. ʿAṭṭār, *MN*, 160, ll. 940–942. The obstinate human, created from a sperm-drop, appears in Q 16:4, as well as Q 36:77. Many verses mention that humans were made from earth or "clay," including Q 6:2.

6. ʿAṭṭār, *MN*, 163, 996–999.

7. ʿAṭṭār, *MN*, 161, ll. 967–968.

8. Kermani, *The Terror of God*, 67.

9. The irony here is that *ghuluww*, literally "exaggeration," is usually a trait attributed to Shiʿi admirers of ʿAlī ibn Abī Ṭālib. Here the exaggeration seems to be applied to the eponyms of the various Sunni legal schools, whose adherents seek to disprove one another. *Khilāfī* (or *ʿilm al-khilāf*, sometimes *ʿilm al-ikhtilāf*) was a comparative venture by which one studied differences and disagreements among the major Sunni schools of jurisprudence. George Makdisi calls it a "dialectic method" that was supposed to be markedly different from polemical disputation, though it seems—at least in Nishapur—to have devolved at times to the latter. See

Makdisi, *The Rise of Colleges: Institutions of Learning in Islam and the West* (Edinburgh: Edinburgh University Press, 1981), 108–111.

10. ʿAṭṭār, *MN*, 163, ll. 1005–1014.

11. ʿAṭṭār, *MN*, 11, l. 960.

12. ʿAṭṭār, *MN*, 161, ll. 954–955.

13. ʿAṭṭār, *MN*, 448, l. 7122.

14. Ilya Pavlovich Petrushevsky, *Islam in Iran*, trans. Hubert Evans (Albany: State University of New York Press, 1985), 294.

15. Omid Safi has studied premodern Sufi involvement in the political scene, arguing that, often, European-language scholarship betrays "a post-Enlightenment conception of religion" that leads us "to think of Sufis as Muslim 'mystics,' that is, Muslims who seek after a private, emotional, nonrational experience of God in their hearts," when, in fact, there has long been an interlacing relationship between Sufi networks and political networks. See Safi, *The Politics of Knowledge in Premodern Islam: Negotiating Ideology and Religious Inquiry* (Chapel Hill: University of North Carolina Press, 2006), 207.

16. ʿAṭṭār, *MN*, 447, l. 7094.

17. ʿAṭṭār, *IN*, 419, ll. 106–108.

18. For an instance of citation see Samʿānī, *The Repose of the Spirits*, 170, as well as Chittick's gloss on 513 n. 521.

19. Hamadānī, *Tamhīdāt*, 90, no. 128.

Conclusion

1. See, for example, the Q 6:2 and Q 23:12.

2. ʿAṭṭār, *TA*, vol. 1, 4. The following quotation comes from this same source.

3. This is a reference to Khiḍr, whom the Qurʾān describes as having a mysterious and immediate sort of knowledge, "a knowledge from Ourselves." See Q 18:65.

4. ʿAṭṭār, *TA*, vol. 1, 4.

5. ʿAṭṭār, *MN*, 288, ll. 3695–3700.

6. ʿAṭṭār, *TA*, vol. 1, 185.

Bibliography

Abbasi, Rushain. "Did Premodern Muslims Distinguish the Religious and Secular? The *Dīn-Dunyā* Binary in Medieval Islamic Thought." *Journal of Islamic Studies* 31, no. 2 (2020): 185–225.

Abū Dāwūd al-Sijistānī, Sulaymān ibn Ashʿath. *Sunan Abī Dāwūd*. Edited by Ibrāhīm Sayyid, with commentary by Sayyid Muhammad Sayyid, 5 vols. Cairo: Dār al-Ḥadīth, 1999.

Aḥmadī-Dārānī, ʿAlī-Akbar. "Darbāra-yi 'Tuḥfat al-mulūk': ba bahāna-yi taṣḥīḥ wa chāp-i mujaddad." *Āyina-yi mīrāth* 4, no. 3 (2001): 60–64.

Ahmed, Shahab. *What Is Islam? The Importance of Being Islamic*. Princeton: Princeton University Press, 2016.

Akasoy, Anna Ayşe. "Al-Ghazālī's Veil Section: Comparative Religion before Religionswissenschaft?" In *Islam and Rationality: The Impact of al-Ghazālī, Papers Collected on His 900th Anniversary*, vol. 2, edited by Frank Griffel, 142–67. Leiden: Brill, 2016.

Albertini, Tamara. "Meanings, Words, and Names: Rābiʿa's Mystical Dance of the Letters." In *Ineffability: An Exercise in Comparative Philosophy of Religion*, edited by Timothy D. Knepper and Leah E. Kalmanson, 219–243. Honolulu: Springer International, 2017.

Anjum, Ovamir. *Politics, Law, and Community in Islamic Thought*. New York: Cambridge University Press, 2012.

Algar, Hamid. "Abu Yaʿqub Hamadāni." *Encyclopædia Iranica* 1, fasc. 4 (1985): 395–396.

———. *Jami*. New Delhi: Oxford University Press, 2013.

Asad, Talal. "Reading a Modern Classic: W. C. Smith's 'The Meaning and End of Religion.'" *History of Religions* 40, no. 3 (2001): 205–222.

ʿAṭṭār, Farīd al-Dīn. *Asrār-nāma*. Edited with an introduction and notes by Muḥammad-Riḍā Shafīʿī-Kadkanī. Tehran: Sukhan, 2007.

———. *Dīwān-i ʿAṭṭār*. Edited by Badīʿ al-Zamān Furūzānfar. Tehran: Nakhustīn, 1997. *Referenced, but not the edition preferred.*

———. *Dīwān-i ʿAṭṭār*. 5th ed. Edited by Taqī Tafaḍḍulī. Tehran: Intishārāt-i ʿIlmī wa Farhangī, 1989 [1962]. *Referenced, but not the edition preferred.*

———. *Dīwān-i ʿAṭṭār-i Nīshābūrī*. Edited by Mahdī Madāyinī and Mihrān Afshārī, supervised by ʿAlī-riḍā Imāmī. Tehran: Charkh, 2013. *Preferred edition.*

———. *Dīwān-i Farīd al-Dīn ʿAṭṭār-i Nīshābūrī*. Edited by Saʿīd Nafīsī. Tehran: Sanāʾī, 1960. *Referenced, but not the edition preferred.*

———. *Farid ad-Din ʿAttār's Memorial of God's Friends: Lives and Sayings of Sufis*. Translated and introduced by Paul Losensky. New York: Paulist Press, 2009.

———. *Ilāhī-nāma*. Edited with an introduction and notes by Muḥammad-Riḍā Shafīʿī-Kadkanī. Tehran: Sukhan, 2008. *Preferred edition.*

———. *Ilāhī-nāma*. Edited with an introduction and notes by Hellmut Ritter. Istanbul: Maʿārif, 1940. *Referenced, but not the edition preferred.*

———. *Manṭiq al-ṭayr*. Edited with an introduction and notes by Muḥammad-Riḍā Shafīʿī-Kadkanī. Tehran: Sukhan, 2012.

———. *Mukhtār-nāma*. Edited with an introduction and notes by Muḥammad-Riḍā Shafīʿī-Kadkanī. Tehran: Sukhan, 1996.

———. *Muṣībat-nāma*. Edited with an introduction and notes by Muḥammad-Riḍā Shafīʿī-Kadkanī. Tehran: Sukhan, 2007.

———. *Tadhkirat al-awliyāʾ*. 2 vols. Edited with an introduction and notes by Muḥammad-Riḍā Shafīʿī-Kadkanī. Tehran: Sukhan, 2018.

Ayubi, Zahra. *Gendered Morality: Classical Islamic Ethics of the Self, Family, and Society*. New York: Columbia University Press, 2019.

Barton, Carlin A., and Daniel Boyarin. *Imagine No Religion: How Modern Abstractions Hide Ancient Realities*. New York: Fordham University Press, 2016.

Bashir, Shahzad. *Sufi Bodies: Religion and Society in Medieval Islam*. New York: Columbia University Press, 2011.

Beelaert, Anna Livia. "Ḵāqāni Šervāni i. Life." *Encyclopædia Iranica* 15, fasc. 5 (2011): 522–523.

Bell, Joseph Norment. *Love Theory in Later Ḥanbalite Islam*. Albany: State University of New York Press, 1979.

Bosworth, C. Edmund. "Nishapur i. Historical Geography and History to the Beginning of the 20th Century." *Encyclopædia Iranica* (2010). https://iranicaonline.org/articles/nishapur-i.

Boyarin, Daniel. *Judaism: The Genealogy of a Modern Nation*. New Brunswick, NJ: Rutgers University Press, 2019.

———. "Rethinking Jewish Christianity: An Argument for Dismantling a Dubious Category (to which is appended a correction of my *Border Lines*)." *Jewish Quarterly Review* 99, no. 1 (2009): 7–36.

Boylen, Michael. "The Galenic and Hippocratic Challenges to Aristotle's Conception Theory." *Journal of the History of Biology* 17, no. 1 (1984): 83–112.

Boylston, Nicholas John. "Writing the Kaleidoscope of Reality: The Significance of Diversity in the 6th/12th Century Persian Metaphysical Literature of Sanāʾī, ʿAyn al-Quḍāt, and ʿAṭṭār." PhD dissertation, Georgetown University, 2017.

Boysen, Benjamin. *The Ethics of Love: An Essay on James Joyce*. Odense: University of Southern Denmark, 2013.

al-Bukhārī, Muḥammad ibn Ismāʿīl. *Ṣaḥīḥ al-Bukhārī*. Damascus: Dār Ibn Kathīr, 2002.

Bulliet, Richard W. "The Age Structure of Medieval Islamic Education." *Studia Islamica*, no. 57 (1983): 105–117.

———. "The Druggist of Nishapur." Unpublished. Accessed May 12, 2021 at Academia.edu.

———. "Medieval Nishapur: A Topographic and Demographic Reconstruction." *Studia Iranica*, no. 5 (1976): 67–89.

———. *The Patricians of Nishapur: A Study in Medieval Islamic Social History*. Cambridge, MA: Harvard University Press, 1972.

Chabbi, J. "Abū Ḥafṣ Ḥaddād." *Encyclopædia Iranica* 1, fasc. 3 (1985): 293–294.

Chittick, William C. "ʿĀql ii. In Persian Literature." *Encyclopædia Iranica* 2, fasc. 2 (1986): 195–198.

———. *Divine Love: Islamic Literature and the Path to God*. New Haven, CT: Yale University Press, 2013.

———. "Moses and the Religion of Love: Thoughts on Methodology in the Study of Sufism." In *Islamic Studies and the Study of Sufism in Academia: Rethinking Methodologies*, edited by Tonaga Yasushi and Fujii Chiaki, 101–118. Kyoto: Kenan Rifai Center for Sufi Studies, Kyoto University, 2018.

———. "Review of *Of Piety and Poetry: The Interaction of Religion and Literature in the Life and Works of Ḥakīm Sanāʾī* by J. T. P de Bruijn." *Journal of the American Oriental Society* 105, no. 2 (1985): 347–350.

Colby, Frederick S. *Narrating Muhammad's Night Journey: Tracing the Development of the Ibn ʿAbbās Ascension Discourse*. Albany: State University of New York Press, 2008.

Cornell, Rkia Elaroui. *Rabiʿa from Narrative to Myth: The Many Faces of Islam's Most Famous Woman Saint, Rabiʿa al-ʿAdawiyya*. London: Oneworld, 2019.

———. "'Soul of a Woman Was Created Below': Woman as the Lower Soul (*Nafs*) in Islam." In *World Religions and Evil: Religious and Phil-*

osophical Perspectives, edited by Hendrik M. Vroom, 257–280. New York: Rodopi, 2007.

Dabiri, Ghazzal. "Reading ʿAṭṭār's *Elāhināma* as Sufi Practical Ethics: Between Genre, Reception and Muslim and Christian Audiences." *Journal of Persianate Studies* 11, no. 1 (2018): 29–55.

———. "'When a Lion Is Chided by an Ant': Everyday Saints and the Making of Sufi Kings in ʿAṭṭār's *Elāhi-nāma*." *Journal of Persianate Studies* 12, no. 1 (2019): 62–102.

Dawlatshāh b. Amīr ʿAlāʾ al-Dawla Bukhtīsha al-Ghāzī al-Samarqandī, Amīr. *Kitāb-i tadhkirat al-shuʿarāʾ*. Edited by Edward G. Brown. Leiden: Brill, 1901.

de Blois, François. "Dīvān, iii. Collected Works of a Poet." *Encyclopædia Iranica* 7, fasc. 4 (1995): 432–438.

de Bruijn, J. T. P. *Persian Sufi Poetry: An Introduction to the Mystical Use of Classical Poems*. Surrey, UK: Curzon Press, 1997.

Dihkhudā, ʿAlī-Akbar. *Lughat-nāma*. 2nd ed., 16 vols. Edited by Muḥammad Muʿīn and Jaʿfar Shahīdī. Tehran: University of Tehran Press, 1998.

El Cheikh, Nadia Maria. *Byzantium Viewed by the Arabs*. Cambridge, MA: Harvard University Center for Middle Eastern Studies, Harvard University Press, 2004.

al-Fārābī, Abū Naṣr Muḥammad. *Kitāb ārā ahl al-madīna al-fāḍila*. Edited by Albayr Naṣrī Nādir. Beirut: Dār al-Mashriq, 1986.

Foucault, Michel. "A Preface to Transgression." In *Language, Counter-Memory, Practice: Selected Essays and Interviews*, edited by Donald F. Bouchard, translated by Donald F. Bouchard and Sherry Simon, 29–52. Ithaca, NY: Cornell University Press, 1977.

Faruque, Muhammad U. *Sculpting the Self: Islam, Selfhood, and Human Flourishing*. Ann Arbor: University of Michigan Press, 2021.

Furūzānfar, Badīʿ al-Zamān. *Aḥādīth wa qiṣaṣ-i mathnawī: talfīqī az du kitāb-i* Aḥādīth-i mathnawī *wa* Maʾākhidh-i qiṣaṣ wa tamthīlāt-i mathnawī. 5th ed. Edited by Ḥusayn Dāwūdī. Tehran: Amīr Kabīr, 2011 [1997].

———. *Sharḥ-i aḥwāl wa naqd wa taḥlīl-i āthār-i Shaykh Farīd al-Dīn ʿAṭṭār-i Nīshābūrī*. Tehran: Dihkhudā, 1975.

al-Ghazālī, Abū Ḥāmid Muḥammad. *Deliverance from Error: An Annotated Translation of* al-Munqidh min al-Ḍalāl *and Other Relevant Works of al-Ghazālī*. Translated by Richard Joseph McCarthy. Louisville, KY: Fons Vitae, 1999.

———. *Iḥyāʾ ʿulūm al-dīn*. Edited by Badawī Ṭabāna. Cairo: Dār Iḥyāʾ al-Kutub al-ʿArabiyya, 1957.

———. *The Incoherence of the Philosophers (Tahāfut al-falāsifa).* Translated by Michael E. Marmura. Provo, UT: Brigham Young University Press, 2000.

———. *Kīmīyā-yi saʿādat.* 9th ed. Edited by Ḥusayn Khadīwjam. Tehran: Shirkat-i Intishārāt-i ʿIlmī wa Farhangī, 2001.

———. *The Marvels of the Heart: Book Twenty-One of the Iḥyāʾ ʿUlūm al-Dīn (Kitāb Sharḥ ʿAjāʾib al-Qalb).* Translated by Walter James Skellie. Edited by T. J. Winter. Louisville, KY: Fons Vitae, 2010.

——— (attributed). *Tuḥfat al-mulūk-i Imām Abū Ḥāmid Muḥammad Ghazālī.* Edited by Muḥammad-Taqī Dānish-pazhūh. *Majalla-yi Dānishkada-yi Adabīyāt-i Mashhad* 1, no. 2–3 (1965): 249–300.

Ghazālī, Aḥmad. *Majmūʿa-yi āthār-i fārsī-i Aḥmad Ghazālī.* 3rd ed. Edited by Aḥmad Mujāhid. Tehran: University of Tehran Press, 1997.

Gorji, Ali, and Maryam Khaleghi Ghadiri. "History of Headache in Medieval Persian Medicine." *Lancet Neurology* 1 (December 2002): 510–515.

Griffel, Frank. *Al-Ghazālī's Philosophical Theology.* New York: Oxford University Press, 2009.

———. "Al-Ghazālī's (d. 1111) *Incoherence of the Philosophers.*" In *The Oxford Handbook of Islamic Philosophy,* edited by Khaled El-Rouayheb and Sabine Schmidtke, 191–209. New York: Oxford University Press, 2017.

Gutas, Dimitri. *Avicenna and the Aristotelian Tradition: Introduction to Reading Avicenna's Philosophical Works.* 2nd ed. Leiden: Brill, 2014.

Haddad, Yvonne Yazbeck. "The Conception of the Term *dīn* in the Qurʾān." *Muslim World* 64, no. 2 (1974): 114–123.

(al-)Hamadānī, ʿAyn al-Quḍāt. *The Essence of Reality: A Defense of Philosophical Sufism.* Translated by Mohammed Rustom. New York: Library of Arabic Literature, New York University Press, 2022.

———. *Tamhīdāt.* 4th ed. Edited by ʿAfīf ʿUsayrān. Tehran: Manūchihrī, 2004 [1994].

Hammersholt, Torben. "Steven T. Katz's Philosophy of Mysticism Revisited." *Journal of the American Academy of Religion* 81, no. 2 (2013): 467–490.

Heath, Peter. *Allegory and Philosophy in Avicenna (Ibn Sînâ), with a translation of the Book of the Prophet Muḥammad's Ascent to Heaven.* Philadelphia: University of Pennsylvania Press, 1992.

Hughes, Aaron W. *The Texture of the Divine: Imagination in Medieval Islamic and Jewish Thought.* Bloomington: Indiana University Press, 2004.

Hujwīrī, Abū al-Ḥasan ʿAlī. *Kashf al-maḥjūb.* Edited by Valentin Alekseevich Zhukovskiĭ. Tehran: Ṭahūrī, 2008 [1926].

Hume, David. *A Treatise of Human Nature: Volume I.* Edited by David Fate Norton and Mary J. Norton. Oxford: Oxford University Press, Clarendon Press, 2007.

Ibn ʿArabī, Muḥyī al-Dīn. *al-Futūḥāt al-makkiyya*. Beirut: Dār Ṣādir, 1968.

Ibn Khaldūn, ʿAbd al-Raḥmān. *al-Muqaddima*. 5 vols. Edited by ʿAbd al-Salām al-Shaddādī. Casablanca: Khizānat Ibn Khaldūn, Bayt al-Funūn wa al-ʿUlūm wa al-Ādāb, 2005.

Ibn al-Qaysarānī, Muḥammad ibn Ṭāhir al-Maqdisī. *Maʿrifat al-tadhkira fī al-aḥādīth al-mawḍūʿa*. Edited by ʿImād al-Dīn Aḥmad Ḥaydar. Beirut: Muʾassasat al-Kitāb al-Thiqāfiyya, 1985.

Ibn Qayyim al-Jawziyya, Shams al-Dīn. *Madārij al-sālikīn bayn manāzil iyyāka naʿbud wa iyyāka nastaʿīn*. 3 vols. Edited by Muḥammad al-Muʿtaṣim bi-llāh al-Baghdādī. Beirut: Dār al-Kitāb al-ʿArabī, 2003.

Ibn Sīnā, Abū ʿAlī Ḥusayn. *The Metaphysics of* The Healing (*al-Shifāʾ: al-Ilāhīyāt*). Translated by Michael E. Marmura. Provo, UT: Brigham Young University Press, 2005.

———. *Miʿrāj-nāma*. 2nd ed. Edited by Najīb Māyil-Hirawī. Mashhad: Āstān-i Quds-i Raḍawī, 1987 [1986].

James, William. *The Varieties of Religious Experience: A Study in Human Nature (The Gifford Lectures on Natural Religion Delivered at Edinburgh in 1901–1902)*. London: Longmans, Green, 1902.

Jāmī, Nūr al-Dīn ʿAbd al-Raḥmān. *Nafaḥāt al-uns min ḥaḍarāt al-quds*. Edited by Maḥmūd ʿĀbidī. Tehran: Sukhan, 2007.

Johnson, Kathryn V. "A Mystic's Response to the Claims of Philosophy: Abū'l Majd Majdūd Sanāʾī's *Sayr al-ʿIbād ilā'l-Maʿād*." *Islamic Studies* 34, no. 3 (1995): 253–295.

Josephson-Storm, Jason Ā. *The Myth of Disenchantment: Magic, Modernity, and the Birth of the Human Sciences*. Chicago: University of Chicago Press, 2017.

Juwaynī, ʿAlāʾ al-Dīn ʿAṭā Malik b. Bahāʾ al-Dīn Muḥammad b. Muḥammad. *Genghis Khan: The History of the World Conqueror*. Translated by John Andrew Boyle from the text of Mizra Muhammad Qazvini. Manchester: Manchester University Press, 1997.

———. *Tārīkh-i jahāngushāy-i Juwaynī*. 1 vol. Edited by Muḥammad Qazwīnī and Sayyid Shāhrukh Mūsawīyān. Tehran: Dastān, 2006.

al-Kalābādhī, Abū Bakr Muḥammad ibn Isḥāq. *al-Taʿarruf li-madhhab ahl al-taṣawwuf*. Edited by ʿAbd al-Ḥalīm Maḥmūd Ṭāhā ʿAbd al-Bāqī Surūr. Tehran: Asāṭīr, 1992.

Karamustafa, Ahmed T. *God's Unruly Friends: Dervish Groups in the Islamic Middle Period, 1200–1550*. Salt Lake City: University of Utah Press, 1994.

Katz, Steven T. "Language, Epistemology, and Mysticism." In *Mysticism and Philosophical Analysis*, edited by Steven T. Katz, 22–74. New York: Oxford University Press, 1978.

Kaukua, Jari. "Self, Agent, Soul: Abū al-Barakāt al-Baghdādī's Critical Reception of Avicennian Psychology." In *Subjectivity and Selfhood in Medieval and Early Modern Philosophy*, edited by Jari Kaukua and Tomas Ekenberg, 75–89. Cham, Switzerland: Springer, 2016.

Kāẓim-Baygī, Muḥammad-ʿAlī. "Akhlāq-i ḥirfa-ī wa bāwarhā-yi dīnī dar bāzārhā-yi īrānī, sadahā-yi 8–12 hijrī-qamarī." In *Akhlāq-i ḥirfa-ī dar tamaddun-i īrān wa islām*, edited by Aḥad-Farāmarz Qarāmalikī, 491–513. Tehran: Pizhūhishkada-i Muṭālaʿāt-i Farhangī wa Ijtimāʿī, 2008.

Keeler, Annabel. "Abū Yazīd al-Bisṭāmī and Discussions about Intoxicated Sufism." In *Routledge Handbook on Sufism*, edited by Lloyd Ridgeon, 46–62. London: Routledge, 2021.

Kermani, Navid. *The Terror of God: Attar, Job and the Metaphysical Revolt*. Cambridge: Polity Press, 2011.

Keshavarz, Fatemeh. "Flight of the Birds: The Poetic Animating the Spiritual in ʿAṭṭār's *Manṭiq al-ṭayr*." In *ʿAṭṭār and the Persian Sufi Tradition: The Art of Spiritual Flight*, edited by Leonard Lewisohn and Christopher Shackle, 112–134. London: I. B. Tauris, 2006.

———. *Recite in the Name of the Red Rose: Poetic Sacred Making in Twentieth-Century Iran*. Columbia: University of South Carolina Press, 2006.

Kröger, Jens. *Nishapur: Glass of the Early Islamic Period*. New York: Metropolitan Museum of Art, 1995.

Kugle, Scott. *Sufis and Saints' Bodies: Mysticism, Corporeality, and Sacred Power in Islam*. Chapel Hill: University of North Carolina Press, 2007.

Kukkonen, Taneli. "The Self as Enemy, the Self as Divine: A Crossroads in the Development of Islamic Anthropology." In *Ancient Philosophy of the Self*, edited by Pauliina Remes and Juha Sihvola, 205–224. Dordrecht, Netherlands: Springer.

Landolt, Hermann. "Ghazālī and 'Religionswissenschaft': Some Notes on the *Mishkāt al-Anwār*." *Asiatische Studien* 45 (1991): 19–72.

Latour, Bruno. *We Have Never Been Modern*. Translated by Catherine Porter. Cambridge, MA: Harvard University Press, 1993.

Lewis, Franklin D. "Reading, Writing and Recitation: Sanāʾī and the Origins of the Persian Ghazal." PhD dissertation, University of Chicago, 1995.

———. "Sexual Occidentation: The Politics of Conversion, Christian-Love and Boy-Love in ʿAṭṭār." *Iranian Studies* 42, no. 5 (2009): 693–723.

Lewisohn, Leonard. "Sufism's Religion of Love, from Rābiʿa to Ibn ʿArabī." In *The Cambridge Companion to Sufism*, edited by Lloyd Ridgeon, 150–180. New York: Cambridge University Press, 2015.

Lipton, Gregory A. *Rethinking Ibn ʿArabi*. New York: Oxford University Press, 2018.

Lumbard, Joseph E. B. *Aḥmad al-Ghazālī, Remembrance, and the Metaphysics of Love*. Albany: State University of New York Press, 2016.

———. "From Ḥubb to ʿIshq: The Development of Love in Early Sufism." *Journal of Islamic Studies* 18, no. 3 (2007): 345–385.

Madelung, Wilferd. "Al-Ghazālī's Changing Attitude to Philosophy." In *Islam and Rationality: The Impact of al-Ghazālī, Papers Collected on His 900th Anniversary*, vol. 1, edited by Georges Tamer, 23–34. Leiden: Brill, 2015.

Makdisi, George. *The Rise of Colleges: Institutions of Learning in Islam and the West*. Edinburgh: Edinburgh University Press, 1981.

Malamud, Margaret. "The Politics of Heresy in Medieval Khurasan: The Karramiyya in Nishapur." *Iranian Studies* 27, no. 1/4 (1994): 37–51.

Mansouri, Mohamed Tahar. *Du Voile et du Zunnār*. Tunis: l'Or du Temps, 2007.

Markwith, Zachary. "And When I Love Him: The *Ḥadīth al-Nawāfil* and the Formation of Sufism." PhD dissertation, Graduate Theological Union, Berkeley, 2020.

Marmura, Michael E. "Some Questions Regarding Avicenna's Theory of the Temporal Origination of the Human Rational Soul." *Arabic Sciences and Philosophy* 18 (2008): 121–138.

Meier, Fritz. *Abū Saʿīd Abū al-Khayr: ḥaqīqat wa afsāna* [a Persian translation of *Abū Saʿīd-i Abū l-Ḫayr: Wirklichkeit und Legende*. Tehran: Bibliothèque Pahlavi, 1976]. Translated by Mihr-Āfāq Bāyburdī. Tehran: Markaz-i Nashr-i Dānishgāhī, 1999.

———. *Essays on Islamic Piety and Mysticism*. Translated by John O'Kane. Leiden: Brill, 1999.

Meisami, Julie Scott. *Medieval Persian Court Poetry*. Princeton: Princeton University Press, 1987.

———. *Structure and Meaning in Medieval Arabic and Persian Poetry: Orient Pearls*. London: RoutledgeCurzon, 2003.

Melville, Charles. "Earthquakes in the History of Nishapur." *Iran* 18 (1980): 103–120.

Miller, Matthew Thomas. "Poetics of the Sufi Carnival: The 'Rogue Lyrics' (Qalandariyāt) of Sanāʾi, ʿAttār, and ʿErāqi." PhD dissertation, Washington University, St. Louis, 2016.

Morris, James Winston. "The Spiritual Ascension: Ibn ʿArabī and the Miʿrāj." *Journal of the American Oriental Society* 107 (1987): 629–652, and 108 (1988): 63–77.

Mourad, Suleiman Ali. *Early Islam between Myth and History: al-Ḥasan al-Baṣrī (d. 110H/728CE) and the Formation of His Legacy in Classical Islamic Scholarship*. Leiden: Brill, 2006.

Muslim ibn al-Ḥajjāj. *Ṣaḥīḥ Muslim*. Riyadh: Dār al-Mughnī, 1998.

Mustawfī Qazwīnī, Ḥamdallāh b. Abī Bakr b. Aḥmad b. Naṣr (d. after 740/1339–1340). *Tārīkh-i guzīda*. Edited by ʿAbd al-Ḥusayn Nawāʾī. Tehran: Amīr Kabīr, 1983.

Myrne, Pernilla. *Female Sexuality in the Early Medieval Islamic World: Gender and Sex in Arabic Literature*. London: I. B. Tauris, 2020.

Nafīsī, Saʿīd. *Zindigīnāma-yi Shaykh Farīd al-Dīn ʿAṭṭār*. Tehran: Iqbāl, 2005.

Nguyen, Martin. *Sufi Master and Qurʾan Scholar: Abū'l-Qāsim al-Qushayrī and the Laṭāʾif al-Ishārāt*. Oxford: Oxford University Press, 2012.

Nongbri, Brent. *Before Religion: A History of a Modern Concept*. New Haven, CT: Yale University Press, 2013.

Ogunnaike, Oludamini. "'Shining of the Lights and the Veil of the Sights in the Secret Bright': An Akbarī Approach to the Problem of Pure Consciousness." *Journal of the Muhyiddin Ibn ʿArabi Society* 61 (2017): 17–42.

O'Malley, Austin. *The Poetics of Spiritual Instruction: Farid al-Din ʿAttar and Persian Sufi Didacticism*. Edinburgh: Edinburgh University Press, 2023.

Payāmī, Bihnāz, and Fāṭima Farhūdī-Pūr. "Bar-rasī-i taṭbīqī-i sākhtār-i rawāʾī-i *Muṣībat-nāma*-yi ʿAṭṭār wa *Sayr al-ʿibād*-i Sanāʾī bih mathāba-yi 'tamthīl-i ruʾyā.'" *Muṭālaʿāt-i ʿirfānī* (University of Kashan) 19, no. 1393 (2014): 55–84.

Petrushevsky, Ilya Pavlovich. *Islam in Iran*. Translated by Hubert Evans. Albany: State University of New York Press, 1985.

Pourjavady, Nasrollah. "'Tuḥfat al-mulūk' wa dāstān-i Shaykh-i Ṣanʿān." *Maʿārif* 17, no. 1 (2000): 3–20.

Pūrnāmdārīyān, Taqī. *Dīdār bā Sīmurgh: shiʿr wa ʿirfān wa andīsha-hā-yi ʿAṭṭār*. Tehran: Institute for Humanities and Cultural Studies, 2011.

Qummī, Najm al-Dīn Abū al-Rajāʾ. *Tārīkh al-wuzarāʾ*. Edited by Muḥammad-Taqī Dānish-pazhūh. Tehran: Muʾassasa-yi Muṭālaʿāt wa Taḥqīqāt-i Farhangī, 1984.

al-Qushayrī, Abū al-Qāsim. *Al-Qushayrī's Epistle on Sufism*. Translated by Alexander D. Knysh. Reading: Garnet, 2007.

Reinert, B. "ʿAṭṭār, Farīd al-Dīn." *Encyclopædia Iranica* 3, fasc. 1 (1989): 20–25.

Renard, John. *Friends of God: Islamic Images of Piety, Commitment, and Servanthood*. Berkeley: University of California Press, 2008.

Ritter, Hellmut. *The Ocean of the Soul: Man, the World and God in the Stories of Farīd al-Dīn ʿAṭṭārī*. Translated by John O'Kane. Leiden: Brill, 2003.

Rustom, Mohammed. *Inrushes of the Heart: The Sufi Philosophy of ʿAyn al-Quḍāt*. Albany: State University of New York Press, 2023.

Ṣafā, Dhabīḥallāh. "Dawlatšāh Samarqandī." *Encyclopædia Iranica* 7, fasc. 2 (1994): 149–150.

Safi, Omid. "Bargaining with *Baraka*: Persian Sufism, 'Mysticism,' and Pre-modern Politics." *Muslim World* 90 (Fall 2000): 259–287.

———. *The Politics of Knowledge in Premodern Islam: Negotiating Ideology and Religious Inquiry*. Chapel Hill: University of North Carolina Press, 2006.

Samʿānī, Aḥmad. *The Repose of the Spirits: A Sufi Commentary on the Divine Names*. Translated by William C. Chittick. Albany: State University of New York Press, 2019.

Sanāʾī, Majdūd ibn Ādam Ghaznawī. *Dīwān-i Ḥakīm Sanāʾī*. 2 vols. Edited by Muḥammad-Riḍā Barzigar-Khāliqī. Tehran: Zawwār, 2015.

———. *Ḥadīqat al-ḥaqīqa wa sharīʿat al-ṭārīqa*. 6th ed. Edited by Muḥammad-Taqī Mudarris-Raḍawī. Tehran: University of Tehran Press, 2004.

———. *Sayr al-ʿibād ilā al-maʿād*. Edited by Maryam al-Sādāt Ranjbar. Tehran: Mānī, 1999.

Ṣanʿatī-Nīā, Fāṭima. *Maʾākhidh-i qiṣaṣ wa tamthīlāt-i mathnawī-hā-yi ʿAṭṭār-i Nīshābūrī*. Tehran: 1990, Zawwār.

al-Ṣanʿānī, Abū Bakr ʿAbd al-Razzāq. *al-Muṣannaf*. Edited by Ḥabīb al-Raḥmān al-Aʿẓamī. Beirut: al-Maktaba al-Islāmī, 1983.

al-Sarrāj al-Ṭūsī, Abū Naṣr ʿAbdallāh ibn ʿAlī. *Kitāb al-lumaʿ fī al-taṣawwuf*. Edited by Reynold Alleyne Nicholson. Leiden: Brill, 1914.

Sells, Michael. *Early Islamic Mysticism: Sufi, Qurʾan, Miʿraj, Poetic, and Theological Writings*. New York: Paulist Press, 1996.

Sevincer, A. Timur, Gabriele Oettingen, and Tobias Lerner. "Alcohol Affects Goal Commitment by Explicitly and Implicitly Induced Myopia." *Journal of Abnormal Psychology* 121, no. 2 (2012): 524–529.

Shackle, Christopher. "Representations of ʿAṭṭār in the West and in the East: Translations of the *Manṭiq al-ṭayr* and the Tale of Shaykh Ṣanʿān." In *ʿAṭṭār and the Persian Sufi Tradition: The Art of Spiritual Flight*, edited by Leonard Lewisohn and Christopher Shackle, 165–193. London: I. B. Tauris, 2006.

Shafīʿī-Kadkanī, Muḥammad-Riḍā. *Qalandariyya dar tārīkh: digardīsīhā-yi yik īdiʾūlūzhī*. Tehran: Sukhan, 2007.

———. *Zabūr-i pārsī: nigāhī bi zindigī wa ghazal-hā-yi ʿAṭṭār*. Tehran: Āgāh, 1999.

Shah-Kazemi, Reza. *Paths to Transcendence: According to Shankara, Ibn Arabi, and Meister Eckhart*. Bloomington, IN: World Wisdom, 2006.

Shajīʿī, Pūrān. *Jahān bīnī-i ʿAṭṭār*. Tehran: Wīrāyish, 1995.

Shamīsā, Sīrūs. *Sayr-i ghazal dar shiʿr fārsī: az āghāz tā imrūz*. Tehran: Firdawsī, 1983.

Siddiqui, Sohaira Z. M. *Law and Politics under the Abbasids: An Intellectual Portrait of al-Juwayni*. Cambridge: Cambridge University Press, 2019.

Sizgorich, Thomas. "Monks and Their Daughters: Monasteries as Muslim-Christian Boundaries." In *Muslims and Others in Sacred Space*, edited by Margaret Cormack, 193–216. Oxford: Oxford University Press, 2013.

Smith, Margaret. *Rabiʿa: The Life and Work of Rabiʿa and Other Women Mystics in Islam*. Oxford: Oneworld, 1994.

———. *Rābiʿa the Mystic, A.D. 717–801 and Her Fellow Saints in Islam, Being the Life and Teachings of Rābiʿa al-ʿAdawiyya al-Qaysiyya of Basra, Sufi Saint ca. A.H. 99–185, A.D. 717–801, Together with Some Account of the Place of the Women Saints in Islam*. Cambridge: Cambridge University Press, 1928.

———. *Studies in Early Mysticism in the Near and Middle East*. Oxford: Oneworld, 1995.

Stone, Lucian. "Blessed Perplexity: The Topos of *Ḥayrat* in ʿAṭṭār's *Manṭiq al-ṭayr*." In *ʿAṭṭār and the Persian Sufi Tradition: The Art of Spiritual Flight*, edited by Leonard Lewisohn and Christopher Shackle, 95–111. London: I. B. Tauris, 2006.

al-Sulamī, Abū ʿAbd al-Raḥmān. *Majmūʿat āthār ʿAbd al-Raḥmān Sulamī*. 3 vols. Edited by Nasrollah Pourjavady and Muḥammad Sūrī. Tehran: Iranian Institute of Philosophy and the Institute of Islamic Studies at the Free University of Berlin, 2009.

Sviri, Sara. "Ḥakīm Tirmidhī and the *Malāmatī* Movement in Early Sufism." In *The Heritage of Sufism*, vol. 1, *Classical Persian Sufism from Its Origins to Rumi (700–1300)*, edited by Leonard Lewisohn, 583–613. Oxford: Oneworld, 1999.

Ṭabīb, Rashīd al-Dīn Faḍlallāh Hamadānī. *Jāmiʿ al-tawārīkh* (*Tārīkh-i mubārak-i ghāzānī*). 4 vols. Edited by Muḥammad Rawshan and Muṣṭafā Mūsawī. Tehran: Mīrāth-i Maktūb, 2015.

Taves, Ann. *Religious Experience Reconsidered: A Building-Block Approach to the Study of Religion and Other Special Things*. Princeton: Princeton University Press, 2009.

al-Tirmidhī, Abū ʿIsā Muḥammad ibn ʿĪsā. *al-Jāmiʿ al-ṣaḥīḥ, wa huwa Sunan al-Tirmidhī*. 5 vols. with an introductory volume. Edited by Aḥmad Muḥammad Shākir, Muḥammad Fuʾād ʿAbd al-Bāqī, and Ibrāhīm ʿAṭwa ʿAwaḍ. Cairo: Muṣṭafā al-Bābī al-Ḥalabī, 1978 [1962–1978].

Tugendhat, Ernst. *Egocentricity and Mysticism: An Anthropological Study*. Translated by Alexei Procyshyn and Mario Wenning. New York: Columbia University Press, 2016.

———. *Self-Consciousness and Self-Determination*. Translated by Paul Stern. Cambridge, MA: MIT Press, 1986.

Vaziri, Mostafa. *Iran as Imagined Nation: The Construction of National Identity*. New York: Paragon House, 1993.

Walker, Paul E. "Philosophy of Religion in al-Fārābī, Ibn Sīnā, and Ibn Ṭufayl." In *Reason and Inspiration in Islam: Theology, Philosophy and Mysticism in Muslim Thought, Essays in Honour of Hermann Landolt*, edited by Todd Lawson, 85–101. London: I. B. Tauris, 2005.

Yaghoobi, Claudia. *Subjectivity in ʿAṭṭār, Persian Sufism, and European Mysticism*. West Lafayette, IN: Purdue University Press, 2017.

Zahiremami, Parisa. "Cosmopolitanism, Poetry, and Kingship: The Ideal Ruler in Sanāʾī's (d. 1131 or 1135) Poetry." PhD dissertation, University of Toronto, 2021.

Zargar, Cyrus Ali. *The Polished Mirror: Storytelling and the Pursuit of Virtue in Islamic Philosophy and Sufism*. London: Oneworld, 2017.

———. "Sober in Mecca, Drunk in Byzantium: Antinomian Space in the Poetry of ʿAṭṭār." *Journal of the American Academy of Religion* 89, no. 1 (2021): 272–297.

Zarrīn-kūb, ʿAbd al-Ḥusayn. *Na sharqī, na gharbī, insānī: majmūʿa-yi maqālāt, taḥqīqāt, naqd-hā, wa namāyishwāra-hā*. Tehran: Amīr Kabīr, 1974.

Zysow, Aron. "Karrāmiya." *Encyclopædia Iranica* 15, fasc. 6 (2011): 590–601.

Index

āb-i ḥayāt (Water of Eternal Life), 15
Abraham, 98, 107, 137, 165
Abū Saʿīd b. Abī al-Khayr, 9, 26, 29, 87
Adam, 137, 139, 151–152, 165
Ādamī, Ibn ʿAṭāʾ Aḥmad, 28
ʿAdawiyya, Muʿādha bint ʿAbdallāh al-, 70
ʿAdawiyya, Rābiʿa al-. *See* Rābiʿa
Ādharī-Ṭūsī, Shaykh, 30
ahl al-dhimma (protected non-Muslims), 98
Aḥmad b. Ḥanbal, 26, 172n27
Aḥmad b. Ḥarb, 25
Ahmed, Shahab, 86
aḥwāl (states), 17, 111, 119, 145, 164
āʾīn (custom), 45
ʿĀʾisha bt. Abū Bakr, 69–70, 181n5
ʿajūz (old lady), 67, 72
ākhira, al- (the hereafter), 46, 141
Akkāf, Rukn al-Dīn, 31
Albertini, Tamara, 71
alchemy, 15
allusions (*ishārāt*), 3, 101, 103
ʿAmmūriyya, 108
annihilation. See *fanāʾ*
Anṣārī, Khwāja ʿAbdallāh, 87
Anwarī, Awḥad al-Dīn, 16
ʿaql. *See* intellect
asceticism (*zuhd*), 17, 25–26, 47, 88, 91, 99, 113, 158
Ashʿarī school, 11–12, 27, 178n2, 199n36
aṣl (foundation), 79, 95
Avicenna. *See* Ibn Sīnā
awliyāʾ (saints), 9, 10, 18, 27, 29, 55, 126, 164–165, 180n13
Ayubi, Zahra, 71

Baghdad, 24, 27–28, 108
Baghdādī, Majd al-Dīn, 30–31
Balkh, 24
Balkhī, Shaqīq al-, 87
baqāʾ (remaining), 119, 123
Barton, Carlin, 41
Baṣrī, al-Ḥasan al-, 48, 70, 86–87
Basṭāmī, Bāyazīd, 63, 87, 125–128
bāṭin (inner), 142, 151
bayt (line of poetry), 14, 169n2
Beckett, Samuel, 157
bewilderment, 18, 82, 87–88, 98
Boyarin, Daniel, 41
Boylston, Nicholas, 134
Boysen, Benjamin, 3–4
Brown, Edward, 35
Bruijn, J. T. P. de, 134, 196n16
Buddhism, 100, 121, 123

butkhāna (idol temple), 93, 97–98, 114
Buyid(s), 27
Byzantium, 107–109, 111

Chāchī, Abū al-Rajāʾ, 86
Chittick, William, 87
Christ. *See* Jesus
Christian(ity), 4, 40, 42, 51, 98, 105, 121, 123; beautiful-faced, 99; –child, 106; girls/women, 108, 110–114; and Judaism, 41, 88; Nestorian, 107; Protestant, 39; spaces, 99, 105, 109; and the *zunnār*, 68, 97–98, 111
Constantinople, 107–109, 113
Cornell, Rkia Elaroui, 69–71
cosmology, 2, 15, 85
Crusades, the, 51, 106
Cup of Jamshīd, 14–15

ḍaʿīfa (weak woman), 71–72. See also *ʿajūz*
David, 80, 137, 161
Dawlatshāh, Amīr, 3, 21, 31–32, 34–36
Daylamī, Abū al-Ḥasan al-, 87
dervish(es), 8, 32–33, 160
dhikr (the remembrance of God), 26, 56, 97, 138
dil (heart), 17, 146, 150–151, 198n31, 200n54; conflated with spirit (*rūḥ*) in al-Ghazālī's writings, 198n31; eyes as most direct portal to, 191n20; prophetic typology of, 165; purification and unveiling of, 56–57; relationship with *tajrīd*, 192n2; superior to intellect (*ʿaql*), 63, 145, 146
dīn (religion), 4, 39–43, 45–70, 72, 74–75, 82, 96, 146
dīwān, 14, 16, 81
dunyā (worldly), 45–51, 60

egocentricity, 4, 155
Eliade, Mircea, 122
exegesis (*tafsīr*), 55–56
existence (*hastī*), 142

faith (*īmān*), 81–83; simple, 62
falsafa. *See* philosophy
fanāʾ (annihilation of selfhood), 18, 119, 123, 126, 140–141
faqīh (legal scholar), 24, 43, 56
faqr. *See* poverty
Fārābī, al-, 61
Fārmadī, Abū ʿAlī, 9
faylasūf. *See* philosopher
fiqh, 55–56
firqa (sect), 88–89
Fitzgerald, Edward, 18
Foucault, Michel, 102

Genghis Khan, 34
ghazal, 30, 100, 105
Ghazālī, Abū Ḥāmid al-, 9–11, 28, 62–65, 75, 107, 144–146
Ghazālī, Aḥmad al-, 9, 28, 85, 88, 99, 107, 135
Ghazna, 19

Ḥadīth, 2, 46, 53, 55, 62, 69–70, 73, 161, 164, 178n2
Ḥaddād, Abū Ḥafṣ al-, 27
Ḥafiẓ, 35
Hajj, 31, 108
ḥakīm (sage), 3
Ḥallāj, Manṣūr al-, 19, 26, 28, 31, 87, 96, 139, 169n4, 191n20
Hamadānī, ʿAyn al-Quḍāt, 85, 88, 99, 161
Hamadānī Ṭabīb, Rashīd al-Dīn Faḍlallāh, 100
Ḥamdūn al-Qaṣṣār, 27
Ḥanafī school, 23–24, 133–134

ḥaqq (Real/Truth): amorous relationship with, 145; drawing closer to, 120, 126–127, 140–141, 158–160, 165, 167; God as Reality, 28–29, 33, 48, 72, 82; I am the, 96; reflected in humans, 103; religious sciences, 159; as Truth, 146; understanding through intelligence, 75
Harawī, Amīr Ḥusaynī, 35
hastī (existence), 142
Ḥaydar, Quṭb al-Dīn, 8
ḥayrat (perplexity), 82, 148
heart. See *dil*
Hell, 4, 128, 137, 154
Herat, 24, 87
hereafter, the, 46, 141
heresy, 19, 41, 157
Ḥīrī, Abū ʿUthmān al-, 27
ḥiss (sense), 17, 137, 142–145, 146, 151, 154, 155, 198n26
Homer, 1
ḥubb (healthy love). *See* love
hudhud (hoopoe), 16, 105, 131, 134
Hujwīrī, ʿAlī b. ʿUthmān, 19
Hume, David, 59–60

Iblīs (Satan), 47–48, 137, 139–140
Ibn Abī al-Dunyā, 71
Ibn Abī al-Khayr, Abū Saʿīd, 9, 26, 29, 87
Ibn al-Jawzī, 71
Ibn ʿArabī, 130, 183n30, 193n17
Ibn Karrām, 25
Ibn Khafīf, 87
Ibn Manṣūr, Sayf al-Dīn Muḥammad, 133–134
Ibn Qayyim al-Jawziyya, 67
Ibn Sīnā, 54–56, 60–62, 87, 129–132, 134, 144–146, 149, 178n4, 195n8, 197n5, 201n4
Ibn Taymiyya, 67
idol temple, 93, 97–98, 114
idolatry, 96, 108, 114
ikhlāṣ (sincerity), 8, 26–27, 67, 69, 72, 80, 95
ilhām (inspiration), 62, 180n13
Il-khanid(s), 100
imagination. See *khayāl*
īmān (faith), 81–83; simple, 62
I-ness (*man-ī*), 128, 142–144, 155, 165, 198n27
infidelity: devotion and, 99; and faith, 82–83, 166; *kufr*, 82; love and, 5, 92, 111; metaphorical, 18–19, 82, 165; piety and, 90; places of, 105, 108–109, 111, 190n12; symbols of, 16, 84, 105
inspiration (*ilhām*), 62, 180n13
intellect, 53–55, 137, 139, 142, 147–150, 155, 159; Active, 54–55, 132; *ʿaql*, 17, 45, 63, 179n8; compared to the heart, 63, 145, 150; compared to love, 15, 43, 54; and *dīn*, 68; and imagination, 146; *khirad*, 148; philosophical, 63, 65, 68; and the soul, 60–61, 130–134; Universal, 53–54, 178n4
intelligence. See *khirad*
intoxication, 70–71, 80, 95, 114, 132
Iran, 7, 22, 24, 26–28, 42, 62, 88, 149
Iṣfahānī, Kamāl Ismāʿīl, 35
Iṣfahānī, ʿAlī b. Abī Ḥafṣ Maḥmūd al-, 107
ishārāt (allusions), 3, 101, 103
ʿishq (passionate love). *See* love
Islamic law, 24, 55. *See also* Sharīʿa
Ismāʿīlīsm, 11, 196n11
istidlāl (reasoning), 55, 79, 180n13

Jaʿfar al-Ṣādiq, 19, 87, 173n17
Jāḥiẓ, al-, 71
James, William, 120–122
Jāmī, ʿAbd al-Raḥmān, 29–32, 34–35, 167

Jesus, 41, 47, 69, 107, 137, 165
jinn, 15, 17, 137
Josephson-Storm, Jason, 42
Joyce, James, 3–4
Judaism, 4, 41, 51, 88, 121, 123
Junayd, al-, 27–28
Juwaynī, Abū Maʿālī al-, 11–12, 24, 62–63, 171n25
Juwaynī, ʿAṭā-Malik, 100

Kaaba: beautiful vision, 93–95, 112; Constantinople as anti-, 108–109; sobriety of, 114; spurning the, 92–93; compared to tavern, 97, 99
Karrāmiyya, 25–27
kashf (unveiling), 56, 63, 97, 132, 161, 180n13
Katz, Steven, 122–123
Keeler, Annabel, 87
Kempe, Margery, 71
Kermani, Navid, 157, 169n1
Keshavarz, Fatemeh, 92, 177n5
khalwa (meditative retreat), 56, 113
khānaqāh, 25–26
Khāqānī Shirwānī, Afḍal al-Dīn, 107, 125
kharābāt (ruins), 51; as brothel, 100, 189n28–30; *khūr-ābād* (sun temple), 100; as ruins, 98–99; *pīr-i*, 91
Kharrāz, Abū Saʿīd al-, 87
khayāl (imagination), 17, 61, 137, 144–146, 149, 154–155, 169n4, 198n26, 199n35
Khayyām, ʿUmar al-, 10, 18
Khiḍr, 148
khirad (intelligence), 45, 80–81, 148, 184n4. *See also* intellect
Khorasan, 23–24, 27, 86, 133
Kirmānī, Shams al-Dīn Muḥammad Bardsīrī, 130
kīsh (confession), 45
Kubrā, Najm al-Dīn, 14, 130
Kubrawīyya, 30–31
kufr. *See* infidelity
Kurrakānī, Abū al-Qāsim, 9
Khwarazm, 30
Khwārī, Aḥmad, 30

Laylā and Majnūn, 93
Lewis, Franklin, 106, 195n9
Lewisohn, Leonard, 86
Losensky, Paul, 18, 71
love: cosmology of, 15, 85; of God, 40, 49, 59, 70, 72, 79, 83, 85–86, 89, 103, 112, 114, 147, 166; *ḥubb* (healthy), 86; human, 79; and infidelity, 5, 82, 105, 111; and intellect, 43, 54, 80–81; *ʿishq* (passionate), 40, 45, 86–87, 89; language of, 16, 71, 80, 84, 86, 90; poetry, 16–17, 33, 96–97, 160; Psalms of, 80; religion of, 2–3, 19, 39, 42–43, 79, 112, 115, 165; School of, 86, 88–89, 91–92; Sharīʿa of, 88; soul in, 130, 161; transgressive, 102; and union, 40, 85, 87, 119; Valley of, 145; worldly, 48, 50

madhhab (way), 45, 68, 88–89
madhhab-i ʿishq (School of Love), 86, 88–89, 91–92. *See also* love
Majnūn and Laylā, 93
Malāmatiyya, 26–27, 96
man-ī (ego state). *See* I-ness
maqāmāt (stations), 17, 101, 119
martyrdom, 34
Marv, 23–24
Mary (Mother of Jesus), 47, 69
master paradigm, 42
mathnawī, 15, 105, 130
Maybudī, Rashīd al-Dīn, 87

maykhāna (tavern), 16, 91–97, 99–100, 114
Mecca, 11, 109, 111–112, 114
Medina, 11, 31
millat (nation), 45, 63
miʿrāj (night journey and ascent), 17, 124–126, 129–131, 140
Miṣrī, Dhū al-Nūn al-, 87
Mithra (Mītrā), 100, 189n27
modernity, 41–42
Mongols, 7, 23–24, 34–36, 100, 160
Moses, 18, 72, 75, 101–102, 137, 148, 165, 183n27, 189n32
Muhammad (Prophet of God), 8, 62–64, 67, 69, 88, 108, 128, 137–138; chain (*silsila*), 28, 30; companions of, 31; in dreams, 108, 110, 190n12; family of, 19, 178n1; intercession of, 165; light of, 79; night journey and ascent, see *miʿrāj*; revelation, 54–55, 164; sayings of, 62, 67, 88, 128, 132; way (*sunna*), 53, 134
Munkir and Nakīr, 73
muṣībat (affliction), 139
Muslim b. al-Ḥajjāj, 24
Muʿtazilīs, 178n2
mutafakkir (thinker), 2

nafs (self), 128
Najm al-Dīn Kubrā, 14, 130
Nawāʾī, ʿAlī-shīr, 21, 34
Neoplatonism, 54, 121, 129
night journey and ascent. See *miʿrāj*
Nīsābūrī, ʿUmar b. al-Ḥasan al-, 108
Nishapur, 7, 9–12, 19, 22–28, 30–31, 34–36, 48, 62, 86, 96, 102, 107, 160, 163, 167
nīstī (nonexistence), 142
Niẓāmī, 125, 184n4
Noah, 137
Nongbri, Brent, 39
nubuwwa (prophethood), 61, 75
Nūrī, Abū al-Ḥusayn al-, 87

Oghuz, 23–24
O'Malley, Austin, 3
Otto, Rudolf, 122

Paradise, 48, 108, 128, 137, 154
Petrushevsky, Ilya Pavlovich, 160
perplexity (*ḥayrat*), 82, 148
Pharaoh, 18, 75, 101
philosophy, 10–11, 54, 56, 60–63, 131–132, 135, 171n23, 199n36
philosopher(s), 2–5, 54–55, 59–62, 64, 67, 73, 75, 87, 129–131, 146, 148–149, 164, 178n1
pīr-i kharābāt (master of the ruins), 91
poverty, 8, 26, 70, 93, 97, 119, 140, 160
Prophet, the. *See* Muhammad
prophethood. See *nubuwwa*
prophets, 17, 40, 45–46, 61, 69, 125, 128, 148, 163, 165, 180n13

Qāf, Mount, 4, 105, 130–131
qalandar, 91
Qaranī, Uways al-, 31
qaṣīda, 13
Qaṣṣār, Ḥamdūn al-, 27
quatrain. See *rubāʿīyāt*
Qurʾān, 133–134, 138, 140, 145, 150, 152, 164
Qushayrī, Abū al-Qāsim al-, 19, 27, 71

Rabbānī, Imām al-, 9
Rābiʿa, 9, 69–75, 87, 92–93, 114, 147
religion. See *dīn*

Ritter, Hellmut, 2, 8, 92, 108
riyāʾ (pietistic ostentation), 26
rubāʿīyāt, 13, 18
rūḥ (spirit), 17, 103, 127–128, 138, 145, 152–155, 157, 164, 179n6, 198n31
Rūmī, Jalāl al-Dīn, 1, 14, 26, 31, 35, 54, 107, 131, 134–135, 167
rumūz (clues), 103

Saʿdī, 29
Ṣādiq, Jaʿfar al-, 19, 87, 173n17
Ṣadrā, Mulla, 198n26
saints. See *awliyāʾ*
samāʿ (music), 96–97
Samʿānī, Aḥmad, 88
Sanāʾī, Majdūd b. Ādam Ghaznawī, 16, 29, 35, 54, 86–88, 92, 99, 125, 129–135, 143, 146
Ṣanʿānī, Abū Bakr ʿAbd al-Razzāq al-, 108–109
Sanjar, Aḥmad b. Malikshāh (Sultan), 23
Sarrāj, Abū Naṣr al-, 28
Satan, (Iblīs), 47–48, 137, 139–140
School of Love. *See* love
Schopenhauer, Arthur, 157
science, 41–42, 120–121, 164, 166; Islamic, 19, 53, 55, 159; rational, 11, 53–55, 59, 62–63, 73; three, 56; philosophical, 60; Sufi, 10
secular, 4, 46, 49
sect (*firqa*), 88–89
Seljuk(s), 23, 100, 174n9
Sells, Michael, 71
sense. See *ḥiss*
Shabistarī, Maḥmūd, 35
Shādyākh, 21, 23
Shāfiʿī school, 11–12, 23–24, 27
Shafīʿī-Kadkanī, Muḥammad-Riḍā, 35, 99
shāh-i parīyān (fairy king), 14
shāhid (witness), 96–97
Sharīʿa, 87–88, 158, 166–167. *See also* Islamic law
Sharīʿa of Love, 88
Shaykh of Ṣanʿān, 103, 105, 109
Shiblī, Abū Bakr al-, 87, 93, 108
silsila (chain), 30
Sīmurgh, 16, 81, 105, 115, 119, 130–131, 165
sincerity. See *ikhlāṣ*
Smart, Ninian, 122
Smith, Margaret, 71
Solomon, 15
Sophist(s), 2, 64–65, 159
spirit. See *rūḥ*
Stace, Walter, 122
states. See *aḥwāl*
stations. See *maqāmāt*
sūfisṭānī. *See* Sophist(s)
Suhrawardī, Shihāb al-Dīn Yaḥyā, 130
Suhrawardiyya, 85
Sulamī, Abū ʿAbd al-Raḥmān, 19, 27, 29, 70, 72
sunna, 53
sūnyatā (emptiness), 123
superstition, 41–42, 166

taʿabbud (selfless servitude), 72
tafsīr (exegesis), 55–56
ṭāʾifa (band), 9–10
taṣawwuf, 24, 27–28
taslīm (surrender), 63–64
tavern. See *maykhāna*
Taves, Ann, 121–123
tawḥīd (God's oneness), 15, 18, 119, 125, 127, 143, 148, 152, 168, 192nn1–2
theologian(s), 3, 42, 61–62, 73
Timurid(s), 31, 160
Tugendhat, Ernst, 155
Ṭūs, 9, 23–24, 27

Ṭūsī, ʿAbbāsa, 69
Ṭūsī, Jamāl al-Dīn Muḥammad, 9
Ṭūsī, Naṣīr al-Dīn, 10

union, 2, 5, 17–18, 34, 40, 85, 87, 114, 119–120, 123–129, 131–134, 138–141, 145, 152–157, 160
Universal Intellect. *See* intellect
unveiling. See *kashf*
Uwaysī connection, 31

waḥdāniyyat (Unity), 127
wahm (estimation), 63–64, 68, 145, 181n20
Walad, Bahāʾ al-Dīn Muḥammad, 134
wayfarer(s), 17, 120, 123–124, 127, 137–160, 165
wine, 16–18, 80, 91, 94–96, 98, 101–102, 107–108, 110, 114, 143, 151
winehouse. See *maykhāna*

Yaghoobi, Claudia, 71, 102

Zaehner, Robert Charles, 122
zāhid-i khushk (dry ascetic), 91
zāhidān (ascetics), 158. *See also* asceticism
ẓāhir (outer), 142
Zoroastrian(s), 53, 100, 178n2
zuhd. See asceticism
zunnār (Christian girdle), 68, 97–98, 111

www.ingramcontent.com/pod-product-compliance
Ingram Content Group UK Ltd.
Pitfield, Milton Keynes, MK11 3LW, UK
UKHW041002010525
458084UK00002B/30

9 781438 498669